412324

Japan's Economic Diplomacy
with China, 1945–1978

Studies on Contemporary China

The Contemporary China Institute at the School of Oriental and African Studies (University of London) has, since its establishment in in 1968, been an international centre for research and publications on twentieth-century China. *Studies on Contemporary China*, which is edited at the Institute, seeks to maintain and extend that tradition by making available the best work of scholars and China specialists throughout the world. It embraces a wide variety of subjects relating to Nationalist and Communist China, including social, political, and economic change, intellectual and culture developments, foreign relations, and national security.

SERIES EDITOR

Dr Frank Dikötter, Director of the Contemporary China Institute

Japan's Economic Diplomacy with China, 1945–1978

YOSHIHIDE SOEYA

CLARENDON PRESS · OXFORD
1998

Oxford University Press, Great Clarendon Street, Oxford OX2 6DP

Oxford New York

Athens Auckland Bangkok Bogotá Buenos Aires Calcutta
Cape Town Chennai Dar es Salaam Delhi Florence Hong Kong Istanbul
Karachi Kuala Lumpur Madrid Melbourne Mexico City Mumbai
Nairobi Paris São Paulo Singapore Taipei Tokyo Toronto Warsaw
and associated companies in
Berlin Ibadan

Oxford is a trade mark of Oxford University Press

Published in the United States
by Oxford University Press Inc., New York

British Library Cataloguing in Publication Data
Data available

Library of Congress Cataloging in Publication Data
Data available

ISBN 0–19–829219–8

1 3 5 7 9 10 8 6 4 2

Typeset by Alliance Phototypesetters, Pondicherry
Printed in Great Britain on acid-free paper by
Biddles Limited, Guildford and
King's Lynn

ACKNOWLEDGEMENTS

Writing a book is a long and lonely process, and yet this study has not been finished without the help and encouragement of many people. Acknowledging those who have guided me in various ways would provide a dynamic account of the evolution of research, conceptualization, and writing of this book, but I am indebted to too many people to name all. I can only mention a few here.

Substantial research on Japan–China trade relations was originally conducted as part of my Ph.D. dissertation submitted to The University of Michigan in 1987. In particular, Professors John Campbell and Michel Oksenberg furnished extensive and penetrating comments on my draft at various stages. While writing the dissertation, I was fortunate to be given a post at the Institute of International Relations of Sophia University in Tokyo, where Professors Ogaka Sadako and Royama Michio gave me invaluable assistance and guidance in the research.

In developing a conceptual framework for the analysis of Japanese diplomacy and Japan–China relations, I am also indebted to many people who gave me intellectual inspirations and guidance before and after joining Keio University in 1988; Professors Ikei Masaru, the late Kosaka Masataka, Watanabe Akio, Nishihara Masashi, Iokibe Makoto, and Tanaka Akihiko, to name a few. I would also like to express my gratitude to David Shambaugh for his long-term friendship and for facilitating the publication of this book.

Most of the writing of the book was done when I was a visiting fellow at the East–West Center in Honolulu in 1993–95, partly supported by the Abe fellowship of the Center for Global Partnership of the Japan Foundation. In particular, I would like to thank Michel Oksenberg, Charles Morrison, and Muthiah Alagappa for providing me with a comfortable environment as well as intellectual stimuli.

I dedicate this work to my wife, Kazuko.

CONVENTIONS

In this book, Japanese names are given in the Japanese order, with the surname preceding the given name. Macrons to indicate long vowels are omitted.

CONTENTS

LIST OF TABLES

LIST OF ABBREVIATIONS

AAPSG	Asia–African Problem Study Group; Ajia Ahurica Mondai Kenkyu-kai
AKJ	Ajia Keizai Junpo
APSG	Asian Problem Study Group; Ajia Mondai Kenkyu-kai
ASEAN	Association of South East Asian Nations
CCP	Chinese Communist Party
CCPIT	China Committee for the Promotion of International Trade
CHINCOM	China Committee, the Consultative Group, the Organization for European Economic Cooperation
COCOM	Coordinating Committee, the Consultative Group, the Organization for European Economic Cooperation
JAPIT	Japan Association for the Promotion of International Trade; Nihon Kokusai Boeki Sokushin Kyokai
JCAET	Japan–China Association on Economy and Trade; Nitchu Keizai Kyokai
JCFA	Japan–China Friendship Association; Nitchu Yuko Kyokai
JCIEA	Japan–China Importers and Exporters Association; Nitchu Yushutsunyu Kumiai
JCOTLC	Japan–China Overall Trade Liaison Council; Nitchu Sogo Boeki Renraku Kyogi-kai
JCP	Japan Communist Party; Nihon Kyosan-to
JCTPA	Japan–China Trade Promotion Association; Nitchu Boeki Sokushin-kai
JCTPDML	Japan–China Trade Promotion Diet Members League Nitchu Boeki Sokushin Giin Renmei
JETRO	Japan External Trade Organization
JSP	Japan Socialist Party; Nihon Shakai-to
LDP	Liberal Democratic Party; Jiyuminshu-to
LT	Liao–Takasaki
LTTA	Long Term Trade Agreement; Choki Boeki Kyotei
MITI	Ministry of International Trade and Industry; Tsusho Sangyo-sho
MT	Memorandum Trade; Oboegaki Boeki
NKKK	Nitchu Keizai Kyokai Kaiho
NREA	Natural Resources and Energy Agency; Shigen Enerugi-cho
PARC	Policy Affairs Research Council; Seimu Chosa-kai
PTBT	Partial Test Ban Treaty.

1
Introduction

This study traces the evolution of the structure and process of Japan's trade relations with China in the 1950s, the 1960s, and the 1970s. It illuminates the pluralistic structure of postwar Japan–China trade which survived the three politically turbulent decades after the end of World War II, and thus highlights continuity in the bilateral trade relationship amid political discontinuity.

The conventional wisdom on postwar Japan–China relations stresses the predominance of strategic concerns and fluctuations in the overall bilateral relationship. Despite significant political fluctuations, however, the records of Japan–China trade were impressive when viewed in relative terms. A few statistics demonstrate the point. As a share of Japan's total trade with North East Asian countries (China, Taiwan, Hong Kong, South Korea, North Korea, and the Soviet Union), Japan–China trade occupied as much as 29.8 per cent in 1956, which made China the leading trade partner of Japan in the region (Table 2.3 on page 43). From 1964 to 1967, Japan's trade with China was larger than that with Taiwan and South Korea, and not until 1980 did it 'recover' to the level of the 26 per cent share recorded in 1966. Moreover, while its average yearly share in Japan's North East Asian trade from 1967 to 1971 was 18.4 per cent, from 1972 to 1976 it increased by only 2 per cent to 20.4 per cent. This is not a big difference, considering the fact that the first five-year period corresponds to the period affected by the Chinese Cultural Revolution, and the second to the post-normalization years (Tables 3.1 and 7.1 on pages 45 and 143).

We need to understand why Japan–China trade was relatively substantial and constant in the three postwar decades amid strategic and political fluctuations. This study argues that three distinct foreign policy orientations of postwar Japan (policy lines to seek 'collaboration' with the United States, to emphasize diplomatic 'autonomy' *vis-à-vis* the United States, and to aspire for 'independence' from the system controlled by the United States)[1] and the activities of Japan's non-governmental pro-China actors gave rise to a pluralistic structure in Japan–China trade, which produced relative stability and continuity in the bilateral trade relationship.

Before proceeding to a detailed discussion on this analytical perspective, three qualifications are in order. First, while Japan–China trade in the three

[1] For an earlier discussion of mine in more detail on these diplomatic orientations in Japanese, see Soeya Yoshihide, *Nihon-gaiko to Chugoku, 1945–1972 [Japanese Diplomacy and China, 1945–1972]* (Tokyo: Keio University Press, 1995).

postwar decades was relatively substantial within North East Asia, its share in Japan's world trade was small: the highest shares in each of the three decades were 2.62 per cent recorded in 1956, 3.22 per cent in 1966, and 3.34 per cent in 1975. Our argument, therefore, does not imply the predominance of trade dimensions in postwar Japan–China relations; an explanation of why Japan–China trade was not higher would lie in general political constraints and the overall pattern of Japan's world trade. Our central concern is the inherent momentum in postwar Japan–China relations, as indicated by the trade figures noted above, which cannot be explained as a function of fluctuating international politics.

Second, we do not argue that bilateral trade was entirely unaffected by strategic and political factors. Chinese reactions to the Nagasaki flag incident of May 1958 (Chapter 2) was a highly political act and had an enormous impact on trade (Table 2.3 on page 43). The Cultural Revolution and the heightening tension in East Asia during the second half of the 1960s halted the previous rapid upturn in bilateral trade (Table 3.1 on page 45). The overall trend of continuity described above, however, is still impressive. Moreover, it is quite noteworthy that diplomatic normalization, the single most important political event in the bilateral relationship in the postwar years, apparently did not affect the trend of Japan's China trade very much. In relative terms, the peaks in Japan–China trade in the 1960s and the 1970s were the 26.0 per cent and 3.22 per cent shares in North East Asia and the world in 1966, and the 25.9 per cent and 3.34 per cent shares in 1975. This is a clear indication that the postwar Japan–China trade relationship had its own momentum, which did not necessarily predominate over all the political factors but yet had a significant impact.

Third, our analysis does not cover the period beyond the 1970s. This is because the Chinese new open-door policy introduced completely new economic elements at the beginning of the 1980s, including Japanese governmental loans and grants, private financing, and direct investment.[2] These new moves spurred trade: in 1984, Japan's trade with China reached 4.30 per cent of its world trade. An analysis of these new elements and their effects would require a different framework from the one used in this study. Without going into this new period, this study focuses on the continuity in the bilateral relationship through the 1950s, the 1960s, and the 1970s.

1.2. ANALYTICAL PERSPECTIVE

In Japan, reflecting the importance of the China issue, numerous articles and books covering a whole range of the aspects of the relationship have been

---

[2] For an analysis on the new aspects of Japan–China economic relations, see Chae-Jin Lee, *China and Japan: New Economic Diplomacy* (Stanford: The Hoover Institution Press, 1984).

published by a variety of China watchers including scholars, researchers, journalists, politicians, and pro-China activists.[3] Several scholarly works treat China policy as a case of Japan's foreign policy-making, the scope of these studies being carefully confined to a specific issue area or period of time. Another approach specifically focuses on the structure and process of Japan's China policy-making from various angles such as the LDP, the governmental policy-making community, and the business community. Also, serious attempts to portray the entire picture of postwar Japan–China relations has begun to emerge in recent years, which provide a balanced perspective incorporating domestic, bilateral, and international factors, or give a detailed account of the entire process of development of events.[4]

A skewed perspective prevails, however, in several efforts by non-academic writers to recapitulate the postwar history of Japan–China relations. For example, in his thorough study of the history of postwar Japan–China relations, an Asahi newsman denounces Yoshida's choice of Taipei as a legitimate government of China as an intervention into Chinese domestic affairs, and thus an 'undisguised' anti-China action, a 'fiction', and the 'original sin' which plagued succeeding Prime Ministers of Japan.[5] Another book by a former executive of a pro-China organization, which contains detailed information on postwar Japan–China trade, equally denounces the governments of the United States and Japan for their anti-China policy and for constructing 'artificial' barriers of all kinds to the development of Japan–China trade.[6] These skewed interpretations emphasize the role of non-governmental pro-China Japanese who are portrayed as the true architects of Japan–China relations.

In contrast, neither of the two representative interpretations in western scholarly writings recognizes the role of Japan's pro-China organizations and individuals. One approach treats Japanese policy as a derivative of Japan's security framework within which the United States was the primary actor. The basic argument reads: 'the domestic environment throughout the period

3 For a bibliographical study in this area, see Kida Shojiro, *Gendai Chugoku-Gaiko Kenkyu Bunken Mokuroku, 1949–1980 [Bibliography of Studies on Contemporary China's Foreign Policy in Japan]* (Tokyo: Ryukei Shosha, 1982). This lists 341 books and pamphlets and 1,437 articles under the heading of Japan–China relations. Many of them are, however, descriptions of events and personal experiences, expressions of particular viewpoints, or a combination of both.

4 Ogata Sadako, *Sengo Nitchu-Beichu Kankei [Postwar Japan–China/US–China Relations]* (Tokyo: University of Tokyo Press, 1992), translated by Soeya Yoshihide from Ogata Sadako, *Normalization with China: A Comparative Study of US and Japanese Processes* (Berkeley: Institute of East Asian Studies, University of California, 1988); Tanaka Akihiko, *Nitchu Kankei, 1945–1990 [Japan–China Relations, 1945–1990]* (Tokyo: Tokyo-daigaku Shuppan-kai, 1991); Nagano Nobutoshi, *Tenno to To Shohei no Akushu [Handshake by the Emperor and Deng Xiaoping]* (Tokyo: Gyosei Mondai Kenkyu-jo, 1983).

5 Furukawa Mantaro, *Nitchu Sengo Kankei-shi [History of Postwar Japan–China Relations]* (Tokyo: Hara Shobo, 1981) [Revised Version, 1988], p. 4.

6 Okamoto Saburo, *Nitchu Boeki Ron [Japan–China Trade]* (Tokyo: Toyo Keizai Shinpo-sha, 1971), p. i.

from 1955 to 1970 had less of an influence on [Japan's] China policy than the foreign environment', and 'the Japan–China associations . . . had little direct influence on the decision-makers'.[7]

These studies do not recognize significant initiatives on the part of Japan, as represented most typically by an argument that 'Bilateral relations [between Japan and China] were determined almost entirely by [Japanese] responses to American diplomatic pressures or Chinese policies, or to the drift of world politics.'[8] This perspective considers Japan–China trade relations as a reflection of the Chinese capacity to force the Japanese into concessions.[9] Here Japan is treated as an object, not a subject.

Yet, the other approach basically depicts Japan's China policy as an effort to seek foreign policy autonomy. One study, for example, argues that the decision to enter into the LT Trade agreement (Chapter 5) arose from the Japanese determination to pursue a more independent foreign policy. It states, 'The Japanese policy-makers were willing to accept the US policy toward the PRC as a political constraint, but they were equally determined to pursue a more independent policy in the non-political issue areas, specifically in Japan's economic and cultural relations with the PRC.'[10] Another study also characterizes Japan's China policy in the postwar period as a 'search for an adjustment to the new realities of China . . . that had to be independent of American policy'.[11]

A little more aggressive interpretation along the same line of thinking says:

> The key to Japan's strategy toward China down to the Nixon Shocks was the use of pro-Beijing members of the ruling Liberal Democratic Party (LDP) to open separate channels to the mainland, while simultaneously having the leaders of the party take pro-Taiwan positions in order to placate the Americans. . . .
>
> . . . this strategy was one of the most skillfully executed foreign policies pursued by Japan in the postwar era–a clever, covert adaptation by Japan to the Cold War and a good example of Japan's essentially neo-mercantilist foreign policy.[12]

Both of these two approaches in the western writings basically treat the Japanese government as a unitary actor in Japan's conduct of China policy.

---

[7] Nathan Newby White, *An Analysis of Japan's China Policy Under the Liberal Democratic Party, 1955–1970* (Ph.D. Dissertation, University of California, Berkeley, 1971), pp. 665, 668.

[8] Donald C. Hellmann, 'Japan and China: Competitors in a Multipolar World?' in Priscilla Clapp and Morton H. Halperin (eds.) *United States–Japanese Relations: The 1970s* (Cambridge: Harvard University Press, 1974), p. 173.

[9] David G. Brown, 'Chinese Economic Leverage in Sino-Japanese Relations', *Asian Survey*, 12 (1972); Chae-Jin Lee, 'The Politics of Sino-Japanese Trade Relations', *Pacific Affairs*, 42 (1969).

[10] Alexander C. Yang, *The Policy-Making Process in Japan's Policy Toward The People's Republic of China: The Making of The Liao–Takasaki Trade Agreement* (Ph.D. Dissertation, Columbia University, 1969), p. 148.

[11] Wolf Mendl, *Issues in Japan's China Policy* (London: MacMillan, 1978), p. 123.

[12] Chalmers Johnson, 'The Patterns of Japanese Relations with China, 1952–1982', *Pacific Affairs*, 59 (1986), p. 405.

Under this assumption, the Japanese government is portrayed either as a passive actor conforming to the external constraints, or as an independent actor determined to pursue its autonomy despite the external constraints. But which is the true picture?

This study argues that neither picture is true; both of them simplify the relationship between the government and non-governmental actors and fail to take into account the overall complex structure in which Japan's China policy evolved. One is often tempted to interpret international developments from the standpoint of governmental policy *post factum*. But this does not mean that real forces causing particular developments are always governmental. This study does not subscribe to the notion that Japan's pursuit of China trade resulted from coherent governmental initiatives. Instead it highlights three distinct foreign policy orientations of postwar Japan, and the rise of Japanese non-governmental actors as chief initiators of Japan–China trade. The combination of these two sets of factors gave birth to the pluralistic structure of Japan's trade relations with China, which was the key to Japan's flexible response.

To further clarify this analytical perspective, overviews of the three foreign policy orientations, and of the pluralistic structure of Japan's trade relations with China are next in order.

1.3. THREE FOREIGN POLICY ORIENTATIONS

The way that World War II ended in the Pacific proved conducive to the United States virtually monopolizing the power to mould a new Japan. When the United States contemplated the idea of constructing a postwar world order with a sustained US–Soviet cooperation and a stable and democratic China as its central components, it thought that the world would be better off if Japan were converted into a demilitarized and neutralist dwarf. The legacy of Japanese aggression to China and the Pacific War was playing a vital role in this conceptualization of Japan's status in the postwar international system. The 1946 Constitution, which in its Article 9 prohibits Japan from possessing any land, sea, and air forces for purposes of settling international disputes and thus is commonly known as the Peace Constitution, reflected such a principle.

The world, however, witnessed the proclamation of the Truman Doctrine and the Marshall Plan in 1947, and saw the outbreak of the Cold War between the United States and the Soviet Union in the European theatre. The eruption of the Korean War in 1950 convinced the United States of the Moscow–Beijing monolith, and the United States and China fought a war in Korea. The Cold War thus developed into a world-wide phenomenon engulfing Asia, with Japan being redefined by George Kennan as one of the five power centres in the world, on top of the two superpowers, Great Britain and Germany.[13] The legacy of the Pacific War was thus overshadowed by the new postwar realities, and Japan was now to be converted into a US stronghold in Asia.

These shifting American occupation policies gave rise to three distinct foreign policy orientations among Japanese political élites, respectively advocating 'compliance' with the United States, 'autonomy' *vis-à-vis* the United States but within the framework of Pax Americana, and 'independence' from American control.

The diplomatic orientation of 'collaboration' with the United States was an expression of determination to live in Pax Americana and to regenerate war-torn Japan with a minimum level of armament. Prime Minister Yoshida Shigeru, who laid the groundwork for the 'collaboration' policy which thus came to be commonly known as the Yoshida Doctrine, was reluctant to revise the Peace Constitution, but complied with the US Cold War strategy and agreed to light rearmament.

Two political forces opposed Yoshida's realism from two different ends. One group argued for the revision of the Peace Constitution and the full-fledged rearmament of Japan, while the other committed itself to the cause of the Peace Constitution and attacked Yoshida's pro-US stance which they thought was instrumental in reinstating prewar elements of militarism and authoritarianism in Japan's domestic politics. The former assumed the 'autonomy' orientation, while the latter advanced the 'independence' line.

We will now examine these three policy orientations and the place of China in them in more detail.

1.3.1. Collaboration with the United States

The collaboration line, as laid out by Yoshida Shigeru, aimed at Japan's postwar recovery and development within Pax Americana, i.e., the international order of peace and prosperity led by the United States. Yoshida resisted American pressure for rearmament in his famous meeting with John F. Dulles in late January 1951, arguing that Japan's economic capability did not allow it. If Japan embarked on full-fledged rearmament, Yoshida insisted, social unrest would ensue which the communist forces would be tempted to take advantage of, Asian countries would strongly oppose it, and elements of prewar militarism might regain their power in Japanese society.[14]

Yoshida, however, was not an advocate of disarmament. His resistance to rearmament was an essential part of his overall policy to pursue Japan's national interests under the given circumstances, which he thought would be

[13] George F. Kennan, *Memoirs 1925–1950* (Boston: Little, Brown, 1967), p. 359.
[14] Ministry of Foreign Affairs, 'Daresu-komon Honichi ni Kansuru Ken' [On the Japan Visit by Mr. Dulles] (5 January 1951), Foreign Ministry Archive, Microfilm B'-0009.

best realized by the basic policy of collaboration with the United States. For Yoshida, therefore, the total disarmament of Japan was unrealistic under the reality of the Cold War. He knew that it would be inevitable to compromise with the US demand for rearmament, and thus proposed to Dulles in early February 1951 to set up security forces with 50,000 troops. These came into existence in August 1951, further developing into the Self Defense Forces in July 1954.

Of course, the United States was not totally happy with Yoshida's reluctance about rearmament, but was more concerned about possible consequences of the autonomy orientation and the independence line gaining weight. To some extent, these two diplomatic orientations were both motivated by anti-US nationalism, although the directions in which they discharged their nationalism were completely opposite, with the former advocating traditional nationalist goals such as full-fledged rearmament and the latter advancing pro-Soviet/China pacifism. The consequences of either of these policy lines would have been devastating for US strategy in Asia. Thus, the interests of the United States and the Yoshida administration converged (for a discussion on the place of China in this equation, see Chapter 2).

As seen below, the collaboration line was challenged by succeeding administrations under Hatoyama Ichiro, Ishibashi Tanzan, and Kishi Nobusuke. However, it became firmly rooted in Japanese diplomacy under the leadership of Prime Minister Ikeda Hayato who formed the cabinet from July 1960 to November 1964. Ikeda's assertive economic policies represented by his income-doubling plan would have been impossible without close economic relations with the United States. In this spirit, Ikeda had criticized Hatoyama's policy of normalizing diplomatic relations with the Soviet Union as 'dual diplomacy', and opposed the revision of the Japan–US Security Treaty by Kishi by arguing that Japan had neither defence nor economic capabilities to seek an 'equal partnership' with the United States.[15]

As seen in Chapter 3, the United States did not express great concern about Ikeda's China policy concerning LT Trade, which perhaps reflected a US trust in Ikeda's collaboration orientation. For Ikeda's high-growth policy, the meaning of China trade was almost nil. Ikeda did not have the intention to approach China in the context of seeking diplomatic autonomy, either. Ikeda looked at China from a long-term perspective, outside of the framework of collaboration with the United States. Ikeda's attitude toward China was that of a natural posture, which formed a sharp contrast to the cases of the autonomy advocates who tended to regard China as a target of opportunity from which to gain short-term political points.

---

[15] Hiwatari Yumi, *Sengo-seiji to Nichibei-kankei [Postwar Politics and Japan–US Relations]* (Tokyo: Tokyo-daigaku Shuppan-kai, 1990).

1.3.2. Autonomy vis-à-vis the US and 'Autonomous Diplomacy'

The advocates of diplomatic autonomy aspired to achieve something which was not a derivative of US strategy. They, however, did not have any intention to circumvent or outdo the United States, nor to challenge the logic of the Cold War or Pax Americana. The primary motives were to satisfy their sense of nationalism and to oppose the policy of collaboration with the United States in domestic politics. They were not much concerned about the implications of their policies for the state of the Cold War or Pax Americana; the US-centred international order was so dominant and was far beyond Japan's control anyway. Therefore, the policy outcome of the autonomy orientation was simply the expansion of the margins of autonomy within Pax Americana, stopping short of affecting the prevailing structure of international relations.

The autonomy orientation emerged from political resistance to the collaboration line of Yoshida Shigeru, and advocated 'autonomous defence' by full-fledged rearmament with the revision of the Constitution, an 'equal partnership' with the United States with the revision of the Japan–US Security Treaty, and the expansion of the 'diplomatic horizon' to the Soviet Union and Asia.

During his tenure as Prime Minister (November 1954 to December 1956), Hatoyama Ichiro, strongly motivated by his sense of political rivalry against Yoshida, attempted to revise the Peace Constitution to achieve rearmament, and to normalize relations with the Soviet Union and China to modify Yoshida's unilateral dependence on the United States. In the general elections in February 1955, Hatoyama proclaimed that he would seek the revision of the Constitution if he received enough support, but failed in gaining the two-thirds majority needed for the revision. When Hatoyama sent his Foreign Minister Shigemitsu Mamoru to Washington in August 1958, Hatoyama conveyed his request for the withdrawal of the American troops from Japan and the revision of the Japan–US Security Treaty, but in vain.[16]

Obviously, diplomatic normalization with China was much more popular among the Japanese than that with the Soviet Union as a diplomatic agenda. The former, however, would have meant a major modification of the international order in Asia led by the United States. As it turned out, diplomatic normalization with the Soviet Union in October 1956 was Hatoyama's only achievement from his diplomatic agenda seeking autonomy, which was a telling indication that Japan's search for diplomatic autonomy was possible only within the confines of Pax Americana. The United States had diplomatic relations with the Soviet Union, and therefore did not oppose Japan's normalization *per se*, although it was concerned about the possibility of Japan's unnecessary concessions on the issue of the Northern Territories.[17] Naturally,

[16] *Ibid.*, p. 121.
[17] Tanaka Takahiko, *Nisso Kokko-kaifuku no Shiteki-kenkyu [A Historical Study of Japan–Soviet Diplomatic Normalization]* (Tokyo: Yuhikaku, 1993).

the Yoshida group was strongly opposed to normalization with the Soviet Union, and the 82 members of the Yoshida group boycotted the National Diet when the joint communiqué to establish normalization with the Soviet Union was ratified in November.

In December 1956, Ishibashi Tanzan succeeded Hatoyama. Ishibashi was a strong advocate of alignment with China as a key to Asian stability. This perspective was of course in conflict with the logic of the Cold War, which encouraged Ishibashi in later years to advance the concept of a 'peace alliance among Japan, China, the United States and the Soviet Union'. As a Prime Minister, however, even Ishibashi knew the tenacity of the Cold War constraints, and simply wished to advance Japan–China trade without endangering basic political relations with the United States. The Ishibashi cabinet, however, was short lived because of Ishibashi's illness, descending from power in February 1957. Ishibashi's peculiar perspective on international relations became much more invigorated in his dedication to the promotion of Japan–China relations after retiring from Prime Minister.

The Kishi cabinet (February 1957 to July 1960) stressed the invigoration of Asian diplomacy and the revision of the Japan–US Security Treaty as major foreign policy goals. Kishi did not look to China in a non-ideological fashion as Ishibashi did. This was because Kishi had the intention to foster Japan's relations with Asia as a leverage with which to establish an 'equal partnership' with the United States.[18] In order for this strategy to be accepted by the United States, approaching China was out of the question and appealing his anti-communist stance in Asia was more effective. It was with these considerations in mind that Kishi visited South East Asia in May 1957, his first overseas trip as Prime Minister, prior to his trip to the United States in June. Specifically, Kishi cherished the idea of a South East Asia Development Fund as the central component of his strategy, attempting to solicit necessary funds from the United States 'under Japanese leadership'. Here lay the true significance of his making trips to South East Asia and the United States 'as a package deal'.[19] The time was not yet ripe, however, for Kishi's ambition to be supported by the United States.

Closely related to this Asian diplomacy was Kishi's desire for an 'equal partnership' with the United States, or what Kishi himself liked to call a 'new era' in Japan–US relations. Kishi's aspiration for autonomy *vis-à-vis* the United States was demonstrated by his eagerness to revise the Japan–US Security Treaty. For the advocates of diplomatic autonomy, the security treaty signed in 1951 had several flaws: there was no explicit stipulation of US obligation to defend Japan, it did not specify an expiration date or stipulations for

---

[18] Kishi Nobusuke, *Kishi Nobusuke Kaikoroku: Hoshu Godo to Anpo Kaitei [Memoirs of Kishi Nobusuke: Unification of Conservative Parties and Revision of Japan–US Security Treaty]* (Tokyo: Kosaido Shuppan, 1983), p. 312.

[19] *Ibid.*, p. 321.

revision and termination, and it allowed for an intervention by US forces in Japan's domestic unrest.

Initially, the United States had been reluctant to revise the security treaty, but eventually accepted Kishi's requests judging that it was important for the stability of the relationship to accommodate Japan's aspiration for autonomy.[20] The revision, therefore, was a reflection of the American generosity as a 'big brother', rather than a result of the Japanese aspiration of an equal partnership. Kishi later recalled himself: 'Thank God, the United States accepted such revisions.'[21] In short, Pax Americana was stable.

When Pax Americana was strong, Japan's pursuit of diplomatic autonomy did not affect the structure of the East Asian international order very much. As Pax Americana began to transform itself toward the end of the 1960s, however, Japan's autonomous efforts began to become an integral part of the regional system. We will call Japan's aspiration for diplomatic autonomy in such a new age 'autonomous diplomacy'.

This process of transformation had two aspects. First, by the time Sato Eisaku formed his cabinet in November 1964, the rivalry between the collaboration school and the autonomy school became less of an issue in domestic politics, with a generational change in the political leadership and with the steady economic growth of Japan. Second, as Japan became economically affluent, Japan's rise as an economic power became an important source of the transformation of Pax Americana. As the economic gap between Japan and the United States became narrower, Japan's importance in the international system rose with the substance of Japan's autonomous diplomacy becoming an important constituent of an international order.

The fundamental defect of this diplomacy was, as explored in detail in Chapter 7 which examines Japanese diplomacy in the 1970s, that Japan's aspiration was not backed by its readiness to become a full-fledged political player of regional politics. Japan's diplomatic agenda basically continued to be conditioned by peculiar constraints originating from its domestic politics and political norms of non-military pacifism.

Diplomacy by Sato Eisaku embodied such a transition in postwar Japanese diplomacy. In the initial phase of the Sato administration (November 1964 to July 1972), Prime Minister Sato Eisaku exhibited a forward-looking posture toward China (Chapter 3). Also, Sato vigorously promoted Japan's role in Asian economic development, as exemplified by his commitment to the Ministerial Conference for the Economic Development of South East Asia and the Asian Development Bank, both of which were inaugurated in 1966. This could be explained as an expression of his aspiration of diplomatic autonomy *vis-à-vis* the United States, which typically sought to expand the margins of Japan's Asian diplomacy within the confines of Pax Americana but did

---

[20] Hiwatari, *Sengo-seiji to Nichibei-kankei*, pp. 160–63.
[21] Kishi, *Kishi Nobusuke Kaikoroku*, p. 567.

not have a significant impact on the nature of the dominant environment in the region.

In the second half of Sato's tenure, however, Sato's diplomacy began to have regional implications, although in the mind of Sato himself the attainment of diplomatic autonomy itself still continued to motivate him. The most illustrative case was Sato's commitment to the reversion of the administrative rights of Okinawa, which Sato himself characterized as a central component of his autonomous diplomacy.[22] The reversion was promised in the Sato–Nixon joint communiqué in November 1969, but only in exchange for Sato's commitment to the 'Korea clause' and the 'Taiwan clause' stating a linkage between the security of Japan, on the one hand, and that of South Korea and Taiwan, on the other (Chapters 3 and 6). In short, the realization of Sato's autonomous diplomacy in the reversion of Okinawa promoted Japan's involvement in the security environment of East Asia.

It became all the more apparent under the Tanaka Kakuei administration (July 1972 to December 1974) that Japan's diplomatic response would have significant implications for a regional order in the Asia-Pacific. Normalization of diplomatic relations with China was the most conspicuous case, as examined in Chapter 6. For many Japanese both in the policy-making circle and outside, China was important in demonstrating that Japan had a diplomacy of its own, and Japan was not necessarily inspired by the calculation of strategic interests as was the case with the United States and China. Nonetheless, Japan–China diplomatic normalization was a major event affecting the configuration of major power relations in East Asia.

The same pattern was more or less repeated in negotiations over the Japan–China Peace and Friendship Treaty signed in August 1978. The Miki Takeo cabinet (December 1974 to December 1976) was eager to promote the negotiations but was bogged down in the handling of the political scandals of Tanaka Kakuei. Chinese domestic politics was also in flux in the same period. During the tenure of Fukuda Takeo (December 1976 to December 1978), however, Deng Xiaoping came back to power in July 1977 and the Chinese leadership became eager to conclude the treaty, to which Fukuda responded swiftly. Fukuda's preference, however, was to conclude the treaty as part of his 'omni-directional' diplomacy, trying to stay away from the dynamism of the US–China–Soviet strategic triangle, thus in effect executing an autonomous diplomacy of a kind. Fukuda carried out the same type of diplomacy toward Indo-China, as seen in Chapter 7.

This autonomous diplomacy reflected a Japanese hope to remain independent of the military-strategic imperative of international relations. This propensity was a reflection of the peculiar pattern of Japan's postwar domestic politics where military-strategic issues as well as those related to World

---

[22] Kamiya Fuji, *Sengo-shi no Naka-no Nichi-bei Kankei [Japan–US Relations in the Postwar History]* (Tokyo: Shincho-sha, 1989), pp. 124–37.

War II became extremely divisive issues between the pro-US conservatives and the pro-Socialist progressives, often paralysing a decision-making process. In this context, a policy to stay away from strategic-military dimensions of regional politics was not only popular for many Japanese but was politically safe for political leaders.

To the extent that Japan was not ready to become a full-fledged political player, however, Japanese diplomacy had to continue to rely on the United States at the very basic level of national security. Japan's autonomous diplomacy, therefore, was not a quest to become an independent security player: to the contrary, Japan had the luxury of indulging itself in autonomous diplomacy as long as it maintained its basic security relationship with the United States. Such a diplomacy, therefore, was often a reflection of Japan's aspiration for a bigger political role in areas where there were no major conflict of interest, or in such a way as to cause no major conflict, with the United States. Paradoxically, the success of such autonomous diplomacy depended much on successful policy coordination with the United States.

1.3.3. Independence from Pax Americana

In clear contrast to the autonomous diplomatic orientation, the independence advocates vigorously strove to dissociate Japan from Pax Americana. They advocated the abrogation of the Japan–US security and political ties, and called for closer ties with the Soviet Union and China.

The fundamental motivating factor of the independence orientation was the conviction that the United States was piloting Japan into a 'reverse course', particularly after the Korean War, facilitating the reinstatement of the very prewar elements in the Japanese society that it had once pledged to renounce. They, therefore, felt that Japan was being betrayed by the United States, and it would need to become independent from the United States in the true sense of the world. Ironically, the 1946 Peace Constitution, which was imposed by the United States when it was still mindful of the prewar elements of militarism, became their bible.

Their motive, therefore, was not so much to side with the Socialist camp as to achieve independence from American control. In fact, the independence proponents refused to recognize the reality of the Cold War by calling it a 'fiction' fabricated by the United States. It was against this backdrop that 'neutrality' became their political ideology. Approaching the Soviet Union and China was not thought to be contradictory to neutrality, to the extent that it was considered effective in freeing themselves from Pax Americana.

The weakness of this line of thinking was that it lacked a realistic understanding of Japan's position in the postwar international system. Neutrality was not a well thought-out diplomatic strategy, but was just a slogan that allowed them to escape from the contradiction between their refusal to deal with the United States and the reality that the United States was almost omnipotent in directing the future course of Japan. The independence line, therefore, had no chance of becoming a central diplomatic orientation of postwar Japan.

But it had some appeal to the public sentiment. An example is a massive popular demonstration against Kishi who signed a revised security treaty with the United States in 1960. The independence advocates interpreted the revised security treaty as entangling Japan further in Pax Americana. Their political opposition was combined with a popular anti-US feeling among the public, culminating in unprecedented anti-government mass demonstrations in Japan. As seen, Kishi's move to revise the 1951 security treaty was inspired by his aspiration for diplomatic autonomy which was motivated by nationalism. The fact that this autonomy nationalism was attacked by the independence nationalism signified a sharp division in Japan's postwar nationalism under the Cold War.

The advocates of the independence orientation were the most outspoken proponents of Japan–China cooperation. Interestingly enough, their actions, in combination with those by the autonomy advocates, gave rise to a pluralistic structure in Japan–China trade before diplomatic normalization. As seen in Chapter 2, they had begun national movements to promote trade and cultural exchanges with China in the late 1940s. In the 1960s, the independence proponents were the primary architects of Friendship Trade, which existed in tandem with LT Trade promoted by the autonomy advocates. For both of these groups, a China which was going its own way was an attractive country, albeit for different diplomatic reasons.

I.4. STRUCTURE AND MOTIVES OF JAPAN'S CHINA TRADE

1.4.1. Pluralistic Structure of Trade Relations with China

The different diplomatic orientations among the Japanese actors as examined above were important sources of a pluralistic structure of Japan's trade relations with China before diplomatic normalization. First, the difference between the collaboration orientation and the autonomy orientation held by Japanese Prime Ministers affected their basic stance toward China. Prime Ministers who were motivated by the political desire for diplomatic autonomy *vis-à-vis* the United States tended to see China as an important target of their diplomacy, with the single exception of Kishi Nobusuke who looked to non-communist Asia to satisfy his diplomatic aspirations.

Second, the difference between the autonomy orientation and the independence orientation among the non-governmental pro-China actors gave rise to a complex structure of China trade in the private sector as well as in the relationship between the government and the non-governmental sector. As seen in the following section in detail, many pro-China Japanese were motivated primarily by deep pro-China feelings and a sense of reciprocity which transcended political ideologies or diplomatic orientations. Nonetheless, they were not necessarily politically homogeneous, gradually splitting into two distinct groupings in trade dealings with China. The most important divisive factor was indeed their difference over diplomatic orientations, which in turn affected their relationships with both the Japanese government and the Chinese government.

Those pro-China Japanese who were motivated by the ambition of diplomatic autonomy included Matsumura Kenzo, Murata Shozo, Takasaki Tatsunosuke, and Okazaki Kaheita, who joined the Japan Association for the Promotion of International Trade (JAPIT) in the 1950s and promoted LT/MT Trade in the 1960s (Chapters 2 and 5). As argued in Chapter 3, it was easier for the Japanese government to establish a pattern of 'division of labour' with these pro-China actors in the conduct of China trade, which constituted one tier of the pluralistic structure of Japan's trade relations with China.

In contrast, those pro-China actors desiring to gain diplomatic independence from US control often complied with Chinese political demands and politically confronted the Japanese government. In China trade, they gathered under the Japan–China Trade Promotion Association (JCTPA) in the 1950s, and gradually extended their influence into the JAPIT, too. Friendship Trade was constructed by this group of pro-China actors, and together with LT/MT Trade constituted the second tier of the pluralistic structure in Japan–China trade in the 1960s (Chapters 4 and 5).

In the 1970s, the independence advocates were quite baffled by the US–China *rapprochement*. They welcomed subsequent diplomatic normalization between Japan and China which in fact had been the major political goal in their movement to promote China trade. Nonetheless, they could not deal with the political situation effectively where Japan's diplomatic normalization with China became compatible with US–China *rapprochement*, which in the previous decades were mutually exclusive in their political agenda. In the 1970s, therefore, their political power shrank rapidly.

For the proponents of the autonomy orientation, on the other hand, these two sets of Japan's bilateral relations were mutually compatible. For them, Japan should have pursued such a diplomacy a long time ago. Therefore, it was natural for them to establish a close relationship with the Japanese government in the conduct of China trade in the post-normalization phase. Promoters of LT/MT Trade in fact made a transition into the Japan–China Association of Economy and Trade (JCAET) created with the support of the Ministry of International Trade and Industry (MITI) in November 1972 (Chapter 6).

Beneath these diplomatic orientations, Japan's non-governmental actors in China trade were motivated by strong pro-China feelings. While differences over diplomatic orientations were important in producing the pluralistic structure in Japan's trade relations with China, they alone cannot explain why these actors were so dedicated to the promotion of China trade. Their pro-China feelings were deep-rooted and genuine, giving rise to a norm of reciprocity in their conduct of China trade.

1.4.2. Reciprocity in Japan's China Trade

Reciprocity has been talked about quite often, sometimes very loosely, in the fields of political science, economics, law, and sociology, by both scholars and practitioners.[23] Robert Keohane sees 'specific reciprocity' and 'diffuse reciprocity' as important principles for eliciting cooperation in international relations. In specific reciprocity, such as in economic exchange, the benefits to be exchanged are specifically set, and obligation is defined in terms of rights and duties. Diffuse reciprocity, by contrast, involves conforming to generally accepted standards of behaviour and entails a general sense of obligation. For international cooperation, diffuse reciprocity is more important because 'specific reciprocity alone cannot account for voluntary cooperation'.[24]

What Keohane calls specific reciprocity corresponds in the case of Japan–China relations to the practice of exchanging goods in such a way as to reflect economic compatibility between the two nations. One person who produced a most concrete result in the 1950s was Inayama Yoshihiro, then managing director of Yawata Iron and Steel Co. The steel industry had been suffering from recession in 1957, and Inayama signed a long-term steel barter trade agreement with China on 26 February 1958. It stipulated that Japan would export 10 million pounds sterling ($27.7 million) of steel in exchange for Chinese iron ore and coal from 1958 to 1962.[25] This agreement, which was aborted along with all other trade transactions by the Chinese after the Nagasaki flag incident in May 1958, reflected the economic compatibility between Japan and China. Over time, Inayama came to believe that trade based on this compatibility would contribute to Chinese economic development, too. His vision was revived twenty years later in the 1978 Long Term Trade Agreement, of which Inayama was a chief architect.

The analysis below shows that other forms of expanded Japan–China trade were also pursued in such a way as to reflect the objective economic conditions of both countries. Indeed, all of the overall trade agreements concluded

---

[23] For a brief discussion on this, see Robert O. Keohane, 'Reciprocity in International Relations', *International Organization*, 40 (1986), pp. 1–5.

[24] Ibid., p. 4.

[25] Inayama Yoshihiro, *Watashi no Showa Tekko-shi [My Showa History of Steel]* (Tokyo: Toyo Keizai Shinpo-sha, 1986), pp. 100–109; *Kokusai Boeki*, 23 April 1974.

between the two countries, from the First Japan–China Private Trade Agreement of 1952 to the Long Term Trade Agreement of 1978, embodied reciprocity in this sense. The basic pattern was that Japan exported industrial inputs to China in exchange for natural resources and agricultural products.

A sense of obligation by pro-China Japanese, however, went beyond the economic exchange embodied by economic compatibility. Diffuse reciprocity was demonstrated in Japan–China relations as a sense of obligation that induced spontaneous cooperation. A deep commitment to Chinese economic reconstruction was unmistakable among many pro-China Japanese. There were three basic elements in this attitude: a belief in 'Asianism', personal experiences with China before and after the war, and the sense of guilt over the war calamities Japan had inflicted on China.

Asianism as a motive was most typically embodied in Ishibashi Tanzan and Matsumura Kenzo, pro-China politicians who laid a groundwork for LT Trade (Chapter 5). On 4 June 1959, Ishibashi wrote to Zhou Enlai that Japan and China should act in concert with each other to protect peace in Asia and to promote world peace. Ishibashi stated before his trip to China in September 1959 that Japan and China were destined to hold hands with each other in the future.[26] Matsumura Kenzo was convinced that Asia ought to be united and that Japan should act as an Asian country to enhance Asian unity and to lead Asia into a new age of prosperity. This belief in Asianism even outweighed the ideological differences between Japan and China. Matsumura believed that a driving force behind the Chinese revolution was not communist ideology but Chinese nationalism.[27]

Matsumura's belief in Asianism was shared by his political followers. Tagawa Seiichi, a pro-China LDP politician and Matsumura's protégé, stated in an interview that he shared the same view on Asia with Matsumura.[28] Furui Yoshimi recalled that without Matsumura's influence, he would not have entered into China trade.[29] He believed that Asia was one, and went so far as to state that the ultimate goal of Japan–China cooperation was to prevent war between the United States and the Soviet Union.[30]

In March 1970, Matsumura Kenzo, hoping to make Fujiyama Aiichiro (LDP Dietman) his heir in Japan–China relations, took Fujiyama to China. Fujiyama had assumed the position of an advisor to the pro-Beijing Asian-African Problem Study Group established in 1965 (Chapter 3). Fujiyama

[26] Ishibashi Tanzan, *Ishibashi Tanzan Zenshu, Dai-14-kan [A Complete Work of Ishibashi Tanzan, Vol. 14]* (Tokyo: Toyo Keizai Shinpo-sha, 1970), pp. 425, 431.

[27] Matsumura Kenzo, 'Watashi no Ajia-kan: Nitchu Kankei wo Chushin-ni' [My View on Asia: In Relation to Japan–China Relations], *Shiso*, 463 (1963), pp. 152–6.

[28] Interview with Tagawa Seiichi, Lower House Dietman, 22 September 1986 (hereafter cited as Tagawa Interview).

[29] Furui Yoshimi, *Nitchu Juhachi-nen: Seijika no Kiseki to Tenbo [Eighteen Years of Japan–China: the Past and the Future of a Politician]* (Tokyo: Makino Shuppan, 1978), p. 71.

[30] Furui Yoshimi, 'Nitchu wa Korekara ga Hajimarida' [Now is the Beginning of Japan–China Relations], *Sekai*, 488 (1986), pp. 172–3.

revisited China in February 1971 with a Memorandum Trade delegation, apparently thinking to himself that he would assume Matsumura's role in Japan–China relations. After diplomatic normalization, he succeeded Ishibashi Tanzan as chairman of the JAPIT in June 1973. Fujiyama also shared Matsumura's view of Asia; he insisted at the time of diplomatic normalization that the real issue for Japan and China in the post-normalization decade was how to attain Asian peace and stability, which was a responsibility of Japan and China and not of the United States or the Soviet Union.[31] Utsunomiya Tokuma was a political protégé of Ishibashi Tanzan, and in 1967 he assumed the vice-chairmanship of the JAPIT at the urging of Ishibashi. He also advocated as early as 1961 that Japan and China should cooperate for the maintenance of peace and the prevention of an arms race between the two superpowers.[32]

The same belief in Asianism was also shared by such non-politicians as Okazaki Kaheita and Watanabe Yaeji, the central promoters of LT/MT Trade. Okazaki believed that Asia should become the third force to prevent a clash between the United States and the Soviet Union; Japan should cooperate with Asian countries, China among others, for Asian peace and prosperity; Japan and China should contribute to the development of all Asia, which in turn would become a basis for world peace.[33]

In essence, this belief in Asianism contradicted a perception that China was a source of instability in the region. Thus, Asianism became a central factor that compelled pro-China individuals to act independently of the security constraints imposed on Japan–China relations.

Personal encounters with China both before and after the end of the war were another factor which turned several Japanese toward bilateral economic cooperation. The case of Takasaki Tatsunosuke presents the most illustrative example. Takasaki became vice-president of Manchu Heavy Industry in March 1941, succeeding Ayukawa Yoshisuke as president at the end of 1942. As the war ended, Takasaki's knowledge of the economy of north east China was utilized by three different occupation authorities for which Takasaki served: the Soviets from August 1945, the Chinese Communists from April 1946, and the Chinese Nationalists from May 1946. Takasaki was bewildered by the plundering of the Soviet Army and the corruption of the Nationalist Army, but was impressed with the discipline, order and high spirits of the Chinese Revolutionary Army.[34] These experiences of Takasaki in north east China from March 1941 until October 1947, when he was sent by the

---

31 Fujiyama Aiichiro, 'Pekin Kosho no Kiso' [Basis of Negotiations in Beijing], *Chuo Koron*, 87 (1972), pp. 147–46.

32 Utsunomiya Tokuma, 'Nitchu Fukko to Kyokuto no Heiwa' [Japan–China Normalization and Peace in the Far East], *Sekai*, 189 (1961), p. 76.

33 Okazaki Kaheita, *Watashi no Kiroku [My Records]* (Tokyo: Toho Shoten, 1979), p. 276.

34 Takasaki Tatsunosuke, *Manshu no Shuen [The Collapse of Manchuria]* (Tokyo: Jitsugyo no Nihon-sha, 1953).

Nationalist authority to Japan for the purpose of investigating the reparation issue, provide the key explanation for his active role in Japan–China trade in the postwar era. He wrote in 1953 that, when he heard the news that economic reconstruction in China was progressing rapidly, he felt as if his child left in China was being raised very soundly.[35]

Some other businessmen also had prewar contacts with China. Murata Shozo, the first chairman of the JAPIT, had stayed in China from 1901 to 1910, working for the Osaka Lines. He accompanied Sun Yatsen on a merchant vessel provided by his company when Sun left Hong Kong for political exile in 1913.[36] Okazaki Kaheita also had prewar contacts with China as a student, a bank officer in Shanghai, and an official of the embassy office in Shanghai.[37]

For these people, however, postwar encounters with Zhou Enlai also had an important impact on their careers in Japan–China trade. When Murata visited postwar China for the first time in 1955, he was still concerned about the nature of communism in China. But conversations with Zhou Enlai dispelled Murata's worries. In fact, some of Murata's views on the nature of the Chinese political system, as recounted after his return from China, quite resemble those explained by Zhou. For example, Zhou told Murata that political movements would rise out of the people's will, and that China was now devoted to national reconstruction.[38] Murata wrote in November 1955 that China was now devoting its whole energy to national reconstruction and that communism was just one form of politics for the welfare of people.[39] Okazaki Kaheita himself was quite influenced by his encounters with Zhou Enlai. Okazaki looked up to Zhou as his 'preceptor of life'. He wrote at the passing of Zhou: 'I was attracted by the clean and noble personality of Premier Zhou and came to admire him as a man of humanity rather than as a respectable Premier.'[40] Zhou's personal charm and his enthusiasm for the development of China even reinforced a belief in Asianism shared by pro-China Japanese.

The commitment to Chinese economic development was strengthened by a feeling of guilt for the war calamities which Japan had caused China. Almost every Japanese devoted to Chinese economic reconstruction was motivated by this consciousness. The most typical case was Ohara Soichiro, president of Kurashiki Rayon, who was very active in arranging for export of chemical fibre plant facilities with Export–Import Bank credits in 1963 (Chapter 5).

35 *Ibid.*, preface, p. 4.
36 Murata Shozo, *Nitchu Kakehashi no Ichi-kiroku [A Record of Bridging Japan and China]* (Tokyo: Osaka Shosen Mitsui Senpaku, 1972), pp. 1, 96.
37 Okazaki Kaheita, *Owari-naki Nitchu no Tabi [Endless Journey between Japan and China]* (Tokyo: Hara Shobo, 1984).
38 Murata, *Nitchu Kakehashi no Ichi-Kiroku*, pp. 37–8.
39 Murata Shozo, 'Nitchu Kankei no Genjo wo Ureu' [Worrying about the Present Situation of Japan–China Relations], *Sekai*, 119 (1955), pp. 20–21.
40 Okazaki Kaheita, 'Shu Onrai Sori no Omoide' [Memories of Premier Zhou Enlai], *Sekai*, 364 (1976), p. 164.

He wrote that the Japanese were obliged to 'do penance' to the Chinese, who were trying to forget their resentment from the past.[41]

The motivations of the Japanese practitioners of diffuse reciprocity were thus complex. In essence, however, all these feelings transcended anti-communist political ideology, and made them distinct actors in postwar Japan–China relations. In a word, they all believed, 'red or white, China is China'.

[41] Ohara Soichiro, 'Tai-Chugoku Puranto Yushutsu ni Tsuite' [About the Plant Export to China], *Sekai*, 213 (1963), p. 107.

2
Japan–China Trade in the 1950s

The structure of Japan–China relations in the 1950s become the prototype of the developments in the following decade in two respects. First, heightened tension between the United States and China in the early 1950s structured the overall political relationship between Japan and China. In order for Japan to construct a new trade relationship with mainland China in this tense political environment, it now had to find a way to promote China trade under the strategic constraints imposed by the highly political objectives of the United States. A conflict between American strategic concerns and the extensive Japanese desire for trade with China had given rise to a specific mechanism of Japan's China trade, which proved resilient throughout the 1960s and, to a significant extent, in the post-normalization decade as well.

Second, the 1950s was the decade when Japan's China trade organizations took shape and major individuals involved in China trade emerged. Not all of these organizations and individuals survived the turbulent decades of Japan–China relations prior to normalization of diplomatic relations in 1972. Nonetheless, all the core elements sustaining the subsequent developments in Japan–China trade had emerged during the first decade after the birth of the communist regime on the China mainland. Very significantly, we can discern already in the early 1950s sources of the pluralistic structure of Japan's China trade mechanisms. Distinct channels of trade did not emerge during the 1950s, but it is significant that the elements behind the two institutionalized channels of Japan–China trade in the 1960s, i.e., Friendship Trade and LT Trade, were already emerging well before their initiation.

In the following sections, we will give an overview of the new patterns of Japan–China relations after World War II, which provided the basic political framework for the specific forms of bilateral trade arrangements. This will be followed by an analysis of the structure and process of Japan–China trade in the 1950s.

2.1. YOSHIDA DOCTRINE AND CHINA

The 1945–1952 occupation of Japan by the United States completely remoulded postwar Japan into a non-military country in the US-led postwar order of Pax Americana. To Prime Minister Yoshida Shigeru, who signed the San Francisco Peace Treaty in September 1951 and thus paved the way for postwar Japanese diplomacy, this international order was given and beyond the control of Japan. Under these circumstances, Yoshida's choice was to pursue a road to Japan's postwar recovery and prosperity by taking advantage of the dominant Pax Americana, which motivated him to cut the military burden to the minimum.[1] This basic policy came to be known as the Yoshida Doctrine, representing the 'collaboration' school of postwar Japanese diplomacy. The Yoshida Doctrine, therefore, was nothing other than a realistic choice measured against the predominant Pax Americana. It was natural, therefore, that Yoshida's policies were affected by the international order surrounding Japan of which the United States was a primary architect.

It is important to recognize, however, that Yoshida's China policy on the basis of the collaboration thinking was not identical with that of the United States. If they appeared similar, this was because Pax Americana was so predominant. Yoshida later recalled that 'we had been defeated in a reckless war which placed Japan under US occupation, and then pursued a road to recovery and reconstruction. Japan's postwar international standing, i.e., its position as a member of the free world, was determined by this fact.' He then continued that to promote contact with China was to 'play the fool who willingly disturbs the balance of power of international politics'.[2] At the same time, however, he also contended in 1957 that 'America has not come near to understanding China truly', and that 'almost all the postwar US policies toward China were a failure'.[3]

Indeed, the signing of the Japan–US Security Treaty and the non-military path of postwar Japan derived from Yoshida's realism. With China, too, Yoshida attempted to cope realistically, trying to remain flexible in areas where China was important for Japan while refusing to deal with it otherwise. Yoshida thought that the policy of collaboration with the United States was the basis for pursuing Japan's national interests. China, however, was also an important country for Japan's national interests as perceived by Yoshida, where lay a source of Yoshida's agony.

In fact, Yoshida thought that for the success of the Yoshida Doctrine, trade with China would be indispensable. Yoshida told an American CBS newsman in 1949, 'I don't care whether China is red or green. China is a natural market, and it has become necessary for Japan to think about markets.' In May 1949, he told the Diet that trade with China, whether communist or not, was indispensable to Japan's regeneration.[4] In 1951, after the outbreak of the Korean War, Yoshida wrote:

[1] John W. Dower, *Empire and Aftermath: Yoshida Shigeru and the Japanese Experiences, 1878–1954* (Cambridge: Harvard University Press, 1979); Michael Schaller, *The American Occupation of Japan: The Origins of the Cold War in Asia* (New York: Oxford University Press, 1985), pp. 276–7, 293–4.

[2] Yoshida Shigeru, *Sekai to Nippon [The World and Japan]* (Tokyo: Bancho Shobo, 1963), pp. 144–5.

[3] Yoshida Shigeru, *Kaiso Junen, Dai-l-kan [Recollections of Ten Years, Vol. 1]* (Tokyo: Shinchosha, 1957), p. 270.

[4] Nancy Bernkopf Tucker, 'American Policy Toward Sino-Japanese Trade in the Postwar Years: Politics and Prosperity', *Diplomatic History*, 8 (1984), pp. 193–5.

In some quarters a fear is entertained that a separate peace might permanently sever Japan's trade with Red China. Red or white, China remains our next-door neighbour. Geography and economic laws will, I believe, prevail in the long run over any ideological differences and artificial trade barriers.[5]

In this context, it was almost a national consensus that Japan's economic development in the postwar era could not be achieved without opening up trade relations with mainland China. In late 1949, for instance, Inagaki Heitaro, Minister of MITI, revealed a governmental expectation that trade with China would eventually reach 25 to 30 per cent of Japan's trade with the world.[6] It may sounds like a wishful thinking in hindsight, but was not necessarily so at the time. Before the Korean War, the United States itself had not abandoned the hope to industrialize Japan with Chinese resources. Moreover, the Chinese communists themselves had sought to trade with Japan, as they told American Consul General O. Edmond Clubb in 1949.[7] It is also important to recall that before the Korean War the United States had still been pursuing a policy to 'Titonize' China, i.e., to make China independent of Soviet influence like Yugoslavia under Marshall Tito, and eventually to establish diplomatic normalization with Communist China.[8]

When the Cold War turned into a hot war in the Korean peninsula, however, Japan's realistic hope to establish substantial relations with China vanished. The policy measures the United States took to detach Japan from China included the strict imposition of the rules of the Coordinating Committee (COCOM) of the Consultative Group, the highest decision-making body of the Organization for European Economic Cooperation, and of the China Committee (CHINCOM) under the Consultative Group, which were established in the winter of 1949/50 and in the summer of 1952 respectively as forums to coordinate embargoes upon the socialist bloc and China;[9] efforts to substitute the South East Asian market for the China market;[10] and Japan's choice of Taipei over Beijing as China's legitimate government by a forced signing of the Japan–Taiwan Peace Treaty on 25 April 1952.

Yoshida's choice of Taiwan merits a brief discussion, because his decision determined the basic political framework of postwar Japan–China relations

---

5 Shigeru Yoshida, 'Japan and the Crisis in Asia', *Foreign Affairs*, 29 (1951), p. 179.

6 Tucker, 'American Policy Toward Sino-Japanese Trade in the Postwar Years', pp. 193–5.

7 Ibid., pp. 87, 192.

8 Iriye Akira, *The Cold War in Asia: A Historical Introduction* (Englewood Cliffs: Prentice-Hall, 1974).

9 Gunner Akler-Karlson, *Western Economic Warfare, 1947–1969: A Case Study in Foreign Economic Policy* (Stockholm: Almquist & Wiksell, 1968); Yasuhara Yoko, 'Amerika no Taikyosanken Kinyu Seisaku to Chugoku Boeki no Kinshi, 1945–50' [American Policy of Embargo Against the Communist Bloc and Prohibition of China Trade, 1945–50], *Kokusai Seiji*, 70 (1982); Yasuhara Yoko, *Myth of Free Trade: Cocom and Chincom, 1945–1952* (Ph.D. Dissertation, University of Wisconsin-Madison, 1984); Yasuhara Yoko, 'Japan, Communist China, and Export Controls in Asia, 1948–52', *Diplomatic History*, 10 (1986).

10 William S. Borden, *The Pacific Alliance: United States Foreign Economic Policy and Japanese Trade Recovery, 1947–1955* (Madison: University of Wisconsin Press, 1984).

until diplomatic normalization in 1972. Several historical studies now reveal that Yoshida's true intention was to keep Japan's future alternatives as wide as possible.[11] The reason Yoshida thought that he had flexibility even under the realities of the Cold War was two-fold: one derived from Yoshida's insight into Sino-Soviet relations, and the other came from a disagreement between the United States and Great Britain over their China policies.

Yoshida thought that the civilizations, national characters, and political conditions of China and the Soviet Union were mutually incompatible.[12] Before signing the Yoshida letter of 24 December 1951, which was drafted by Dulles himself and was forced upon Yoshida, therefore, Yoshida had attempted to convince Dulles that Japan could play an important role in detaching China from the control of the Soviet politburo, but to no avail.[13] Yoshida had also been encouraged by the agreement between John F. Dulles and Herbert S. Morrison (British Foreign Minister), signed on 19 June 1951, to the effect that no Chinese representative would be invited to the San Francisco Peace Conference and that it would be up to Japan to decide its own attitude toward the China question. Yoshida thus insisted to Dulles in December 1951 that he was prepared to 'begin negotiations' to 'normalize relations with the Nationalist Government within the area where it is exercising its de facto power of control', but that he wanted to postpone the question of a peace treaty until the China question was solved internationally.[14]

But the American pressure prevailed. The Yoshida letter (1951), addressed to Dulles, ended with the sentence: 'I can assure you that the Japanese government has no intention to conclude a bilateral treaty with the Communist regime in China.'[15]

It is obvious that this China policy was not identical with that of the United States. Yoshida, however, was a political realist to the backbone. He rejected any sentimental attitude toward China on the grounds that Japan's international status and its economic prosperity depended on its close relationship with the United States, in which he saw 'the balance of power in world politics'.[16] Yoshida later recalled that he had wanted to avoid a hasty decision, but that there had been no alternative to signing the peace treaty with Taipei under the given situation surrounding Japan.[17]

---

[11] Dower, *Empire and Aftermath*; William J. Sebald and Russel Brines, *With MacArthur in Japan: A Personal History of the Occupation* (New York: W. W. Norton, 1965); Hosoya Chihiro, 'Yoshida Shokan to Bei-Ei-Chu no Kozo' [The Yoshida Letter and the Structure of US–Britain–China Relations], *Chuo Koron*, 97 (1982).

[12] Yoshida Shigeru, *Kaiso Junen, Dai-3-kan [Recollections of Ten Years, Vol. 3]* (Tokyo: Shincho-sha, 1957), p. 72.

[13] Hosoya, 'Yoshida Shokan to Bei-Ei-Chu no Kozo', p. 83.

[14] Ibid., pp. 74, 82.

[15] 'Sori no Daresu-ate Shokan' [Prime Minister's Letter to Dulles] (24 December 1951), Foreign Ministry Archive, Microfilm B'-0009.

[16] Yoshida, *Sekai to Nippon*, pp. 144–5, 147.

[17] Yoshida, *Kaiso Junen, Dai-3-kan*, p. 73.

The course of Japan's postwar China policy was thus directed by the United States as the architect of international relations in East Asia. As American policies proved successful in reducing the attraction of the China market to Japan, the government lost both the rationale and the incentive to risk Japan–US relations for the revival of Japan–China trade. Against this backdrop, the Japanese government chose to tie Japan's economic growth to 'a triangular integration with the United States and South East Asia'.[18]

In this context, it was non-governmental pro-China Japanese that endeavoured to promote Japan–China trade. Many of them were advocates of the diplomacy of autonomy *vis-à-vis* the United States or independence from American control. These pro-China elements were not homogeneous, but they all shared a belief that without peace with China there would be no peace in Asia, and without trade with China there could be no peace with China. They also strongly believed that China was not an aggressive country. Many of them had opposed the signing of the San Francisco Peace Treaty on grounds that a 'one-sided' peace treaty excluding China would foreclose a sound basis for the promotion of Japan–China trade and peace in Asia.[19]

Thus, the 1950s became a decade when the chances for governmental reconciliation between Japan and China became remote, and instead, non-governmental actors appeared on stage in the role of architects of bilateral trade.

2.2. JAPAN'S CHINA TRADE ORGANIZATIONS

We will now review several institutions which were active in Japan–China trade in the 1950s. Their organizational characteristics were diverse, which in turn became a source of 'structural pluralism' in Japan's trade relations with China.

In short, the 1950s was a decade of trial and error for both Japanese and Chinese interested in bilateral trade. On the Japanese side, advocates of autonomy and independent lines of diplomacy promoted movements to trade with China, through which several pro-China organizations emerged. They even included government-related institutions such as the Japan–China Importers and Exporters Association under MITI and the Japan–China Trade Promotion Diet Members League in the National Diet. As the US policy to 'contain' China came to determine the basic political framework of Japan–China relations, however, the role of organizations with institutionalized channels with the Japanese government also began to decline.

[18] Dower, *Empire and Aftermath*, p. 419.
[19] Sakata Masatoshi, 'Kowa to Kokunai-seiji: Nitchu Boeki Mondai tono Kanren wo Chushin ni' [Peace Treaty and Domestic Politics: In Relation to Japan–China Trade Issue], in Watanabe Akio and Miyazato Seigen (eds.) *Sanfuranshisuko Kowa [San Francisco Peace Treaty]* (Tokyo: Tokyo Daigaku Shuppan-kai, 1986), pp. 87–112.

Nonetheless, the establishment of these government-related institutions reflected a wide national consensus on the necessity to trade with China, and the Chinese government attempted to take advantage of such Japanese political conditions. Judging from circumstantial evidence, the political purpose of China's trade policy in the 1950s was to lure the Japanese government into actual trade arrangements, and thus to drive a wedge in the Japan–US relationship as well as between Tokyo and Taipei. The pro-China attitudes of the Hatoyama and Ishibashi cabinets in the mid-1950s also raised such Chinese expectations.

The Chinese experiences in the 1950s, however, reminded Beijing of its difficulty. As the role of the Japanese government was curtailed, the role of the government-related China trade organizations also diminished. The Chinese announcement of 'three trade principles' in 1960, which, as examined in Chapter 4, was intended to make a distinction between the Japanese government and the non-governmental sector in trading with Japan, was a direct response to the frustrating experiences in the 1950s.

Despite these experiences of trial and error, most Japanese individuals and organizations which were actively engaged in China trade before diplomatic normalization emerged onto the stage by the mid-1950s. Their political motives and sources of pro-China feelings were diverse, giving rise to a complex structure and process of Japan–China trade in the 1950s and beyond.

2.2.1. Japan–China Trade Promotion Association

With the communist victory in view on the Chinese mainland, pro-China Japanese immediately started to make efforts to promote exchanges with the new regime. These movements arose as 'united-front' activities to establish a new relationship with the new China, and an effort to resume China trade was an important component of those efforts.[20]

On 8 January 1949, occasioned by the communist takeover of Beijing in early January, labour unions, overseas Chinese associations in Japan, small and medium firms, intellectuals, and progressive Dietmen gathered in Tokyo and started an effort to mobilize nation-wide movements to establish good-neighbour relations with mainland China. On 4 May 1949, commemorating the Chinese May 4th Movement of 1919, they formed the 'China–Japan Trade Discussion Group', which decided to establish a 'China–Japan Trade Promotion Association' and elected about thirty core members to prepare for its inauguration, mostly heads of small and medium firms and progressive

[20] The following paragraph is based, unless otherwise noted, on Hirano Yoshitaro, 'Nitchu Boeki Undo no Hajimari: "Chunichi Boeki Sokushin-kai" no Junbi Jidai' [The Beginning of Japan–China Trade Movements: Preparation Years of 'China–Japan Trade Promotion Association'], *Ajia Keizai Junpo* (hereafter cited as *AKJ*), 526–7 (1963), pp. 34–9.

organizations.[21] On 30 May, they formally established the China–Japan Trade Promotion Association, later to be renamed the Japan–China Trade Promotion Association (JCTPA).

It merits emphasis that, as shown in this process, promoters of trade relations with China were those political forces opposing the policy of collaboration with the United States pursued by the Yoshida cabinet. This was vividly demonstrated by the keynote speeches given by Hirano Yoshitaro, director of the China Research Institute, and the Japan Communist Party's leader Nosaka Sanzo on 4 May. They stressed the following: Japan–China trade should be so conducted as to help Chinese industrialization; Japan's independence and autonomy depend on China trade; Japan–China trade ought to be conducted on a people-to-people basis and monopolistic capitalists must be excluded; China trade is to be pursued as a national movement including small and medium firms, labour unions, and democratic parties.

These pro-China movements then led to the establishment of the Japan–China Friendship Association (JCFA). A preparation group for the establishment of the JCFA was formed on 10 October 1949, when pro-China Japanese gathered to celebrate the establishment of the People's Republic of China (PRC) on 1 October. After a year's preparation, the JCFA was formally established on 1 October 1950, commemorating the first anniversary of the PRC government.[22] The nature of the JCFA, which was concerned with overall Japan–China friendship, was clearly demonstrated by the four major aims of the organization adopted on 1 October 1950: (1) to correct misperceptions of China; (2) to promote cultural exchanges in order to establish cooperative relations and mutual understanding between the two peoples; (3) to promote trade relations in order to enhance people's living and help the economic construction of the two countries; and (4) to contribute to world peace by promoting friendly relations between the two peoples.[23]

The establishment of the JCFA as a general 'united front' pro-China organization induced the JCTPA to concentrate more on trade business. Moreover, the outbreak of the Korean War in June 1950 necessitated reorganization of the JCTPA as a purely economic organization, so that it could survive the red purge and continue to remain active in China trade. The JCTPA reorganized itself to represent only business industries and firms shortly before the Chinese army crossed the Yalu in October 1950.[24] Thereafter, the

[21] Individual names of directors and members of the Association are found in Furukawa, *Nitchu Sengo Kankei-shi*, pp. 25–6.

[22] For the process of establishment of the JCFA, see Nitchu Yuko Kyokai Zenkoku Honbu [National Headquarters of the JCFA] (ed.) *Nitchu Yuko Undo-shi [History of Japan–China Friendship Movements]* (Tokyo: Seinen Shuppan-sha, 1980), pp. 28–38.

[23] *Ibid.*, p. 35.

[24] 'Bosoku Undo ga Ayunda Michi: Suzuki Kazuo Shi ni Kiku (3)' [Looking Back on Trade Promotion Movements: Interview with Mr. Suzuki Kazuo] (hereafter cited as Suzuki Interview), *AKJ*, 622 (1965), p. 21.

JCTPA grew into an organization particularly strong on practical trade matters. More firms joined the JCTPA as it began to provide them with practical services in trade with China, and its daily business was occupied with such arrangements as shipment of goods, cabling to China, and so forth.[25]

It merits emphasis that these pro-China movements started in Japan almost spontaneously before the establishment of the PRC government. As will be examined in detail in Chapter 4, the JCTPA became a core organization in the Friendship Trade arrangements in the 1960s. Suzuki Kazuo, who gradually moved into the central position in the JCTPA and became a most active intermediary in Friendship Trade in the 1960s, had formerly been working for Mitsubishi Corporation. One practical reason for his joining the JCTPA was his expertise in trade business.[26] More importantly, however, he was convinced that the key to Japan's prosperity was economic exchange with China.[27] Suzuki later stated that it was 'faith in China as a reliable country' that made him and other staff endure the unendurable in hard times.[28] This deeply embedded pro-China sentiment must be remembered when one assesses the role of Japan's pro-China organizations throughout the postwar era.

Also, it is noteworthy that these pro-China individuals joined together as anti-America political forces. Their movements were not necessarily directed against the China policy of the United States alone. Rather, they were united in opposing Japan's diplomatic course of collaboration with the US Cold War strategy, which had revived some prewar elements in Japanese domestic politics, made the Japanese economy dependent on the US economy, and brought the 'fiction' of the Cold War into Asia. Thus, they called for gaining independence from Pax Americana, and thought that approaching China would be the most effective way to do so.

2.2.2. Japan Association for the Promotion of International Trade

While the JCTPA had grown out of the movements to establish good-neighbour relations with China, the Japan Association for the Promotion of International Trade (JAPIT) was established in response to the international call for enhancing economic exchanges between the Eastern and Western blocs. Therefore, whereas the promoters of the movements leading to the creation of the JCTPA had been typical pro-China activists, those who came to be involved in the JAPIT included, although not exclusively, internationalists

---

[25] Interview with Tanaka Shujiro, vice-chairman of the Japan–China North East Development Association, Tokyo, 17 September 1986 (hereafter cited as Tanaka Interview). Tanaka was an associate of Suzuki Kazuo at the JCTPA from 1950 to 1955.

[26] 'Suzuki Interview (1)', *AKJ*, 619 (1965), pp. 18–19.

[27] Ibid.

[28] Suzuki Kazuo, 'Kakezuri Mawatta Nitchu Boeki "Sosoki" no Koto' [About the Beginning Years of Japan–China Trade], *Gekkan Ekonomisuto*, 3 (1972), p. 67.

who were deeply concerned about the division of the world into two camps under the progressing Cold War.

In April 1952, an International Economic Conference was held in Moscow with a view to enhancing economic and trade exchanges between socialist and capitalist countries. The socialist camp took the initiative, and it was Nan Hanchen, president of the Chinese People's Bank, who took the lead in attempting to draw Japan into the Conference. In early January 1952, Nan had sent letters to Japanese businessmen, politicians, and intellectuals inviting them to participate. In response to this Chinese initiative, several leaders who later came to occupy the core of the JAPIT formed, on 27 January 1952, the International Economic Discussion Group, which promoted a plan to send representatives to the Moscow International Economic Conference.[29] This group included Ishibashi Tanzan (Lower House Dietman, Liberal Party), Murata Shozo (chairman of Osaka Lines), Kitamura Tokutaro (president of Shinwa Bank), Hoashi Kei (former Upper House Dietman, Ryokuhu-kai), Ayukawa Yoshisuke (former president of the Manchu Heavy Industry), and others. The group, however, did not succeed in sending a delegation to Moscow because the Japanese government refused to issue passports.

One of the concrete results of the Moscow International Economic Conference was the creation of International Trade Promotion Committees in twenty-one countries (including England and France). The Chinese committee was labelled the China Committee for the Promotion of International Trade (CCPIT). The first Japanese group created in response to the Moscow Conference was the Japan–China Trade Promotion Conference, which was inaugurated on 22 May 1952. The Conference was a nation-wide group embracing such pro-China organizations as the JCFA and the JCTPA, chaired by Yamamoto Kumaichi (former Vice-Minister of Foreign Affairs) and Hirano Yoshitaro.

Not having been very successful in the promotion of China trade, members of the International Economic Discussion Group of Japan, including Ishibashi Tanzan, Murata Shozo, and Kitamura Tokutaro, joined in August 1954 with such well-known businessmen as Takasaki Tatsunosuke (president of Toyo Seikan) and Kan Reinosuke (chairman of Tokyo Electric Power), as well as Yamamoto Kumaichi and Suzuki Kazuo (managing director of the JCTPA). They decided to join the international movement by creating the JAPIT, which was formally established on 22 September 1954.[30]

The JAPIT was headed by Murata as chairman, and included Kitamura, Yamamoto, and Tajima Masao (president of Daiichi Kisen) as vice-chairmen.

[29] Kawakatsu Den, *Yuko Ichiro: Watashi no 'Nitchu' Kaiso-ki [The Way to Friendship: My Memoirs of 'Japan–China']* (Tokyo: Mainichi Shinbun-sha, 1985), pp. 20–21; Furukawa, *Nitchu Sengo Kankei-shi*, pp. 36–7.

[30] Hayashi Shigeru, 'Nitchu Boeki 15-nen-shi (Jo)' [Fifteen-year History of Japan–China Trade (1)], *AKJ*, 566 (1964), p. 24; Furukawa, *Nitchu Sengo Kankei-shi*, p. 112.

This top leadership clearly demonstrated the orientation of the JAPIT as free from communist ideology, and the composition of the steering committee further illustrates the point. The fourteen standing committee members included Takasaki Tatsunosuke, Okazaki Kaheita (president of Ikegai Tekko), Matsubara Yosomatsu (president of Hitachi Shipbuilding Co.), Kawakatsu Den (president of Nippon Spindle), and others. Included among the committee members were Ishibashi Tanzan, Ayukawa Yoshisuke, Ikeda Masanosuke (Lower House Dietman, Liberal Party), Sugi Michisuke (chairman of the Osaka Chamber of Commerce), Kosuga Uichiro (president of Nissho Corporation), Hara Kichihei (president of Nichibo), and so on. The JAPIT decided that its purpose would be to enhance, and remove obstacles to, economic and trade exchanges with countries with which Japan did not have diplomatic relations, including China, the Soviet Union, Korea, and other socialist countries. Murata characterized the nature of the JAPIT as being an 'economic Red Cross' that would apply the power of the private sector to what the government would be unable to accomplish.[31]

Many of the leaders of the JAPIT were executives of big companies, and in that respect were distinct from the leaders of the JCTPA. The JAPIT thus found itself at odds with the JCTPA. Suzuki Kazuo, a former Mitsubishi man who came to lead the JCTPA, himself admitted that the initial movements concerning his organization had been led by the Japan Communist Party (JCP).[32] At the creation of the JAPIT in September 1954, in which Suzuki participated (and was elected a standing committee member), it was initially decided that the JCTPA would be absorbed by the JAPIT. But when strong opposition developed among members of the JCTPA, the merger was abandoned.[33] This marked the beginning of a strained tandem relationship between the JAPIT and the JCTPA which persisted into the 1960s. This uncongenial relationship between the two major pro-China trade organizations constituted one element of structural pluralism in Japan's trade relations with China.

2.2.3. *Japan–China Importers and Exporters Association*

The history of the Japan–China Importers and Exporters Association (JCIEA) from 1955 to 1968 underscores the limited ability of the government to lead China trade. The JCIEA was established in December 1955 as a civilian corporate body, on the basis of the Import and Export Transaction Law. This Transaction Law had been revised in September 1955 to allow an association

---

[31] Yonezawa Hideo, 'Kokusai Boeki Sokushin Kyokai no Jigyo' [Business of the JAPIT], *AKJ*, 231 (1954).
[32] 'Suzuki Interview (3)', *AKJ*, 622 (1965), p. 23.
[33] 'Suzuki Interview (4)', *AKJ*, 637 (1966), p. 24.

of firms for the purpose of coordinating import and export business with a particular country or region.[34]

The JCIEA was established in order to solve three fundamental problems in trade with China as perceived by MITI, which initiated the revision of the Transaction Law. First, whereas nationally controlled corporations were the central trade organs on the Chinese side, the Japanese side had been plagued by harsh competition among numerous firms, and this situation had been disadvantageous to Japan. Second, with the lack of direct governmental contacts between Japan and China, it was desirable from MITI's point of view to have an authoritative organization that would reflect governmental policies and function as a coordinator of Japan–China trade. Third, the current barter trade system applied to Japan–China trade required each individual firm to balance imports with exports in its yearly account, a restriction which hindered further expansion of Japan–China trade. Therefore, an organization was needed to coordinate an overall import–export balance, within which individual firms would trade in their strong fields.

The two tasks of the JCIEA were to coordinate and promote Japan–China trade. Coordination would be carried out by setting rules which member firms would follow in terms of trading commodities, price, volume, quality, and forms of payments. The standardized level of each category, however, was never set, because small and medium firms resisted the move for fear that the coordination measures would lead to a *de facto* cartel among big firms.[35] Therefore, the JCIEA's major function was limited to promoting Japan–China trade in general and the benefits to its members in particular. Concrete measures taken in this connection included: (1) a 'special approval system' which allowed members, upon applications and approval, to export limited commodities from the embargo list; and (2) 'major commodities coordination measures' which allowed members to deal in one-way transactions without balancing imports and exports.[36] All these measures were certainly attractive to Japan–China trade firms, and the membership jumped from the original 125 at the time of inauguration to 370 in July 1957, covering almost all firms engaged in China trade.

The establishment of a Japan–China trade organization enjoying authoritative privileges was naturally perceived by pro-China organizations as a threat posed by the Japanese government and big firms. They would deal in major commodities which only the JCIEA could authorize with MITI's blessing. An article in *Ajia Keizai Junpo*, a journal of the China Research Institute, whose president Hirano Yoshitaro was quite active in the creation of the

34 Nitchu Yushutsunyu Kumiai [JCIEA], *Nitchu Boeki Jitsumu Dokuhon [Trade with China: A Practical Guide]* (Tokyo: Nitchu Yushutsunyu Kumiai, 1957), pp. 27–9. The information following on the JCIEA is based on this source unless otherwise noted.

35 Okamoto, *Nitchu Boeki Ron*, pp. 59–60.

36 JCIEA, *Nitchu Boeki Jitsumu Dokuhon*, pp. 203–14, 226–8.

JCTPA, even stated, 'The JCIEA is a most undemocratic organization. It was established as a corporate association reflecting the government's intentions, and is being led by big capital.'[37]

Substantiating the fears of a decreasing role in Japan–China trade on the part of small and medium firms, the JCIEA's activities proved conducive to an increasing share for large trading firms. In 1956, for instance, 61 per cent of overall trade transactions between Japan and China was recorded by the top ten leading trading firms active in China trade; and 85 per cent and 94 per cent of the bilateral trade were handled by twenty and thirty firms, respectively.[38]

Succeeding developments, however, vividly showed the limitations of governmental involvement. This pattern involving the JCIEA came to a sudden end due to rapidly deteriorating relations between the governments of Japan and China, as signified by the Nagasaki flag incident of May 1958, as will be seen below. As an organization closely linked to MITI, the JCIEA proved very susceptible to the climate of governmental relations. And as the mutual exchange of goods and people was suspended in 1958, its membership declined over three years from 398 to 196 in November 1961. Moreover, a third of the members stopped paying membership dues, which constituted a major portion of its budget, and the JCIEA faced a deadlock in its management. As a consequence, MITI chose to cut its subsidy to the JCIEA in the second half of 1960.[39]

When a plan for what came to be called LT Trade emerged in 1962, the Japanese government decided to revitalize the JCIEA as an organ to promote a new form of trade with China.[40] By this time, however, Friendship Trade had already started, which emphasized a clear distinction between the Japanese government and the private sector. Therefore, MITI's intention to revitalize the JCIEA was met with resistance from both Japan's pro-China forces and the Chinese government. The function of the JCIEA was reduced to a role of coordinating the imports of commodities requiring approval by MITI.[41]

Consequently, MITI's influence over the JCIEA was weakened and the influence of 'friendly firms', designated by China as such, began to prevail within the JCIEA. The top leadership positions were filled, for instance, by presidents of influential friendly firms, such as Daiichi Tsusho, Wako Koeki, and Toko Bussan.[42] The JCIEA's role in Japan–China trade now became nominal. When the Friendship Trade system underwent a massive transformation

---

[37] Yonezawa Hideo, 'Saikin no Nitchu Boeki Sokushin Undo' [Japan–China Trade Promotion Movements in Recent Years], *AKJ*, 279 (1956), p. 13.

[38] Sugioka Isao, 'Nitchu Boeki to "Kato Kyoso" ' [Japan–China Trade and 'Excessive Competition'], *AKJ*, 331 (1957), p. 7.

[39] *Nihon Keizai Shinbun*, 21 November 1961.

[40] *Asahi Shinbun*, 7 August 1962; *Nihon Keizai Shinbun*, 7 August 1962, 23 September 1962.

[41] *Nihon Keizai Shinbun*, 13 January 1963.

[42] *Nihon Keizai Shinbun*, 5 September 1962.

in 1966, its member firms disengaged themselves from the JCIEA, and having lost its support, the JCIEA eventually dissolved itself in August 1968.[43]

2.2.4. Japan–China Trade Promotion Diet Members League

The Japan–China Trade Promotion Diet Members League (JCTPDML) was not a trade-conducting organization but merits a brief mention because it became a signatory of the four private trade agreements concluded in the 1950s. Its Chinese counterpart was the CCPIT. Chinese acknowledgement of the JCTPDML as a Japanese signatory of the four trade agreements reflected its intention to use trade as a means to influence Japanese governmental policy. The history of the JCTPDML activities, however, again demonstrated the limited capacity of a government-related institution to become a central actor in Japan–China trade.

The JCTPDML was established as early as May 1949 as a supra-partisan organization by about ninety Dietmen from both the Upper and Lower Houses. There were twenty-six members from the Liberal Party from both houses, seventeen from the Democratic Party, twenty-one from the Japan Socialist Party (JSP), ten from the JCP, twelve from Ryokufu-kai, and six independents.[44] In ten years' time, the number increased to about 360, representing approximately 50 per cent of the total Diet members.[45]

Aside from being a signatory of Japan–China private trade agreements, the JCTPDML endeavoured to promote mutual exchanges of people, to present resolutions on Japan–China trade to the Diet, and to urge the government to take measures to improve Japan–China trade. Twelve Diet resolutions concerning promotion of Japan–China trade were presented during the 1950s, with only four not being passed due to the time limit in the Diet sessions.[46]

As trade transactions came to a halt after the Nagasaki flag incident, the LDP decided to withdraw from the JCTPDML, and its supra-partisan nature was lost momentarily. But the organization continued to exist, if only nominally, and about fifty LDP Dietmen rejoined the JCTPDML by the beginning of 1964. In 1970, the JCTPDML embraced seventy members from the LDP, eighty-four from the JSP, nineteen from the Socialist Democratic Party, and eleven from the Clean Government Party. But the JCTPDML was

43 Okamoto, *Nitchu Boeki Ron*, p. 219; Nitchu Keizai Kyokai [Japan–China Association on Economy and Trade], *Nitchu Oboegaki no 11-nen [Eleven Years of Japan–China Memorandum]* (Tokyo: Nitchu Keizai Kyokai, 1975), p. 113.

44 Fukui Haruhiro, *Jiyuminshu-to to Seisaku Kettei [LDP and Policy-making]* (Tokyo: Fukumura Shuppan, 1970), pp. 294–5.

45 Yamamoto Kumaichi, 'Trade Problems with People's Republic of China', *Contemporary Japan*, 25 (1958), p. 364.

46 Nitchu Kokko Kaihuku Sokushin Giin Renmei [Diet Members League for the Promotion of Japan–China Diplomatic Normalization] (ed.) *Nitchu Kokko Kaihuku Kankei Shiryo-shu [Compilation of Materials Related to Japan–China Diplomatic Normalization]* (hereafter cited as *Kankei Shiryo*) (Tokyo: Nitchu Kokko Shiryo Iinkai, 1972), pp. 3–6.

not active after 1958, as indicated by the fact that not a single resolution was presented to the Diet throughout the 1960s.[47]

The creation of the JCTPDML in the national Diet as early as 1949, and its signing the four private trade agreements, indicate that the promotion of Japan–China trade had received national support. Its inability to contribute to Japan–China trade after 1958, however, signifies that the 1950s was a decade of trial and error for Japan–China trade, through which viable actors had been sorted out and a new structure gradually emerged.

2.3. JAPAN–CHINA PRIVATE TRADE AGREEMENTS

2.3.1. First Agreement

The first Japan–China private trade agreement was concluded as a by-product of the Moscow International Economic Conference in April 1952.[48] As seen above, those who were eager to participate in the Conference in order to break the deadlock in East-West trade formed the International Economic Discussion Group and began the task of forming a delegation to Moscow. But the Japanese government refused to issue passports for them. Having failed to get the government's permission, Hoashi Kei and Miyakoshi Kisuke (Lower House Dietman, Kokumin Kyodo Party) planned to enter the Soviet Union by way of Europe. They applied for passports to go to Denmark for a study trip. Although the government was suspicious of their true intentions, and waited until the Moscow Conference ended before issuing passports, they chose to visit Moscow and Beijing on their way back to Japan.[49] Hoashi and Miyakoshi joined Kora Tomi (Upper House Dietwoman, Ryokufu-kai) who had already been in the Soviet Union to attend the Moscow Conference, and all three successfully entered China on 15 May 1952.

Kora had been asked by Hoashi to go to Moscow with him. Kora, being vice-chair of the Diet committee on the repatriation of overseas Japanese, seized upon the occasion to negotiate with the Soviet Union and China about repatriation matters.[50] Kora could leave Japan because she had already obtained a passport in order to attend a UNESCO conference in Paris. She entered the Soviet Union in early April and gave a speech at the Moscow Conference. The Moscow Conference was attended by 471 representatives from forty-nine countries, including twelve from the United States and twenty-five from England, but Kora was the only Japanese.[51]

47 Fukui, *Jiyuminshu-to to Seisaku Kettei*, p. 295; Furukawa, *Nitchu Sengo Kankei-shi*, p. 307.
48 Kawakatsu, *Yuko Ichiro*, pp. 20–21.
49 Hoashi Kei, *Soren-Chugoku Kiko [A Trip to the Soviet Union and China]* (Tokyo: Kawade Shobo, 1952), pp. 20–21, 57.
50 Kora Tomi, *Ahinsa wo Ikiru: Kora Tomi Jiden [Living Non-Violence: Autobiography of Kora Tomi]* (Tokyo: Domesu Shuppan, 1983), pp. 140–41.
51 *Ibid.*, p. 146.

As the above episode shows, the Japanese government had nothing to do with, but rather was deeply concerned about, the China visit by the three Japanese as well as the first private trade agreement with China. In this context, it was Hoashi, a progressive Dietman, who was the central person pursuing that aim. Before becoming a member of Ryokufu-kai and later the JSP, he had started his prewar career as an economist, and had also been active in the business field in both prewar and postwar years. Moreover, he actively participated in the movements to promote Japan–China trade, which gave birth to the JCTPA and the JAPIT as seen above. At the time of his trip to the Soviet Union and China, he was a member of the International Economic Discussion Group of Japan, a director of the JCFA, and an advisor to the JCTPA. With this background, Hoashi signed the first Japan–China private trade agreement as a representative of the JCTPA on 1 June 1952. The two other signatories, Kora and Miyakoshi, signed the agreement as a Japanese representative the Moscow Conference and a director of the JCTPDML, respectively.

The trade talks started in Moscow with Lei Renmin, Vice-Minister of Chinese Ministry of Foreign Trade. Three discussions were held while in Moscow on the basic principles of the Japan–China trade agreement. On 16 May 1952 in China, they met Nan Hanchen, president of the Chinese People's Bank and chairman of the newly created CCPIT, and started a two-week negotiation over the trade agreement.

The Chinese side presented a plan which contained three categories of trading commodities. Category A was composed of 'strategic items' whose export from Japan was prohibited by the so-called 'Battle Act' of the United States.[52] The Chinese insisted that the exchange of goods in Category A had to be carried out before less 'strategic' commodities of Categories B and C could be exchanged. Eventually a compromise was reached that trade would start with whatever commodities were possible. The categorization, however, was left intact, with the principle that commodities would be exchanged only within each category.[53] The eight articles of the agreement can be summarized as follows:[54]

1. The total value of trade will be 30 million pounds sterling ($84 million).
2. Commodities of the same categories as classified by the appendix are

[52] Its formal name is the Mutual Defense Assistance Control Act, which connected the United States allies' trade with the socialist bloc with the United States military, financial, and economic assistance to them. This came into force in 1951.

[53] Hoashi Kei and Wakimura Yoshitaro, 'Chukyo Boeki wa Kano ka' [Is China Trade Possible?], *Sekai*, 81 (1952), pp. 133–5; Hoashi, *Soren-Chugoku Kiko*, pp. 323–4.

[54] For the complete text, see Gaimu-sho Ajia-kyoku Chugoku-ka [China Section of the Foreign Ministry of Japan] (ed.) *Nitchu Kankei Kihon Shiryo-shu, 1949–1969 [Compilation of Basic Materials on Japan–China Relations, 1949–1969]* (hereafter cited as *Kihon Shiryo*) (Tokyo: Kazankai, 1970), pp. 43–4; Ishikawa Tadao, Nakajima Mineo, and Ikei Masaru (eds.) *Sengo Shiryo: Nitchu Kankei [Postwar Materials: Japan–China Relations]* (Tokyo: Nihon Hyoron-sha, 1970) (hereafter cited as *Sengo Shiryo*), pp. 23–4; *Kankei Shiryo*, pp. 155–6.

to be exchanged, with Category A occupying 40 per cent, Category B 30 per cent, and Category C 20 per cent of the total value.

3. Trade transactions are to be on a barter basis, to be valued in terms of pounds sterling.
4. A Japanese delegation representing civilian commerce and industry is to visit China to carry out the agreement.
5. Methods of transportation and clearance shall be discussed when the detailed contracts are signed.
6. Arbitration concerning trade contracts shall take place in China.
7. The agreement must be implemented before 31 December 1952. If not completed by then, the time limit may be extended by mutual agreement.
8. The agreement has Japanese and Chinese versions, both of which are equally valid.

The appendix designated coal, soya beans, manganese ore, iron ore, and bristle as Chinese exports, and iron and steel materials as Japanese exports in Category A. Category B included salt, mixed beans, peanuts, and so forth from China, and textile machinery, refrigerated steamers, insecticide and others from Japan, while Category C had less significant commodities.

2.3.2. Second Agreement

The second Japan–China private trade agreement also came about as a by-product of an exchange of people between Japan and China. The JCTPDML dispatched a mission to China in September 1953 with three purposes in mind: to deepen friendly relations between the two peoples, to generate an environment for the furtherance of Japan–China trade, and to study the Chinese situation in order to achieve the above two aims.[55] The mission of thirteen Diet members and twelve business people arrived in Beijing on 30 September, and at a reception held that night, Nan Hanchen quite unexpectedly presented a proposal to negotiate a second trade agreement. Ikeda Masanosuke, who headed the mission to China, was not prepared to respond to such an offer, and thus left the matter to Hoashi Kei, a signatory of the first trade agreement, who joined the mission as a deputy head.[56]

The second agreement was signed on 29 October 1953 by Ikeda Masanosuke, representing the JCTPDML, and Nan Hanchen of the CCPIT. The basic tenor of the second agreement was similar to that of the first agreement, but there were three important developments. First, the ratio of the categories was altered, with Category A occupying 35 per cent, Category B 40 per

55 Furukawa, *Nitchu Sengo Kankei-shi*, p. 55.
56 Ikeda Masanosuke, *Nazo no Kuni: Chukyo Tairiku no Jittai [A Mysterious Country: True Situation in Communist China]* (Tokyo: Jiji Tsushin-sha, 1969), pp. 335–6.

cent, and Category C 25 per cent. Thus the Chinese side became a little more realistic than it had been at the time of the first agreement. Second, the stipulation that required the Japanese side to go to China to negotiate trade contracts was dropped from the second agreement, also demonstrating Chinese flexibility compared with the first agreement. Third, probably most important for the future development of Japan–China trade, a memorandum attached to the agreement stipulated that both sides would establish trade representatives in each other's country.[57]

2.3.3. Third Agreement

Reflecting the stipulations in the second agreement to establish trade representatives in both countries, the Chinese side became quite eager to obtain the Japanese government's endorsement of the third trade agreement. This in part reflected the shift in the Japanese government from the Yoshida cabinet to the Hatoyama cabinet in December 1954. Hatoyama was highly motivated by his political rivalry against Yoshida and Yoshida's diplomacy of collaboration with the United States, and aspired to achieve his diplomatic autonomy *vis-à-vis* the United States by establishing diplomatic normalization with the Soviet Union and China, and by introducing a single-seat district system to carry out the revision of Article Nine of the Peace Constitution. Although Hatoyama eventually staked his political life on normalization of diplomatic relations with the Soviet Union only, China presumably expected some flexibility in Hatoyama's China policy.

In this new political situation, Murata Shozo, chairman of the JAPIT, visited China in January 1955. Murata stayed in Beijing from 10 to 25 January and had a series of talks with Chinese officials, including one with Zhou Enlai over four and a half hours on 23 January. A meeting with Lei Renmin, acting director of the CCPIT, on 17 January led to the following agreements: (1) negotiations over the third trade agreement were to be held in Tokyo, (2) mutual commodity exhibitions were to be held, and (3) both sides would endeavour to establish trade representatives in both countries.

Thus, the newly created JAPIT came to the fore of Japan–China trade arrangements. The JCTPDML supported this new move by passing a resolution in the Diet calling for the invitation of a Chinese trade delegation on 27 December 1954, shortly before Murata departed for China. Also, its director Ikeda Masanosuke later became a signatory of the third agreement, which was signed in Tokyo in May 1955.[58] The Hatoyama government agreed to the entry of the Chinese delegation on condition that the government had nothing to do with it and it would be a purely private matter.

57 For the full text of the second Japan–China private trade agreement, see *Kihon Shiryo*, pp. 57–9; *Sengo Shiryo*, pp. 69–70; *Kankei Shiryo*, pp. 168–70.
58 Murata Shozo, 'Shu Onrai to Atte' [Meeting with Zhou Enlai], *Sekai*, 112 (1955); Murata, *Nitchu Kakehashi no Ichi-kiroku*; Furukawa, *Nitchu Sengo Kankei-shi*, p. 114.

Thus, the Chinese delegation of thirty-eight members headed by Lei Renmin arrived in Japan on 29 March 1955. After prolonged negotiations, mainly over the question of governmental involvement in the agreement, the third Japan–China private trade agreement was signed on 4 May 1955, by the JAPIT and the JCTPDML on the Japanese side, and the CCPIT on the Chinese side. The Chinese choice of the Japanese signatories clearly reflected its intent to influence the governmental policy of Japan; so did the contents of the third agreement.

This was indicated by several major developments that had occurred since the previous agreement. First, Article 5 stipulated that payments would be settled by opening clearance accounts in the Chinese People's Bank and the Bank of Japan, and before such a goal was attained transactions would be settled in pounds sterling. Thus, the barter trade stipulation was removed from the third agreement, although in fact this provision was not implemented. Second, Article 8 declared that arbitration would be conducted in the country of the defendant, not in China as had been stipulated in the previous two agreements. Third, both sides agreed in Article 9 to hold commodity exhibitions in each other's country. Fourth, the establishment of a trade representative office in both capitals, which would enjoy diplomatic privileges, was included in Article 10 of the main body of the agreement as an aim to be pursued. Fifth, Article 11 required both sides to urge their governments to hold negotiations on the question of bilateral trade.[59]

This escalation of political aspects from the first to the third agreement is evidence that both Japanese and Chinese negotiators were very eager to draw the Japanese government into Japan–China trade arrangements. Nonetheless, they could not gain anything more than words of 'support and cooperation' from Prime Minister Hatoyama. Hatoyama, in fact, did not commit himself in a written form, but instead simply spoke to Ikeda Masanosuke when they met on 27 April. On the day the third agreement was signed, therefore, Ikeda and Murata jointly wrote a letter to Lei Renmin confirming Hatoyama's words, and the letter became an important part of the agreement.

Nonetheless, Japan's international environment was not offering any real incentives for the Japanese government to promote Japan–China trade beyond the level of a limited private agreement. Instead, Hatoyama chose to devote himself to normalization of diplomatic relations with the Soviet Union. In December 1956, upon achieving that goal, Hatoyama resigned, and Ishibashi Tanzan, who was a strong advocate of the expansion of Japan–China trade, succeeded him on 23 December. But illness prevented him from putting his belief in Japan–China trade into action, and in only two months' time he gave way to Kishi Nobusuke who succeeded Ishibashi on 25 February 1957.

59 For the full text of the third Japan–China private trade agreement, see *Kihon Shiryo*, pp. 83–7; *Sengo Shiryo*, pp. 71–2; *Kankei Shiryo*, pp. 172–8.

2.3.4. Fourth Agreement

It was under the Kishi cabinet that the Japanese government showed most overtly, in deeds as well as in words, its unambiguous intention to strengthen political ties with Taiwan. Kishi became the first Japanese Prime Minister in the postwar era to make a tour to South East Asian countries, and visited Taiwan on his way back to Japan on 2 June 1957. This Taiwan visit is well known for Kishi's assurance to Chiang Kai-shek that he would support 'the recovery of freedom on the mainland'.[60]

It was when the Japanese government's foreign policy was undergoing these important changes that the fourth private trade agreement was being negotiated. Ironically enough, this agreement, signed on 5 March 1958 after a series of prolonged negotiations both in Japan and China over six months, escalated its political demands upon the Japanese government.[61] Most importantly, the memorandum attached to the agreement replaced the term 'diplomatic privileges' in the previous two agreements with more concrete stipulations, such as assurance of the safety of trade representatives, freedom of travel, the right to fly the national flag, and no finger-printing. Moreover, Article 13 stipulated that the contracting parties, i.e., the JAPIT, the JCTPDML, and the JCIEA on the Japanese side, and the CCPIT on the Chinese side, would endeavour to have both governments begin negotiations and conclude a governmental trade agreement as soon as possible.

The Kishi government responded to this fourth agreement on 9 April by presenting a letter to the three signatory organizations of Japan, which read as follows:

The Government, recognizing the necessity of expanded Japan–China trade, respecting the spirit of the fourth private 'Japan–China trade agreement', within the scope of our national laws and on the basis of the non-recognition of the [Chinese] government, and taking into account the current international relations, gives support and cooperation in order to achieve the aim of trade expansion.[62]

A statement issued by Cabinet Secretary Aichi Kiichi supplemented this announcement as follows:

... Needless to say the Government had no intention to recognize Communist China, nor to give privileged public status to the private trade representative that this private agreement seeks to establish. However, as to the treatment of the agreement by private organizations, the Government, respecting its relations with the Republic of China and other international relations, being cautious so that the establishment of the trade representative would not be misunderstood as de facto recognition, and within the scope of national laws, will give support and cooperation.

---

[60] *Asahi Shinbun*, 4 June 1957.
[61] For the full text of the fourth Japan–China private trade agreement, see *Kihon Shiryo*, pp. 129–34; *Sengo Shiryo*, pp. 248–50; *Kankei Shiryo*, pp. 191–4.
[62] *Kihon Shiryo*, p. 134; *Sengo Shiryo*, p. 251; *Kankei Shiryo*, p. 197.

Since the Japanese Government has not recognized Communist China, it is quite natural that flying the so-called national flag of Communist China by the private trade representative should not be recognized as a right.[63]

Precisely because China attempted to gain political concessions from the Japanese government in the political realm, it was quite frustrated by this outcome. On 9 April, Nan Hanchen sent a letter to the three Japanese signatory organizations of the agreement, expressing the Chinese refusal to accept the Japanese government's statements. Thus, the seeds of conflict had already been sown when the Nagasaki flag incident in early May 1958, the pulling down of a Chinese national flag by a Japanese at the Chinese commodity exhibition in Nagasaki city, turned into a historical event in postwar Japan–China relations. The Chinese side criticized Kishi for his inaction after this incident, and chose to sever almost all exchanges of people and goods with Japan.

Kishi believed that Chinese leaders sought to use trade in order to acquire *de facto* recognition of the PRC government, and thus divide Japanese society as well as its relations with the United States and Taiwan. The Chinese decision to stop exchanges of people and goods in May 1958, according to Kishi, also reflected the Chinese intention to influence Japan's public opinion in the middle of a national election, and thus was an intervention in the election.[64] In fact, the Diet had been dissolved on 25 April 1958, and the election, scheduled for 22 May, was significant because it was the first national election after the merger of the two conservative parties, the Liberal Party and the Democratic Party, into the LDP in November 1955. Incidentally, the LDP lost only three seats from the 290 seats it held before the election.

The Chinese certainly learned from these experiences that affecting the policy course of the Japanese government through trade arrangements was extremely difficult. Severing trade relations with Japan did not produce any concrete results.

What emerged from this context was the so-called three political principles advocated by China. The three political principles were hinted at in the Chinese letter to the Japan Fishery Association dated 11 June 1958 and the *People's Daily* of 7 July, and were conveyed in a complete form through a JSP Dietman Sata Tadataka, who visited China in August. Sata's report summarized three Chinese demands of the Kishi government: Japan should not (1) take a hostile policy against China, (2) take part in a conspiracy to create 'two Chinas', and (3) obstruct diplomatic normalization between the two countries.[65] These points simply expressed Chinese frustration with Kishi's 'anti-China' policy, and eventually became the core political principles in Chinese policy toward Japan.

[63] *Kihon Shiryo*, p. 135; *Sengo Shiryo*, p. 251; *Kankei Shiryo*, p. 197.
[64] Kishi, *Kishi Nobusuke Kaikoroku*, pp. 367–8, 418; Kishi Nobusuke *et al.*, *Kishi Nobusuke no Kaiso [Recollections of Kishi Nobusuke]* (Tokyo: Bungei Shunjyu-sha, 1981), p. 209.
[65] *Kihon Shiryo*, pp. 144–51; *Sengo Shiryo*, pp. 98–101; *Kankei Shiryo*, pp. 204–210.

2.4. STRUCTURE OF JAPAN–CHINA RELATIONS IN THE 1950S

The experiences during the 1950s showed that Chinese efforts to draw the Japanese government into trade arrangements were detrimental to the promotion of Japan–China trade. Japan's choice of Taiwan in 1952 dictated the general pattern of its political interaction with China, which was an integral component of the political structure of Pax Americana into which Yoshida chose to be drawn by way of his collaboration policy with the United States. In parallel, there emerged a policy line to aspire for autonomy within the confines of Pax Americana, and an independence line seeking ultimately to become free from the US-dominated order, both of which challenged Yoshida's diplomatic stance. Advocates of these two policy lines argued for the improvement of Japan–China relations, albeit from different motives. China attempted to take advantage of these political differences to bring about a China tilt of the Japanese government, but to no avail.

Needless to say, objective economic conditions made it unrealistic for the Japanese government to risk its alliance relationship with the United States for the promotion of China trade. The United States became the number-one trade partner of Japan by a large margin, and Japan's trade with South East Asia also came to occupy a central place in Japan's world trade, as shown in Tables 2.1 and 2.2.

TABLE 2.1. Japan's trade with the United States, 1952–1958

	1952	1953	1954	1955	1956	1957	1958
Export[a]	234	234	283	456	550	604	691
%	18.4	18.4	17.4	22.8	22.0	21.1	24.0
Import[a]	768	760	849	774	1067	1623	1056
%	37.9	31.5	35.4	31.3	33.0	37.9	34.8

[a] $ million.
% Share in Japan's overall export and import.

Source: Nihon Boeki Kenkyu-kai (ed.) *Sengo Nihon no Boeki 20-nen-shi [20 Year History of Japan's Postwar Trade]* (Tokyo: Tsusho Sangyo Chosa-kai, 1967), p. 374.

TABLE 2.2. Japan's trade with South East Asia, 1952–1958

	1952	1953	1954	1955	1956	1957	1958
Export[a]	462	606	703	727	868	969	876
%	36.3	47.6	43.2	36.2	34.7	33.9	30.4
Import[a]	496	633	575	663	734	798	591
%	24.4	26.3	23.9	26.8	22.7	18.4	19.5

[a] $ million.
% Share in Japan's overall export and import.

Source: *Ibid.*, pp. 290–91.

In this context, the implications of China trade were largely political for the Japanese government. This was also more or less true for non-governmental pro-China Japanese, except for a group of small firms whose business depended significantly on trade with China. From this overall political perspective, the structural characteristics of Japan–China relations lay in its complexity.

2.4.1. Policy Orientations of the Japanese Government

At the very basic level, no cabinet of the Japanese government intended to expand Japan–China trade to the extent that would undermine Japan–US relations. Within this basic framework, however, the Japanese government's responses to the evolution of Japan–China trade varied depending on two political factors: diplomatic policy orientations of Prime Ministers and China's place in their overall policy preferences.

Of particular importance was a difference between the policy of seeking collaboration with the United States and the diplomatic orientation aspiring for diplomatic autonomy within Pax Americana.

The collaboration line advanced by Yoshida Shigeru complied with the logic of Pax Americana and attempted to take advantage of its dynamism for Japan's recovery. As argued, Yoshida was not preoccupied with the communist ideology when thinking about Japan's relations with China, and was aware of the dynamics of Sino-Soviet uncongenial relations as well as of the folly of US policy to 'contain' China. But for Yoshida, collaboration with the United States was much more important than advancing his own China policy.

Hatoyama Ichiro, however, ascended to the prime ministership with a fierce rivalry with Yoshida. For Hatoyama, too, Pax Americana and the Cold War were the most important international factors dictating the basic course of Japanese diplomacy. His aspiration for autonomy, however, was not necessarily directed against these dominant international imperatives, but primarily against the United States, in general, and Yoshida's policy of collaboration with the United States, in particular. In a way, the international environment was given and beyond the control of Japan at the time, which allowed Hatoyama the 'luxury' of addressing highly international issues from his motivations to confront Yoshida in domestic politics. Hatoyama, therefore, did not feel any contradiction (which he should have felt from the logic of the Cold War) between his policy to seek diplomatic relations with the Soviet Union and China, on the one hand, and a policy to revise the Peace Constitution in order to rearm Japan, on the other. This was because both of these policies were motivated by Hatoyama's aspiration for diplomatic autonomy *vis-à-vis* the United States.

For Hatoyama, China was important in this diplomatic aspiration. China made diplomatic overtures to the conciliatory Hatoyama government, one of which was Zhou Enlai's approach to Takasaki Tatsunosuke, Minister of MITI of the Hatoyama cabinet, at the Bandung Conference in April 1955.[66]

Hatoyama's aspiration, however, could not extend beyond the confines of Pax Americana under the Cold War. This was most vividly shown by the fact that, in order to achieve his goal of gaining membership of the United Nations, which was part of the deal with the Soviet Union in establishing diplomatic normalization, Hatoyama needed the political backing of not only the United States but also of Taiwan. Taiwan, as a permanent member of the Security Council of the United Nations, was equipped with the ultimate power to veto Japan's admission. Hatoyama, therefore, had to use the utmost political caution in expressing his 'cooperation and support' to the third private trade agreement between Japan and China.

Ishibashi Tanzan was also motivated by an aspiration for diplomatic autonomy *vis-à-vis* the United States, and was a strong advocate of improved Japan–China relations, but his cabinet was too short-lived for us to evaluate its actual China policy. As Prime Minister, however, even Ishibashi was fully aware of the importance and the necessity to cooperate with the United States regarding highly political aspects of Japan–China relations.

Kishi Nobusuke was also motivated by his aspiration for diplomatic autonomy *vis-à-vis* the United States Kishi, however, did not look to China to satisfy his aspiration, but instead attempted to take advantage of Japan's strong relations with the United States in advancing his own policies such as the revision of the Japan–US Security Treaty and diplomacy toward South East Asia. In this context, strengthening relations with Taiwan was more important than approaching China, and accordingly governmental relations between Tokyo and Beijing worsened during Kishi's tenure. The end result was the Nagasaki flag incident in May 1958.

Thus, the entire political atmosphere in Japan–China bilateral relations was changed by the differing diplomatic stances of the Japanese government and China's place in them. This is exhibited in Tables 2.3 and 2.4 which show the amounts of bilateral trade and the numbers of mutual visits.

2.4.2. Complexity at the Non-Governmental Level

Encouraged by the end of the Civil War in China, movements to trade with China arose spontaneously among pro-China Japanese, and these crystallized into several pro-China organizations. Because governmental relations froze, trade relations were often used by both the Chinese and the pro-China Japanese as a means for influencing the Japanese government's China policy.

---

[66] For more on Chinese overtures to Hatoyama, see Okada Akira, *Mizudori Gaiko Hiwa: Aru Gaikokan no Shogen [Secret Stories of Waterfowl Diplomacy: Testimony by a Diplomat]* (Tokyo: Chuo Koron-sha, 1983); Chae-Jin Lee, *Japan Faces China: Political and Economic Relations in the Postwar Era* (Baltimore: The Johns Hopkins University Press, 1974), pp. 30–33.

TABLE 2.3. Japan's trade with China, 1952–1959

	1952	1953	1954	1955	1956	1957	1958	1959
Total[a]	16	34	60	109	151	141	105	23
%[b]	0.5	0.9	1.5	2.4	2.6	2.0	1.8	0.3
%[c]	5.2	9.9	17.6	27.2	29.8	26.1	21.4	4.8

[a] $ million.
[b] Share in Japan's trade with the world.
[c] Share in Japan's trade with China, Taiwan, Hong Kong, South Korea, North Korea and the Soviet Union.

Source: *Tsusho Hakusho*, respective years.

TABLE 2.4. Number of visitors between Japan and China, 1952–1959

Year	Japan to China		China to Japan	
	Group	Individual	Group	Individual
1952	11	50	0	0
1953	16	139	0	0
1954	21	192	1	10
1955	52	847	4	100
1956	108	1,182	7	142
1957	133	1,243	16	140
1958	unknown	594	5	93
1959	20	191	0	0

Source: *Chugoku Nenkan 1961*, p. 462.

Although Japan's non-governmental pro-China actors were not powerful enough to force the Japanese government to change its policy course, they were the actual architects of Japan–China trade, while the government found itself fundamentally constrained by international political factors.

The patterns of relations between the Japanese government and the non-governmental pro-China actors were affected by the structure of the pro-China private sector. Among the non-governmental pro-China individuals and organizations, there existed mixed motives of seeking diplomatic autonomy and independence. Those who were strongly motivated by the aspiration for diplomatic independence tended to use the China issue as an instrument to sabotage the basic foreign policy stance of the Japanese government. On the other hand, it was easier for the Japanese government, regardless of whether it was following a policy of collaboration or autonomy, to build a system of 'division of labour' with those advocating improved relations with China from the motives of seeking diplomatic autonomy within the confines of Pax Americana.

The JAPIT included big business people and conservative politicians, whereas the creation of the JCTPA was led primarily by politically progressive forces. The JCIEA was a governmental device created in its attempt to gain control of Japan–China trade. The JCTPDML was formed as a suprapartisan body, but was led by a conservative politician, Ikeda Masanosuke. Accordingly, the Japanese government's attitudes toward these organizations differed from those toward the independence elements. Yoshida was in frequent contact with Murata Shozo of JAPIT. When Hatoyama gave his words of 'support and cooperation' to the third private trade agreement, he conveyed them to Ikeda Masanosuke and Murata Shozo. This distinction in governmental attitudes became clearer when Friendship Trade and LT Trade were installed in the 1960s.

In sum, the complex fabric of structural pluralism in Japan's trade relations with China was thus composed, at one level, of the relationship between the government and the non-governmental sector. The pattern of the relationship was influenced by a further pluralistic structure in the non-governmental group. One tier of actors in this group comprised believers in diplomatic autonomy, while the other was composed of people and organizations motivated by a progressive political ideology calling for independence from Pax Americana.

The experiences of the 1950s did not lead to an institutionalized channel of bilateral trade. This was primarily due to the Chinese use of the four private trade agreements as a means to undermine the Japanese government's foreign policy objectives. This effort was doomed to failure because of Japan's enormous economic and political dependence on the United States. Even the advocates of diplomatic autonomy *vis-à-vis* the United States, who tended to see a 'solution' to the imperfect collaboration policy in an overture to China, had to accept Japan's basic diplomatic stance of reliance on the United States. Under these circumstances, Chinese outright anti-Japanese behaviour often made them feel dubious about Chinese intentions. Okazaki Kaheita, for example, recalled that at one point Chinese behaviour had discouraged him from making any efforts toward Japan–China friendship.[67] Thus, the 1950s was a decade of trial and error for both Japanese and Chinese interested in bilateral trade.

Developments in Japan–China trade in the 1950s, however, gave rise to pluralism as a characteristic of the structure of postwar Japan–China relations. Japan–China relations in the 1960s, including governmental policies by the Ikeda and Sato cabinets as well as Friendship Trade and LT/MT Trade, evolved on this structural pluralism.

[67] Okazaki, *Watashi no Kiroku*, p. 25.

3

Japan–China Relations in the 1960s

The years 1960 and 1962 marked a breakthrough in postwar Japan–China trade. While the mechanisms for bilateral trade in the 1950s did not give rise to an institutionalized channel, the trade system in the 1960s embraced two separate channels with different functions and participants: Friendship Trade (from 1960) and LT Trade (from 1962, which was renamed Memorandum Trade in 1968). In retrospect, Japan–China trade relations survived the turbulent decade of the 1960s because of the existence of these two distinct channels. In a way, trade relations more than survived; Japan's trade with China surpassed that with Taiwan from 1964 to 1967 (Table 3.1).

First, as Tables 3.1 and 3.2 demonstrate, substantial Japan–China trade contacts were constructed during the 1960s despite heavy political constraints. Japan–China trade recorded a marked increase from 1963 to 1966, at a pace exceeding the growth of Japan's trade with any other nation in North East Asia. It increased so rapidly that even a $63 million decline in 1967 left

TABLE 3.1. Japan's trade with China, Taiwan, and South Korea, 1960–1970

Year	China[a]	%	Taiwan[a]	%	South Korea[a]	%
1960	23	3.7	166	26.1	119	18.7
1961	48	6.3	164	21.7	148	19.6
1962	84	8.9	180	19.0	167	17.6
1963	137	11.8	230	19.8	187	16.0
1964	310	20.7	279	18.6	151	10.0
1965	470	25.7	375	20.5	222	12.1
1966	621	26.0	403	16.9	407	17.0
1967	558	21.7	465	18.1	499	19.4
1968	550	17.8	622	20.1	704	22.8
1969	625	16.5	787	20.8	901	23.8
1970	823	18.3	951	21.2	1,047	23.3

[a] $ million.

% Percentage share of Japan's trade with Northeast Asia (China, Taiwan, Hong Kong, South Korea, North Korea, and the Soviet Union).

Source: *Tsusho Hakusho*, respective years.

TABLE 3.2. China's trade with Japan, 1961–1970

	1961	1962	1963	1964	1965	1966	1967	1968	1969	1970
[a]	48	84	137	310	470	621	558	550	625	823
%	1.6	3.1	4.9	9.6	12.1	14.6	14.3	14.6	16.2	19.2

[a] $ million.

% Share of China's trade with Japan out of Japan's world trade.

Source: *Tsusho Hakusho*, respective years.

the level of China trade above that of Taiwan trade. Also, seen from the Chinese side, Japan became China's leading trade partner in 1964. Of course, the overall economic weight of this bilateral contact was much greater for China than for Japan. China, nonetheless, was the fourth largest trading partner of Japan after the United States, Australia, and Canada in 1966. Japan's share in Chinese foreign trade reached as much as 14 per cent by 1966, and maintained that level even during the Cultural Revolution (Table 3.2).

In contrast to these trade records, US East Asian policy determined the Japanese government policy toward China in several highly political and strategic areas: the recognition of Taipei as the sole legitimate government of China, support for the 'important question' formula of the China issue at the United Nations,[1] and careful avoidance by the Japanese government of direct contact with the Chinese government. In these areas, Tokyo could find no room for autonomous actions throughout the 1960s, and the Chinese leaders heavily criticized both Ikeda Hayato and Sato Eisaku for such policies as well as the strengthening of Japan–US security ties.

The first question then arises regarding the role of the Japanese government in overall Japan–China relations, which was severely constrained by the East Asian international environment throughout the 1960s. This issue will be addressed primarily in this chapter, supplemented by an analysis of the Japanese government's involvement in LT/MT Trade in Chapter 5.

The second question asks why the deterioration of political relations between Japan and China in the second half of the 1960s did not affect the volume of Japan–China trade very much. In the 1960s, China upheld the principle of inseparability between politics and economics, from which even pro-China Japanese were not free. In particular, when the governmental relationship rapidly deteriorated shortly before and during the Chinese Cultural Revolution, China made radical political demands on many pro-China individuals and institutions in Japan. How did Japan–China trade survive such extreme politicization of bilateral relations?

[1] This formula was pursued as a UN resolution to designate the issue of Chinese membership in the United Nations as an 'important question' requiring a two-thirds majority in the General Assembly voting. After becoming one of the five promoters of the resolution in 1961, the Japanese government supported the resolution throughout the 1960s.

Analyses in Chapters 4 and 5 reveal that this was due to the dual mechanism of Japan–China trade in the 1960s: Japan–China trade survived bilateral political difficulties because Friendship Trade compensated for the loss inflicted by the deterioration of bilateral relations on LT/MT Trade (see Table 4.2 on page 78). As seen in detail in the following two chapters, China dealt with the trade issue by clearly distinguishing between these two separate trade channels.

Still, the third question remains: why and how could Friendship Trade, which was under the strong influence of the JCP, survive the breakup of the relationship between the JCP and the Chinese Communist Party (CCP)? The answer, as examined in Chapter 4, was because the composition of the promoters of Friendship Trade was further complex. Namely, among the independence school promoting Friendship Trade were pro-JCP actors for whom advancing the Party's independence policy line was more important than friendship with China, and those pro-China actors for whom China was important more than anything else. When the two communist parties broke off their relations, the former group was expelled from Friendship Trade, while the latter actors pledged their allegiance to China.

Thus, the secret of the steady records of Japan–China trade in the politically difficult 1960s lay not in the Japanese government's 'conspiracy' or 'skillfully executed . . . neo-mercantilist foreign policy', but in the structural pluralism in bilateral trade at three levels: (1) the relationship between the Japanese government, which was fundamentally constrained by the international environment, and the non-governmental actors which attempted to promote exchanges with China relatively free from international constraints; (2) the relationship between Friendship Trade and LT/MT Trade; and (3) the relationship between pro-JCP actors and pro-China actors in the Friendship Trade mechanism.

The analysis following in this chapter as well as in Chapter 5 will address the first issue by comparing the China policies of the two Japanese Prime Ministers in the 1960s, i.e., Ikeda Hayato and Sato Eisaku, and by looking at the influence of US and Taiwan factors on their policies. The analysis will reveal the role of the Japanese government and its limits in Japan–China trade, and thus will bring into relief the structure of the relationship between the Japanese government and Japan's non-governmental actors. The second and third issues will be examined in the following two chapters.

3.2. CHINA POLICIES OF IKEDA AND SATO

It is widely held that Ikeda's China policy was positive, whereas Sato's was anti-Chinese. The fact, however, is that at the time when he became Prime Minister Sato's aspiration to improve relations with China was much stronger than that of Ikeda. The difference derived from their different diplomatic orientations: Sato viewed China as an object of his diplomatic aspiration for autonomy *vis-à-vis* the United States and as a target of opportunity to gain a political point in domestic politics, whereas Ikeda tended to see China from a long-term perspective based on his commitment to the policy of collaboration with the United States. Ikeda's basic policy was represented by his income-doubling plan, which required close economic relations with the United States, and he regarded China trade as a long-term possibility. In this sense, Ikeda's attitude toward China trade was that of a natural posture.

This was shown by his remark made to a group of news reporters on 6 October 1962:

Trade with Communist China is to be conducted on a private basis, so there is no need for the government to take a formal stand. If the private sector actively promotes it, the government would make a relevant response. It has been reported that the United States has made reference to Communist China trade, but this is a question that Japan alone should decide.

But, what is trade with Communist China? Mr. Matsumura's visit to China made it evident that it should not be over-evaluated. There is no 'dreaming of another dream', thinking of the old continental trade. The highest point in trade with Communist China was $60 million five years ago. It would not exceed that level even with maximum effort over the coming years. Also, Communist China would want to buy a lot of things from Japan, but what would Japan buy from Communist China?[2]

This statement attracted much publicity and was interpreted by the media as a newly cautious posture by Ikeda.[3] One scholarly work interpreted it as a 'retreat from' or a 'reversal of' Ikeda's earlier posture, brought about by Harriman's speech in late September (see below).[4] These words by Ikeda, however, were nothing other than the expression of his objective assessment of the situation. True, the remark was intended as a response to words of caution in Harriman's statement, and thus was directed primarily toward the conservatives about China trade. The substance of the remark, however, correctly reflected Ikeda's perception. In other words, Ikeda's attitude toward China trade was always carried out within such limits. In contrast, it was Japan's non-governmental pro-China actors that attempted to promote Japan–China trade beyond such limits. As seen in Chapter 5, Ikeda supported the establishment of LT Trade as much as he could. This act, however, was not what he initiated as Prime Minister, but simply an act to support the development initiated by the private sector.

In contrast, Sato Eisaku had been a rather ardent exponent of improved relations with China since shortly before becoming Prime Minister. For

---

[2] *Asahi Shinbun*, 6 October 1962 (evening).

[3] *Asahi Shinbun*, 7 October 1962.

[4] Yang, *The Policy-Making Process in Japan's Policy Toward the People's Republic of China*, pp. 112–16.

example, he appeared at the Chinese Economic and Trade Exhibition in Tokyo in April 1964, and conferred with Nan Hanchen, chairman of the CCPIT, who was visiting Japan as head of the economic friendship delegation to the Exhibition. They met on 14 May at the office of the Sato faction. On this occasion, Sato boldly questioned the validity of the policy of separation of politics from economics, and gave the impression to Nan that his posture on Japan–China relations was more forward-looking than that of Ikeda.[5] The fact that Sato was a member of the Ikeda cabinet as Director of the Hokkaido Development Agency added to the importance of this event. Sato also appeared at Nan Hanchen's farewell party on 20 May. After the party, Nan said to the Japanese press, 'Mr. Sato is a farsighted politician, and impressed me very much.'[6]

At this point, China appeared to be hoping that Sato would succeed Ikeda as Prime Minister. In September 1964, a plan to hold a meeting between Sato and Zhou Enlai in Rangoon, Burma, had been negotiated between Kuno Chuji, a lieutenant of the Sato faction, and Liao Chengzhi. This meeting did not materialize because Ikeda's health worsened and the prospects of Sato's early succession to Ikeda suddenly grew.[7]

Sato's eagerness to meet Nan Hanchen in May 1964 was closely linked to the LDP presidential election scheduled for July. Sato's 'think-tank' grouping, which was set up on 15 January 1964, had been working on a pre-election policy declaration for the coming LDP presidential election. This project, named the 'S Operation' after Sato, took the China question as the most urgent issue facing Japan. In fact, the first draft of the declaration called China policy under a future Sato government 'the most important foreign policy issue', which amounted to a call for fundamental reconsideration of Japan's China policy.[8]

The final version of the declaration, however, was considerably toned down; it simply stated that Sato would deepen Japan–China contacts in all possible areas, including the economic and cultural fronts as well as personal exchanges. The return of Okinawa was another foreign policy issue that the S Operation had listed on the policy agenda, but it too was dropped from the final version, because the team judged it wise to avoid making foreign policy an issue of political contention for the prime ministership.[9]

This did not mean, however, that Sato had given up the idea of promoting Japan–China relations. On 10 November 1964, just one day after the inauguration of his cabinet, Sato stated in a press conference:

5 Tagawa Seiichi, *Nitchu Koryu to Jimin-to Ryoshu-tachi [Japan–China Exchange and the LDP Leaders]* (Tokyo: Yomiuri Shinbun-sha, 1983), pp. 28–9.

6 'Nan Kanshin no 40-nichi' [Forty Days of Nan Hanchen], *Ekonomisuto*, 42 (1964), p. 28.

7 Tagawa, *Nitchu Koryu to Jimin-to Ryoshu-tachi*, pp. 29–32.

8 Kusuda Minoru (ed.), *Sato Seiken 2797-nichi (Jo) [2797 Days of the Sato Government, Vol. 1]* (Tokyo: Gyosei Mondai Kenkyu-jo, 1983), pp. 49, 58.

9 *Ibid.*, pp. 62–3.

... Japan–Korean negotiations and the question of Communist China are fundamental issues of Japanese diplomacy, and therefore important questions that are being imposed on the Sato cabinet. . . . Fortunately or unfortunately, Japan had concluded a peace treaty with the nationalist government. But, I do not think that the goodwill displayed by Generalissimo Chiang at the end of the war will constrain the way Japanese people live. I am very grateful to Generalissimo Chiang, but cannot dispose of this issue by such an emotional argument.[10]

Despite this positive attitude toward China, Sato's China policy gradually turned negative, whereas that of Ikeda, who did not show any of Sato's enthusiasm, appeared forward-looking. This could be explained by the different international and domestic political environments that the two Prime Ministers faced. Internationally, the political environment of Japan–China relations deteriorated during the tenure of Sato due to the Vietnam War and Sato's support of the US military mission. In contrast, Ikeda's China policy was blessed with worsening Sino-Soviet relations and a conciliatory mood in the US China policy during the presidency of John F. Kennedy. At the domestic level, Ikeda's tenure coincided with the period in China when the influence of Chinese radicals subsided because of the failure in the Great Leap Forward, whereas Sato had to deal with China as it embarked on the Cultural Revolution. In Japan, the influence of pro-Taiwan political forces was much stronger on Sato than on Ikeda. We will now turn to an analysis of these factors.

3.3. THE US FACTOR

For the United States, maintaining an effective strategic environment in East Asia was a primary concern; Washington did not interfere with the development of Japan–China relations if it remained within such strategic confines. The crucial policy areas in this connection, as far as Japan was concerned, were Japan–US security ties, Japan's continuous recognition of Taipei, Japan's support of the 'important question' formula at the United Nations, and the imposition of the COCOM restrictions on China trade. No Japanese cabinet ever defied US policies in these areas, and consequently Washington did not appear very concerned about the prospect of a reasonable expansion in Japan–China trade. This clearly contrasted with the case of Tokyo–Taipei relations.

If there were US pressures, they were indirect ones reminding Japan of the importance of complying with the strategic framework. For example, a reminder of the political danger involved in Japan–China trade was issued on 26 September 1962 by Averell Harriman, Assistant Secretary of State for Far Eastern Affairs. The relevant part of the speech, which occupied about a

---

[10] *Asahi Shinbun*, 10 November 1964 (evening).

tenth of the speech delivered at the National Press Club before the Japan–US Society, was as follows:

One interesting aspect of Japan's expansion is that it has been done without, practically without, any trade with mainland China. Some people felt that Japan's future lay in trade with mainland China. Well, the extraordinary result in Japan which we have been discussing has been achieved practically without any trade with mainland China. Such trade has been very small.

I see that there have been some missions which have gone to mainland China, but I hope, Mr. Ambassador, that your government people will recognize that the sound trade you can count on which won't be used for political purposes is trade with the Free World. Moreover, there is a great opportunity for increased development in Free World trade.

Whatever trade is done with the communist countries, one must recognize, might well be used later on for political purposes.

In case of Japan, of course, Red China tried to get political concessions, believing that Japan would give in on political concessions, if you remember. However, Japan stood firm and proved to the Chinese communists that Japan could move forward without them. I think it was a very healthy example and I applaud very much your government and your people for the manner in which you handled it.[11]

The Japanese media reported this statement as American pressure. It, however, should be interpreted not as a warning against Japan's China trade, but as a message reminding Japan that the United States did not wish to see an expansion of Japan–China trade beyond a certain political framework.

Evidence suggests, in fact, that so long as Japan–China trade would not undermine US strategic objectives in East Asia, the United States was well prepared to remain on the sideline. For example, Assistant Secretary of State Roger Hilsman stated in a press conference on 16 April 1963 that allowing deferred payments in Japan–China trade would be equal to providing economic aid, but emphasized at the same time that this was a matter that Japan alone should decide.[12] Moreover, Secretary of Commerce Luther Hodges explicitly stated in a press conference on 7 January 1964—which incidentally was after the Japanese government's decision to allow Export–Import Bank credits for exporting Kurashiki Rayon's plant facilities—that the United States was not very concerned about the report that Japan's China trade had been expanding, because Japan–China trade was on a small scale and did not include strategic commodities.[13]

What converted these moderate US reactions into a larger-than-life obstacle was the hypersensitivity of the Japanese business community. For Ohara Soichiro, president of Kurashiki Rayon, possible repercussions from the United States were his primary concern. To feel out the US reaction to ongoing

11 White, *An Analysis of Japan's China Policy Under the Liberal Democratic Party, 1955–1970*, p. 112.

12 *Asahi Shinbun*, 17 April 1963 (evening).

13 *Asahi Shinbun*, 8 January 1964 (evening).

plant negotiations, Ohara participated in a Japan–US private citizens' conference held in late September 1962 in the United States. There, he found out, much to his relief, that the United States was not against the Japanese export of plant facilities to China. Coming soon after Harriman's statement on Japan–China trade and shortly before the Takasaki mission of late 1962, Ohara's trip had a crucial impact on his subsequent decision to export chemical fibre plant facilities to China as part of the LT Trade agreement negotiated by Takasaki.[14] Developments involving the steel industry and other big business leaders in the preparation stage of the LT arrangements also illustrate the point, as well be recounted in Chapter 5.

In contrast to such hypersensitivity in business circles, the government of Japan, whether under Ikeda or Sato, remained by and large calm and objective in assessing the constraints imposed by US East Asian policy and the meanings of statements by US high officials. Despite their differing basic foreign policy orientations, neither Ikeda nor Sato intended to take the risk of undermining the Japan–US relationship in order to expand Japan–China trade.

Under these circumstances, the Japanese government's involvement in China trade was possible only within the confines delineated by the principle of the separation of politics from economics. The separation of politics from economics did not mean that political matters and economic matters were separable. It meant, most importantly, that the Japanese government would assist or condone trade dealings with China within a certain political framework, but that this would not mean entering into political negotiations with Beijing, let alone recognizing it as the legitimate government of China. This policy of the Japanese government was accepted by the United States, which accounts for its benign reactions to expanded Japan–China trade. For example, the Sato–Johnson communiqué of 13 January 1965 stated:

. . . The Prime Minister stated that it is the fundamental policy of the Japanese Government to maintain friendly ties based on the regular diplomatic relationship with the Government of the Republic of China and at the same time to continue to promote private contact with the Chinese mainland in such matters as trade on the basis of the principle of separation of political matters from economic matters.[15]

Under this policy, Japan–China trade was treated as purely private, which allowed the government of Japan to distance itself from external pressures, including to some extent those from Taipei.

Evidence abounds indicating that this mechanism was effectively at work throughout the 1960s. For instance, in September 1962, when Ikeda conferred with Matsumura before Matsumura's mission to China, Ikeda reportedly said to Matsumura, 'My position compels me to keep my "face" directed

---

[14] Ohara 'Tai-Chugoku Puranto Yushutsu ni Tsuite', p. 104.
[15] Ibid., p. 543.

toward the United States. So will you represent my "face" to China?'[16] Even though Matsumura was a prominent LDP member, he had never officially represented the government in his contacts with China, nor did Ikeda intend to give him such credence. If his China missions had not been conducted in a private capacity, it would have been totally impossible for him to pave the way toward the subsequent Takasaki mission, as explicated in Chapter 5. In fact, on 11 September 1962, Foreign Minister Ohira Masayoshi told a press conference that the visits to China by Matsumura and Takasaki had nothing to do with the government because they were invited as private persons, and that Japan–China trade ought to be conducted purely on a private basis.

It is pertinent to repeat that the separation of politics from economics was not to say that politics and economics were unrelated, but was an expressed determination to carry out economic exchanges within the given political framework. Because of this particular pattern of correlation between politics and economics, the policy proved effective, which in turn allowed non-governmental actors to promote Japan–China trade to the extent which the government alone could not have achieved. This 'division of labour' was the main structural characteristic of the relationship between the Japanese government and the private sector under the given international constraints before diplomatic normalization.

In fact, none of the Japanese participants in bilateral contacts with China officially represented the government in any form. All the LDP politicians involved visited China in a private capacity. And this was effective. Before Tagawa Seiichi visited China in February–March 1968 to negotiate a renewal of the LT arrangements, for example, he resigned his position as Vice-Minister of the Ministry of Welfare.[17] In connection with LT Trade, we will see in Chapter 5 that Watanabe Yaeji also left his position as Bureau Chief of International Trade of the MITI in order to join the Takasaki office, and that Soma Tsunetoshi assumed a position as an advisor to the Japan–China Export–Import Association, cutting his affiliation with the MITI at least formally and temporarily, before leaving for his post in Beijing as chief representative of the Beijing liaison office. Also, bureaucrats dispatched to the liaison office in Beijing assumed posts as members of the Takasaki office, or the Japan–China memorandum trade office as it came to be called later. All of these were rather formal measures, but the formality was the essence of the separation of politics from economics.

It is true that Ikeda, despite his inclination toward collaboration diplomacy, in effect exhibited a much more positive attitude toward expanding Japan–China trade than did Sato, who was quite eager to improve relations

---

[16] Furukawa, *Nitchu Sengo Kankei-shi*, p. 204.

[17] Tagawa Seiichi, *Nitchu Kosho Hiroku: Tagawa Nikki–14-nen no Shogen [Secret Stories of Japan–China Negotiations: Tagawa Diary–Testimony of Fourteen Years]* (Tokyo: Mainichi Shinbun-sha, 1973), p. 72.

with China as part of his pursuit of more autonomy in Japanese diplomacy. The gap is partly explained by domestic politics, where Sato was quite susceptible to pressures from pro-Taiwan forces, as will be seen below. Also, Sato was caught in an unfavourable international development for his China policy. Especially toward the end of the 1960s, the escalation of conflict in Vietnam and the heightening of political radicalism in China during the Cultural Revolution affected Sato's China policy quite significantly. These developments required closer Japan–US cooperation on highly political issues, especially regarding the US engagement in the Vietnam War and efforts to counter the 'China threat'. For example, the joint communiqué between Sato and Johnson signed on 15 November 1967 directly referred to the existence of this 'China threat':

. . . They noted the fact that Communist China is developing its nuclear arsenal and agreed on the importance of creating conditions wherein Asian nations would not be susceptible to threats from Communist China.[18]

The Sato–Nixon communiqué of 21 November 1969 was noted for linking the security of Taiwan with that of Japan:

. . . The Prime Minister said that the maintenance of peace and security in the Taiwan area was also a most important factor for the security of Japan.[19]

All these statements were bitterly criticized by China as a revival of Japanese militarism, and consequently Japan–China relations further deteriorated.[20]

Despite all these so-called 'anti-China' policies by Sato on the political front, Sato kept the overall mechanisms of Japan–China trade basically intact. He continuously adhered to the separation of politics from economics. There was no indication that Sato had discarded this basic policy despite heightening tensions in East Asia during the second half of the 1960s. Sato tolerated heavy criticism directed against him in the MT communiqués negotiated by the MT participants from his own party, and he did not act against Japan–China trade exchanges even though Friendship Trade, with its anti-governmental tone, occupied an increasing portion of trade annually toward the end of the 1960s. In sum, the division of labour continued throughout the 1960s. It remained effective despite changing external conditions, precisely because it was structured to absorb, if not to defy, the external constraints imposed by the strategic environment in East Asia.

Some aspects of Sato's China policy, however, were further constrained by the Taiwan factor. In many ways, it was a much more complicated obstacle than the US factor.

[18] *Nihon Gaiko Shuyo Monjo-Nenpyo (2) 1961–1970 [Major Documents and Chronology of Japanese Diplomacy (2) 1961–1970]* (Tokyo: Hara Shobo, 1984), p. 732.
[19] *Ibid.*, pp. 880–81.
[20] Okabe Tatsumi, *Chugoku no Tai-nichi Seisaku [Chinese Policy toward Japan]* (Tokyo: Tokyo-daigaku Shuppan-kai, 1976).

3.4. THE TAIWAN FACTOR

The United States, as the dominant force in East Asian security, established the basic framework within which the Japan–China economic relationship developed. The resulting policy of the separation of politics from economics by the Japanese government was also in line with the interests of Taiwan. But Taipei had a more intense concern than Washington with the specifics of Japan–China trade, and reacted strongly to any sign of expanded ties. Tokyo's room to manoeuvre was even more circumscribed by the fact that Beijing kept a close eye on the Tokyo–Taipei relationship, or more precisely, on the way Japan would respond to pressures from Taiwan. These factors were reinforced by pro-Taiwan forces within the LDP. For these reasons, the Taiwan factor was at times a more potent influence on the development of Japan–China trade than the Washington factor, albeit at a less fundamental level.

One crucial factor had to do with China policy groups in the LDP and their relationship with Sato. The anti-Beijing, pro-Taipei Asian Problem Study Group (APSG) was formed within the LDP on 16 December 1964, soon after the inauguration of the Sato cabinet. The APSG was led by pronounced pro-Taipei politicians, receiving full support from such influentials as Kishi Nobusuke and Ishii Mitsujiro. They formed the group in a flurry, because they were annoyed by Sato's forward-looking attitude on the China issue and wished to check this tendency before his forthcoming visit to the United States.

The APSG succeeded in drawing up an 'interim report on foreign policy', which was passed by the LDP Policy Affairs Research Council (PARC) Committee on Foreign Affairs on 25 December and was presented to Sato before his departure for Washington. It included four points: (1) China must not be admitted to the United Nations because it is not peace-loving; (2) a small amount of China trade would be condoned, but Chinese political manoeuvring to communize Japan must not be tolerated; (3) Taiwan's seat in the United Nations must be protected, because Taiwan is a lifeline of Japan's security; (4) it is dangerous to expand trade with the communist bloc.[21]

In response to these pro-Taiwan moves, pro-China Diet members established the Asia–African Problem Study Group (AAPSG) on 28 January 1965, a little over a month later than the APSG. This group was led by Utsunomiya Tokuma, Kawasaki Hideji, and Kuno Chuji and included Matsumura Kenzo and Fujiyama Aiichiro as advisors. The AAPSG took the totally opposite posture to the APSG. The AAPSG's basic stance on the China issue could be summarized as follows: (1) China must become a member of the United Nations, which would ease tensions in Asia; (2) therefore, Japan must not support the 'important question' formula of the China issue at the United

---

[21] 'Ajia Mondai Kenkyu-kai' [Asian Problem Study Group], *Ekonomisuto*, 43 (1965), p. 74.

Nations; (3) governmental contacts with China must be pursued through such channels as ambassadorial talks [in a third country]; (4) Japan–China trade must be expanded through governmental contacts.[22]

Table 3.3 shows the distribution of members of the APSG and the AAPSG by LDP factions. Both groups cut across the main factional divisions to some extent, but more significantly, no members of the Kishi–Fukuda and Ishii factions, two major backers of the Sato government, joined the AAPSG in January 1965. Also, in January 1965, 63.0 per cent of the APSG members came from the 'mainstream' factions which supported Prime Minister Sato, including the Sato, Kishi–Fukuda, Ishii, Kawashima, and Miki factions, while 76.8 per cent of the AAPSG members were from the opposing 'non-mainstream' factions.[23] These per centages increased to 67.2 and 86.0 respectively by July 1966, indicating that the cleavage between the mainstream and non-mainstream factions over the China issue became wider as Sato grew more passive in his policy toward China. Also, the total membership of the APSG increased in one and half years, while the membership of the AAPSG showed a reverse trend. It is difficult to judge the causal relationship, but perhaps the increasing predominance of the APSG brought about Sato's passive China policy, which in turn discouraged the activities of the AAPSG.

TABLE 3.3. Distribution of APSG and AAPSG members by factions (Lower House)

Factions	APSG		AAPSG		Total[a]
	Jan. 1965[c]	July 1966[d]	Jan. 1965[c]	July 1966[d]	
Sato[b]	17	19	6	3	44
Kishi–Fukuda[b]	13	11	0	1	20
Ishii[b]	10	12	0	0	14
Kawashima[b]	4	5	1	2	18
Miki[b]	7	16	9	2	30
Matsumura	0	0	6	6	6
Fujiyama	7	6	9	3	18
Maeo	11	12	8	6	47
Ono	7	5	12	8	27
Kono	2	5	17	22	45
Others	3	3	1	4	16
Total	81	94	69	57	

[a] Total of faction members as of July 1966, from Fukui, *Party in Power*, p. 256.
[b] indicates mainstream factions of the Sato cabinet.

Sources: [c] 'Chugoku Seisaku wo Towareru', p. 16; [d] Fukui, *Party in Power*, p. 256.

[22] 'Chugoku Seisaku wo Towareru Hoshu-Kakushin' [Conservative and Progressive Parties Challenged by the China Policy], *Ekonomisuto*, 43 (1965), pp. 15–16.

[23] For more on the implications of the APSG–AAPSG cleavage, see Fukui Haruhiro, *Party in Power: the Japanese Liberal-Democrats and Policy-Making* (Berkeley: University of California Press, 1970), pp. 254–60.

The singular importance of this intra-LDP cleavage can be understood when its different implications for Ikeda and Sato are realized. Only seven and two members from the Ono and Kono factions respectively initially joined the APSG. These two major factions had supported Ikeda, along with the Kawashima and the Miki–Matsumura factions, in the LDP presidential election of 10 July 1964, when Ikeda won his third term against Sato and Fujiyama.

Equally important were the APSG's close personal and institutional ties with Taiwan. A central institution was the Japan–China (Taiwan) Coopera-tion Committee, which originated in 1956 when Ishii Mitsujiro, chairman of the LDP Executive Council, led a friendship delegation to Taipei.[24]

Sixteen meetings were held between April 1957 and October 1971. For the first several meetings, the Japanese participants, largely business-related people and intellectuals, were resentful of the Taiwanese high-handed, self-righteous accusations against what they called the 'pro-communist' attitude of the Japanese government and people.[25]

From the time of the fifth meeting in 1959, however, clear signs emerged that the atmosphere of the Cooperation Committee was changing. Horikoshi Teizo of Keidanren (Federation of Economic Organizations), who was in charge of the administrative matters of the Cooperation Committee, wrote about the fifth meeting that 'Our understanding of one another's domestic conditions has been deepened, and some of the questions which used to re-quire thousands of words can now be solved by an exchange of a few words.'[26]

At the same time, the number of Japanese participants in the Cooperation Committee doubled at this fifth meeting to thirty-one, up from a range of twelve to sixteen members at each of the previous four meetings. More im-portantly, the number of LDP politicians jumped to six, and Nagano Shigeo, president of Fuji Iron and Steel, and Sudo Takujiro, advisor to Toyo Rayon, joined for the first time.[27] These changes were caused by the rupture of Japan–China exchanges after the Nagasaki flag incident of May 1958 and the radicalization of Chinese politics on both domestic and external fronts as signified by the Great Leap Forward and the 1958 offshore islands crisis in the Taiwan strait.

Chang Chun, General Secretary to Chiang Kai-shek, remembered of the Cooperation Committee: 'What we had initially aimed at was to maintain a

[24] Ishii Mitsujiro, *Omoide no Ki, III [Recollections, III]* (Tokyo: Karucha Shuppan, 1976).

[25] Horikoshi Teizo, 'Dai-l-kai Nikka Kyoryoku Iinkai' [The First Japan–China(Taiwan) Cooperation Committee], *Keidanren Geppo*, 5 (1957), p. 15; Horikoshi Teizo, 'Dai-2-kai Nikka Kyoryoku Iinkai Hokoku' [A Report on the Second Japan–China(Taiwan) Cooperation Committee], *Keidanren Geppo*, 6 (1958), p. 39.

[26] Horikoshi Teizo, 'Nikka Keizai Kyoryoku Iinkai Dai-5-kai Sokai Hokoku' [A Report on the Fifth General Meeting of the Japan–China(Taiwan) Economic Cooperation Committee], *Keidanren Geppo*, 7 (1959), p. 40.

[27] For the list of participants in the fifth meeting, see ibid., p. 43.

close working relationship between this institution and governmental diplomacy by using it as a supplement to governmental contacts. We expected that the Japanese members would exert influence on the Japanese government's policy making.'[28] This desire of the Taiwanese side became more and more realistic as influential LDP politicians continued to become involved in the Cooperation Committee. Such LDP elder statesmen as Kishi Nobusuke, Ishii Mitsujiro, and Ono Banboku had been acting as advisors from the initial period, and in the 1960s, Funada Naka, Kaya Okinori, Fukuda Takeo, Aichi Kiichi, Tanaka Tatsuo, and Kitazawa Naokichi were among the participants at several meetings.[29]

As these pro-Taiwan LDP politicians, who later became core members of the APSG, associated themselves with the Cooperation Committee, the Taiwanese side did in fact use the channel in attempting to influence the Japanese government. Following his attendance at the eighth meeting in 1963, for example, Funada Naka conveyed to the Ministers of Foreign Affairs and the MITI Taipei's strong objections to Japan's expected export of industrial plant to China.[30] Also, Chang Chun recalls that he activated the Cooperation Committee channel to transmit Taipei's views to Ono Banboku and Kishi Nobusuke in August 1963 following Ikeda's approval of the Export–Import Bank credits for the export of Kurashiki's plant (Chapter 5). Chiang Kai-shek simultaneously sent a 'full-hearted' telegram to Yoshida Shigeru.[31] In response to these moves by Taipei, Kishi Nobusuke, Ishii Mitsujiro, Adachi Tadashi (chairman of the Japan Chamber of Commerce and Industry), and Horikoshi Teizo visited Ikeda on 7 March 1964, and questioned him about the issue.[32] The resolution adopted at the ninth meeting in December 1964 even declared:

... Japan undertakes to reject government-supported trade in any form with the areas under Communist Chinese control and to deny financial and banking measures to Japanese firms trading with such areas.[33]

These pressures from the Taiwanese side eventually culminated in the Yoshida letter incident in 1964. As seen in Chapter 5, Ikeda thought of the Yoshida letter (1964) as something to give a 'cooling-off' period to Taipei. Sato, however, found himself held entwined in the Taiwan tangle, so he turned his attention away from the China question to the normalization of diplomatic relations with South Korea and the reversion of Okinawa. To

[28] Chang Chun, *Nikka: Huun no 70-nen [Japan–China: Stormy Seventy Years]* (Tokyo: Sankei Shuppan, 1980), p. 242.
[29] Fukui, *Jiyuminshu-to to Seisaku Kettei*, p. 315: Takemi Keizo, 'Kokko Danzetsu-ki ni Okeru Nittai Kosho Channeru no Saihen Katei' [Reorganization Process of the Japan–Taiwan Negotiation Channel at the Rupture of Diplomatic Relations], in Kamiya Fuji (ed.), *Hokuto-Ajia no Kinko to Doyo [Balance and Disturbance in North East Asia]* (Tokyo: Keio Tsushin, 1980), pp. 82–3.
[30] Fukui, *Party in Power*, p. 253.   [31] Chang, *Nikka*, p. 190.
[32] *Asahi Shinbun*, 25 March 1964.   [33] Fukui, *Party in Power*, p. 246.

make things worse, those two foreign policy issues proved quite sensitive ones for Beijing, and so further aggravated already strained relations between Sato and the Chinese leaders.

Recall, however, that Japan–China trade remained at consistent levels, despite the constraint on Sato and the rapid deterioration of Japan–China political relations toward the end of the 1960s. Given the conventional wisdom to the effect that Japan–China relations in the 1960s were a function of high politics, the effectiveness of the division of labour between the government and the non-governmental sector, which constituted one tier of the pluralist structure in Japan's trade relations with China, merits special note. Within this structure, the particular dynamics of trade relations with China developed through the initiatives of non-governmental pro-China actors, which materialized in Friendship Trade and LT Trade.

4
Friendship Trade

The previous chapter explored the China policy of the Japanese government which constituted one layer of the pluralistic structure in Japan's relations with China. This chapter and the following one focus on specific trade arrangements of the 1960s, namely, Friendship Trade and LT/MT Trade, and their relationship. These two forms of trade had quite different characteristics, and constituted the second tier of structural pluralism in Japan's trade relations with China in the 1960s. Also, this chapter will illuminate the third tier of the pluralistic structure, i.e., the structural characteristics of Friendship Trade, and thus explicate how and why Friendship Trade could survive the turbulant era swayed by the conflict between the Japan Communist Party (JCP) and the Chinese Communist Party (CCP).

4.1. BACKGROUND

The foundation of Friendship Trade was established by the 'three trade principles' enunciated on 27 August 1960 by Zhou Enlai in his meeting with Suzuki Kazuo, managing director of the Japan–China Trade Promotion Association (JCTPA). The three principles were the cornerstone upon which three different forms of Japan–China trade would be based, namely, (1) governmental agreement, (2) private contract, and (3) individual consideration. Zhou stated that a governmental agreement must be concluded eventually, but that in the meantime Japanese firms and Chinese corporations could deal with each other on the basis of private contracts. Zhou further referred to the JCTPA and asked it to introduce to the China Committee for the Promotion of International Trade (CCPIT) those transactions which would be friendly, reciprocal, and feasible.[1]

This new development in 1960 was a marked departure from the pattern of the 1950s, in that China clearly distinguished between the Japanese government and the private sector. This policy was a Chinese version of *de facto* 'separation of politics from economics', which ran counter to its official insistance on 'inseparability of politics and economics'. As explained in Chapter 2, China persistently attempted in the 1950s to draw the Japanese government

---

[1] *Kankei Shiryo*, pp. 210–12; *Sengo Shiryo*, pp. 259–60; *Kihon Shiryo*, pp. 178–80. The text of Zhou's remark was handed to a delegation of JSP Diet members during Zhou's talks with the delegation on 10 September (see *Sengo Shiryo*, p. 258), and was published in the *People's Daily* on 13 September.

into bilateral trade arrangements. Zhou's three trade principles now paved the way for Japanese non-governmental elements to establish a new institutionalized channel with the Chinese authorities.

A fortuitous combination of events in early 1960 in both China and Japan facilitated this new development. First, the Sino-Soviet dispute turned into an open rift and escalated sharply at this time. Precipitated most importantly by the offshore islands crisis of 1958 and the Soviet unilateral decision in mid-1959 to tear up the 1957 nuclear agreement, Chinese leaders in mid-1959 felt the necessity to make a critical decision 'whether to extend new pressure on Moscow to alter its policies even at the risk of exacerbating tensions, or to search for compromises in order to try to repair relations'.[2] The domestic political struggle in China over this critical issue eventually led to the purge of the Minister of National Defence Peng Dehuai in late 1959, who had favoured a compromising approach toward the Soviet Union. Thereafter, Mao's more combative view favouring a direct ideological attack prevailed.

On the occasion of the ninetieth anniversary of Lenin's birthday in April 1960, the Chinese took the initiative to bring the dispute into the open. In late June, the Russians moved to the counteroffensive at the Bucharest Conference of communist parties, which led to a bitter clash between Khrushchev and the Chinese representative Peng Zhen. The period after the Bucharest Conference was 'without question the most strained in the long history of the Sino-Soviet alliance'.[3] This tension was highlighted most dramatically by the sudden pullout of almost all Soviet advisors and technical experts in China in July 1960.

The process of China's political disengagement from the Soviet Union could not but influence the pattern of Chinese economic dealings with the world. Moreover, the 'Great Crisis' caused by the failure of the Great Leap Forward did not allow China to disengage itself from outside sources of agricultural and industrial inputs.[4] China's new approach toward Japan took place under these circumstances.

Second, developments in the Japanese political scene also facilitated the resumption of bilateral trade relations. Given the Chinese unyielding opposition to the Kishi government, one could not expect any constructive move from the Chinese side as long as the political situation in Japan remained unchanged. The inauguration of a new Japanese cabinet would, therefore, provide an opportunity for both Japan and China to resume efforts to reopen trade ties with each other. Aptly enough, the new Ikeda cabinet was installed

[2] A. Doak Barnett, *China and the Major Powers in East Asia* (Washington, DC: The Brookings Institution, 1977), p. 39. The author sees a close connection between these two events. See pp. 35–6, 344–6.
[3] Donald S. Zagoria, *The Sino-Soviet Conflict, 1956–1961* (Princeton: Princeton University Press, 1962), p. 320.
[4] Alexander Eckstein, *China's Economic Revolution* (Cambridge: Cambridge University Press, 1977), pp. 58–9.

on 19 July 1960, three days after the Soviet Union announced the withdrawal of its experts in China.

In late July 1960, it was revealed that China would send representatives to the tenth anniversary celebration (opening on 31 July) of the General Council of Trade Unions of Japan (Sohyo), the constituent labour federation of the Japan Socialist Party (JSP), and the Sixth World Congress Against Atomic and Hydrogen Bombs (opening on 6 August).[5] Liu Ningyi, chairman of the All-China Federation of Trade Unions, was to head the delegation, and he reportedly told a Sohyo representative that 'now that Kishi is overthrown, I can meet the people of Japan'.[6] The timing of the announcement, less than a week after Ikeda's inauguration, coupled with the fact that this would be the first delegation to Japan since China had terminated contacts in May 1958, suggested that China was now signalling a change in Japan policy.

The new Ikeda government responded to this Chinese move quite rapidly and favourably. The decision to admit the delegation was announced by Chief Cabinet Secretary Ohira Masayoshi at a press conference on 26 July.[7] Thus, on 29 July 1960, only ten days after Ikeda took office and three days after the Japanese government's decision, the Chinese delegation arrived in Tokyo. The importance of the delegation was unmistakably manifested in its composition, which included Zhao Anbo as deputy head and Sun Pinghua as a member.[8] Both were directors of the Chinese People's Institute of Foreign Affairs and Japan specialists close to Liao Chengzhi, the highest official under Zhou Enlai responsible for China's relations with Japan.

During their two-week stay, the delegation contacted a variety of people and organizations, including the opposition parties, China trade promotion organizations, left-wing organizations, and pro-China LDP politicians.[9] The delegation apparently came away with a favourable impression. In a report on his Japan visit in the *People's Daily* of 27 August (the day when Zhou Enlai conveyed the three trade principles to Suzuki Kazuo), Liu Ningyi attacked Kishi but withheld any comments on the Ikeda cabinet. He affirmed that 'friendly relations between the two peoples are already deep-rooted, and no force can cut them'. This was interpreted in Japan as suggesting that China was now ready to launch new steps to restore bilateral relations.[10] Encouraged by these developments both in China and Japan, and the 'success' of Chinese probes, Zhou Enlai presented the new formula for China's Japan policy to Suzuki Kazuo on 27 August 1960, the same day that the *People's Daily* carried the report of Liu's trip to Japan.

Thus, there were three important aspects in the development leading to the eventual establishment of Friendship Trade. First, the Chinese *de facto*

[5] The information was disclosed in Hong Kong by former secretary-general of the General Council of Trade Unions of Japan (Sohyo) Takano, who arrived in Hong Kong on 24 July.

[6] *Asahi Shinbun*, 25 July 1960.   [7] *Asahi Shinbun*, 27 July 1960.
[8] *Asahi Shinbun*, 30 July 1960.   [9] *Chugoku Nenkan 1961*, pp. 55–6.
[10] *Aschi Shinbun*, 29 August 1960.

policy of separation of politics from economics provided an important new departure. Zhou Enlai, for instance, proposed a formula which clearly distinguished between the Japanese government and the private sector. This meant that while the Japanese government could not deal with the Chinese government owing to international and domestic constraints, Japanese non-governmental sectors would have the leeway to play a practical role in furthering bilateral relations.

Second, the Chinese leaders did not want to give the impression that their new policy contradicted their unyielding official policy of inseparability of politics and economics. The three political principles, which were originally directed against the China policy of the Kishi cabinet, were not necessarily effective toward the Ikeda cabinet with which China was about to establish a new relationship. Thus, the Chinese attached great importance to the three political principles as a yardstick for the definition of 'friendliness' of Japanese firms. By enforcing the same principles on any Japanese firm wishing to engage in Friendship Trade, the Chinese managed to reopen a trade channel to Japan without appearing to discard its previous opposition to the Japanese government.

Third, Ikeda's flexible posture toward China trade was important. This reflected a typical stance toward China held by the promoters of collaboration with the United States. It is worth recalling the place of China in the Yoshida Doctrine. At the core of the collaboration thinking represented by the Yoshida Doctrine was a long-term calculation of Japan's national interests supported by realism to international relations. Ikeda viewed China from this perspective, and the decision to allow the entry of Liu Ningyi was not contrary to the political current at the time nor to his conviction about the collaboration with the United States as the basis of Japanese diplomacy under the Cold War. Rather, it was a decision made from a 'natural posture', and because it was a natural decision, China could take advantage of it to improve relations with Japan without causing much political difficulty in the relationship.

4.2. INSTITUTIONALIZATION OF FRIENDSHIP TRADE

4.2.1. Window Organizations

The Chinese organization responsible for Friendship Trade was the CCPIT, created in the 1950s in order to promote China's trade with western countries. On the Japanese side, however, the designation of a single window organization was not the Chinese intention, nor would it have reflected Japanese realities.

The Chinese intention to diversify Japanese links started to become evident soon after the enunciation of the three trade principles. When Zhou Enlai conveyed the principles to Suzuki Kazuo, he specifically referred to the

JCTPA as a Japanese counterpart to the CCPIT. But, on 12 September 1960, Lei Renmin, Vice-Minister of Foreign Trade, told Hozumi Shichiro, a Japanese Dietman of the JSP, that China needed introductions to friendly firms 'through [Japanese] friends of progressive organizations. We welcome, for example, an introduction by you, Mr. Hozumi.'[11] On 12 October, Takasaki Tatsunosuke, who had been Minister of MITI under the Kishi administration, met with Zhou Enlai. Zhou affirmed at the meeting that even LDP politicians could introduce Japanese firms to China as long as the firms would adhere to the three political principles. Takasaki asked Zhou, 'What if Takasaki, who is a supporter of the Japan–US Security Treaty and is an LDP politician, guarantees them?' Zhou answered, 'That is fine.'[12]

Thus, it became apparent soon after the three trade principles opened the way for a new form of Japan–China trade that it was not the intention of the Chinese to limit their Japanese links to a single entity. Indeed, the Chinese intended to make use of as many pro-China elements in Japan as possible for both economic and political purposes. The Chinese were able to take advantage of domestic 'contradictions' in Japan because of the pluralistic configuration of its pro-China elements. Japanese China trade organizations were competing not only over economic gains but also over power to nominate Japanese firms to the Chinese for designation as friendly firms.

In February 1961, for instance, the Japan Association for the Promotion of International Trade (JAPIT) dispatched a mission to China, whose purpose was indeed to break the monopoly held by the JCTPA. China gave a warm welcome to the mission and, as the JAPIT announced later, this JAPIT mission nominated fifteen firms to China of which fourteen were subsequently designated as friendly firms.[13] This marked the first case in which an organization other than the JCTPA presented friendly firms to China. The Kansai Headquarters of the JAPIT (JAPIT-Kansai) and the Japan–China Friendship Association (JCFA) joined in at the end of March, when they announced that they had received telegrams from China designating five and two friendly firms respectively, with one firm nominated by both.[14]

Thus, in a little over six months after Zhou announced the three trade principles, the organizational contour for Friendship Trade emerged. This pattern was formally institutionalized by the protocol concerning Friendship Trade, which was stimulated by the signing of the LT Trade agreement in November 1962. The protocol was signed on 27 December 1962 by the CCPIT on the Chinese side, and the JCTPA, the JAPIT and the JAPIT-Kansai on the Japanese side. One paragraph of the protocol stated the following:

---

11   *Sengo Shiryo*, p. 260.
12   Takasaki Tatsunosuke, 'Watashi no Mita Chugoku' [China that I Saw], *Asahi Janaru*, 3 (1961), p. 15; *Nihon Keizai Shinbun*, 31 October 1960.
13   *Nihon Keizai Shinbun*, 28 March 1961.
14   *Nihon Keizai Shinbun*, 29 March 1961.

... Both sides reaffirmed their support for the three political principles, the three trade principles, and the principle of inseparability of politics and economics in Japan–China relations, as presented by the Chinese government; and reaffirmed their persistent efforts to strengthen Friendship Trade relations between the peoples of Japan and China and to promote normalization of Japan–China relations, on the basis of preserving these principles.[15]

The conditions for friendliness were publicly enunciated for the first time: the adherence to the three political principles, the three trade principles, and the principle of inseparability of politics and economics. Also, the three central window organizations were designated formally: JCTPA, JAPIT, and JAPIT-Kansai. Another significant aspect of the protocol was that both sides agreed to hold commodities exhibitions in both countries: in Beijing and Shanghai in 1963 and in Tokyo and Osaka in 1964, as specified in a memorandum attached to the protocol. A new channel for Friendship Trade transactions, in addition to the Canton trade fair in which Japanese friendly firms had participated since the spring of 1961, was thus opened.[16]

This protocol had a significant impact on organizational arrangements in Japan. First, a distinction became evident between the three signatories of the protocol, which were all trade-oriented organizations, and the JCFA which was inclined toward more general contacts with China. This was in line with the desire of Kawakatsu Den, chairman of the JAPIT-Kansai, to clarify the 'division of labour' with the JCFA, so that less ideologically oriented firms could join the JAPIT.[17] The JCFA found its Chinese counterpart in October 1963, when China created the China–Japan Friendship Association.

Second, the signing of the protocol marked a turning point in the nature of the relationship between the Tokyo-based JAPIT and the JAPIT-Kansai. From then on, Kimura Ichizo, then managing director of the JAPIT-Kansai and one of the three signatories of the protocol, began to strengthen his contacts with China independently of the Tokyo-based JAPIT headquarters.[18] In fact, for the JAPIT-Kansai the protocol was 'the first international agreement that the Kansai headquarters concluded after it had been detached from, and became independent of, the JAPIT', and thus became a symbol of its independence.[19]

Despite these new developments, Friendship Trade continued to be dominated by the JCTPA until the mid-1960s. Kimura Ichizo even said in an interview that he had not had anything to do at the time, and that everything was

[15] For the entire document, see *Sengo Shiryo*, p. 359; *Kankei Shiryo*, pp. 215–16; *Kihon Shiryo*, pp. 218–19.

[16] For a description of these fairs and exhibitions, see JETRO, *How to Approach the China Market* (Tokyo: Press International CTP, 1972), pp. 139–45.

[17] Kawakatsu, *Yuko Ichiro*, p. 94.

[18] *Ibid.*, p. 95.

[19] Nihon Kokusai Boeki Sokushin Kyokai, Kansai Honbu [The Kansai Headquarters of the JAPIT], *20-nen no Ayumi [Twenty-Year History]*, (1974), p. 9.

taken care of by Suzuki Kazuo of the JCTPA.[20] This is probably an overstatement but clearly conveys a sense of strained relations between them. In addition, the general consensus among the trading corporations was that the JCTPA received more and better transaction offers from China than did the JAPIT.[21]

The basic pattern of Friendship Trade, in which China had the final say in designating friendly firms upon recommendation by the Japanese side, suggests that sources of influence of the Japanese organizations lay almost exclusively in the blessing which the Chinese gave to them. The Chinese decisions were, however, strongly influenced by the Japanese context.

First, the characteristics of these organizations, which were explained in Chapter 2, persisted into the 1960s. That is, the creation of the JCTPA was based on deep-rooted pro-China sentiment mixed with progressive political motives, and this organization was generally oriented toward small and medium-sized trading firms, many of which specialized in trading with China. The JAPIT on the other hand, was created by internationally minded business leaders and targeted not only large trading firms but also manufacturers and banks.[22] This difference in the basic character of the two organizations was most apparent in the selection of personnel in top management positions. The JAPIT tended to select politically and economically prominent figures for its senior managers. In the 1960s, the chairmanship of the JAPIT was held by Yamamoto Kumaichi (former Vice-Minister of the Ministry of Foreign Affairs) and Ishibashi Tanzan (former Prime Minister), and that of the JAPIT-Kansai by two influential businessmen in Kansai, Kawakatsu Den (chairman of Nippon Spindle) and Matsubara Yosomatsu (chairman of Hitachi Shipbuilding Corporation). The JCTPA, on the other hand, was managed almost single-handedly by Suzuki Kazuo. This made it easier for China to deal with the JCTPA than the JAPIT in the system of Friendship Trade. Also, the fact that the JCTPA was under JCP domination (almost all of the administrative staff were JCP members[23]) made it easier for China to handle the JCTPA than the JAPIT.

Second, the opening of another trade channel in November 1962, LT Trade, weakened the JAPIT's role in Friendship Trade. This was because its large member firms, which were interested in larger transactions, gathered under the auspices of the Japan–China Overall Trade Liaison Council, which was established in November 1962 to coordinate business interests in LT Trade.

As the rift between the JCP and the CCP intensified in 1966, however, the connection with the JCP affected the JCTPA adversely. In fact, this rift led to

---

[20] Interview with Kimura Ichizo, vice-president of International Oil, and director of the Japan–China Economic Relations and Trade Center (former JAPIT-Kansai), Tokyo, Japan, 19 April 1985 (hereafter cited as Kimura Interview).

[21] Kawakatsu, *Yuko Ichiro*, p. 115.   [22] *Nihon Keizai Shinbun*, 20 September 1966.

[23] *Shin Chugoku Nenkan 1967*, p. 79.

the dissolution of the JCTPA and a drastic reorganization of the Friendship Trade system as seen below.

4.2.2. Friendly Firms

Just as China did not intend to give an exclusive blessing to a single window organization, it also attempted to draw all kinds of trading firms which adhered to Chinese demands into Friendship Trade. The number of friendly firms was limited to eleven, all privileged members of the JCTPA, for the first six months. The big trading firms supporting the JAPIT were naturally dissatisfied with this situation, which was a main factor behind the JAPIT's China visit in February–March 1961. Therefore, it was a real success for the JAPIT when, on 19 February, Nan Hanchen, chairman of the CCPIT, agreed that any firms could deal with China regardless of their size, if they were not hostile to China.[24] It was revealed later that this JAPIT mission had presented a list of fifteen firms to China for designation as friendly firms, and the JAPIT announced on 27 March that fourteen firms were designated, including the three dummy firms, Kanematsu, Sumitomo Shoji, and Iwai Sangyo.[25]

Several days before this JAPIT announcement, the JCTPA made public that it had received a list of an additional twenty-two friendly firms from the CCPIT, but it withheld identifying them. This was because the list included Nichimen Jitsugyo, a Kansai-based big trading corporation. This designation was considered quite delicate in the light of harsh competition among big trading corporations. But, on 28 March 1961, the day after the JAPIT announcement, an anonymous source revealed that Nichimen had become the first big trading corporation designated as a friendly firm.[26]

It was now clear that the Chinese were serious about expanding the range of friendly firms beyond small-sized, specialized trading firms. With the designation of Nichimen as a friendly firm, there were three different types of friendly firms: (1) small or medium-sized specialized trading firms which were heavily dependent on China trade, (2) dummy firms established or partially funded by big trading corporations specifically for China trade, and (3) large-sized general trading corporations. A great majority were small or medium-sized trading firms, including some which dealt in several commodities, as well as some which specialized in the importation of particular Chinese commodities such as Chinese books, herb medicines, or Tianjin sweet chestnuts.

As for big, general trading corporations, Nichimen presented an exceptional case. In any case, Nichimen uniquely had been using a dummy firm, called Takada Shokai, for Taiwan trade, while it had been directly involved in

---

24 *Nihon Keizai Shinbun*, 22 February 1961.
25 *Nihon Keizai Shinbun*, 28 March 1961.
26 *Nihon Keizai Shinbun*, 29 March 1961.

China trade since the 1950s.[27] This was in clear contrast to such leading trading corporations as Mitsui, Mitsubishi, Marubeni-Iida, and Ito-Chu, which were all directly involved in Taiwan trade and thus had set up dummy firms for China trade. Miyake Takao, then vice-president of Nichimen, looked at China in 1961 from three perspectives: China's potential as the world's largest import–export market, the history of close Japan–China trade relations, and Chinese nationalism as the product of thousands of years of history.[28] The latter two perspectives appear to have been important motives for Nichimen, considering its own historical involvement in China trade; it had already established a branch for cotton trade in 1903, built a spinning mill in Shanghai jointly with the Chinese in 1907, and from then on was a leader in prewar Japan–China trade.[29]

These developments at the end of March 1961 made manifest the potential conflict in the Friendship Trade structure. The JCTPA and the JAPIT had been in a competitive and emotionally bitter relationship since the 1950s.[30] The reasons for their strained relations were both structural and political. Structurally speaking, the fact that two trade organizations with different backgrounds had been contending in China trade since the 1950s (see Chapter 2) explains one aspect of their conflictual relationship in Friendship Trade of the early 1960s. The political aspect of the strain had to do with the difference in their ideological stances. The JAPIT held to a more internationalist view toward China, while the JCTPA was identified with the JCP line.

This difference affected the two organizations' relationships with their member firms. The JCTPA required political combativeness of its member firms, while the JAPIT attempted to stay aloof from anti-governmental activities (until it was affected by the Chinese Cultural Revolution). According to Okamoto Saburo, the expelled JCTPA executive, the criteria for the JCTPA to recommend candidate firms to China included, in addition to the three sets of principles, whether or not, and to what extent, they had participated in political campaigns against the Japan–US Security Treaty, and in favour of unblocking Japan–China relations, reopening Japan–China trade, or realizing a governmental trade agreement.[31]

The JAPIT was unequivocally opposed to these criteria. Shukutani Eiichi, vice-president of the JAPIT, wrote in 1961 that they were not consistent with the true intentions of the Chinese. He explicitly distinguished between those Japanese who were blindly anti-Chinese and those who were relatively object-

[27] *Ibid.*

[28] Miyake Takeo, 'Nitchu Boeki no Genjo to Shorai' [Present and Future States of Japan–China Trade], *Chuo Koron*, 76 (1961).

[29] Takamura Naosuke, *Kindai Nihon Mengyo to Chugoku [Modern Japanese Cotton Industry and China]* (Tokyo: Tokyo-daigaku Shuppan-kai, 1982), pp. 74, 86.

[30] 'Yuko wo Meguru Shosha no Anyaku' [Behind the Scene Movements of Trading Firms over Friendship], *Ekonomisuto*, 39 (1961).

[31] Okamoto, *Nitchu Boeki Ron*, p. 132.

ive but somewhat ambivalent in their judgment of contemporary China. He then asserted that political radicalism by friendly firms would drive people in the latter category unnecessarily in a direction detrimental to friendly relations between Japan and China.[32]

Despite this criticism by the JAPIT, close affiliates of the JCTPA remained the most privileged firms in Friendship Trade in the first half of the 1960s. The most influential were Haga Tsusho, Mutsumi Boeki, and Sanshin Koeki, called the *gosanke* (literally the three branch families of the Tokugawa house in the Edo era) of friendly firms. These three firms alone, for example, handled 16 per cent of Friendship Trade transactions and 12 per cent of total Japan–China trade in 1965, when there were some 300 friendly firms. After the JCP–CCP rift, many less-privileged firms revealed that the *gosanke* had sometimes intruded in their business talks with China to seize their contracts, that the Chinese side had applied pressure to give up part of their trade contracts to the *gosanke*, and that they had had to lower their heads humbly to the *gosanke* even to get a tiny share of the transactions.[33]

This privileged position of the *gosanke* reflected the then congenial relations between the JCP and the CCP. The JCP–*gosanke* connection gains in significance with reference to a speculation by 'a source close to the public security branch of the Japanese government' that there was a 'financial pipeline' between the JCP and the CCP through Friendship Trade transactions.[34] In fact, the Public Security Investigation Agency of the Ministry of Justice (Koan Chosa-cho) estimated in 1967 that the JCP had received more than $100,000 a year from the *gosanke* friendly firms until 1966.[35]

This situation basically persisted until mid-1966, and led to a sense of harsh competition, not only between the JAPIT and the JCTPA, but also among friendly firms. This competition, as well as the Chinese intention to take advantage of it, brought an expansion in the number of friendly firms from the initial eleven in 1960 to about 320 by the dissolution of the JCTPA in October 1966. In 1965, however, only one-third of these—about 100 friendly firms—were in active operation.[36] This diffuse configuration of friendly firms, however, eventually cushioned the repercussions of the JCP–CCP conflict.

4.3. TRANSFORMATION OF FRIENDSHIP TRADE

In the mid-1960s, a great transformation took place in the composition and nature of the Friendship Trade organizations in Japan. This transformation

---

[32] Shukutani Eiichi, 'Nitchu Boeki wo Do Hatten Saseruka' [How to Promote Japan–China Trade], *Sekai*, 189 (1961), p. 85.

[33] 'Kaze ni Soyogu Nitchu Boeki', p. 107.   [34] Ibid., p. 107.

[35] Koan Chosa-cho [Public Security Investigation Agency], *Nihon no Naka no Chukyo* [Communist China in Japan], (1967), p. 18, as cited in Lee, *Japan Faces China*, p. 233, note 59.

[36] 'Kaze ni Soyogu Nitchu Boeki', p. 105.

was a function of the very 'logic' of the Friendship Trade system. As its name indicates, Japanese people and groups wishing to participate in this trade had to prove their friendliness to China by complying with Chinese demands. In other words, the Friendship Trade mechanism would remain effective so long as Japanese participants demonstrated their loyalty by adhering to Chinese demands. The direct cause of the turbulence in the Friendship Trade structure was the breakup of relations between the JCP and the CCP. Simply stated, the JCP elements in Friendship Trade had to be eliminated if Friendship Trade were to survive.

4.3.1. Rift between JCP and CCP

The key factor behind the rift between the two communist parties was 'self-reliance and independence' in the doctrine of the JCP. Thus, the dispute was not a matter of the JCP's choosing either Beijing or Moscow in the Sino-Soviet rift. In fact, until the JCP and the CCP broke up in the spring of 1966, the JCP at first had maintained neutrality between the two communist giants, and somewhat later moved toward the CCP line while preserving the principle of self-reliance and independence. Nonetheless, the Miyamoto regime of the JCP relied on the 'united front' strategy to legitimize its leadership within the party, which included an alignment with the Soviet Union.

As noted above, Khrushchev and Peng Zhen had clashed bitterly at Bucharest in June 1960, which marked the first face-to-face confrontation between the leaders of Beijing and Moscow. In October of the following year, Zhou Enlai, representing the CCP in the 22nd Soviet Communist Party Congress, did not hide his dissatisfaction with Moscow's charges against the leaders of Albania and returned home in the middle of the Congress. At this stage, the JCP remained neutral: in February 1963, it made its position public by passing a resolution calling for 'solidarity among communist parties and labour parties in the world'.[37]

In six month's time, however, two crucial international issues—the prospect of Chinese nuclear testing and the signing of the Partial Test Ban Treaty (PTBT)—put the JCP in a difficult position. Domestically, the JCP's new stance emerged out of its dispute with the Japan Socialist Party (JSP). During preparations for the Ninth World Congress Against Atomic and Hydrogen Bombs, to be held in August 1963 in Hiroshima, Japan's two major progressive parties clashed bitterly over two points.

First, while the JSP and Sohyo, the JSP's constituent labour federation, advocated that the Congress oppose nuclear testing by 'all countries', the JCP, fully aware of the forthcoming Chinese nuclear testing, insisted that a distinction be made between nuclear testing by imperialist and socialist countries.

[37] Asahi Shinbun-sha (ed.), *Nihon Kyosan-to [Japan Communist Party]* (Tokyo: Asahi Shinbun-sha, 1973), pp. 202–4.

Second, the JSP and Sohyo were for the PTBT, but the JCP was against it. In the statement published in *Akahata* (Red Flag, the official newspaper of the JCP) on 4 August 1963, the JCP denounced the position of the JSP and Sohyo by stating that opposition to nuclear testing by all countries would place the Soviet Union in the same category with the United States as enemies of peace, and support for the PTBT would mean confusing the United States with the Soviet Union as champions of peace; this contradiction would be misleading.[38]

The timing of this statement, four days after the Chinese government had issued a statement denouncing the PTBT, seemed to suggest that the JCP had come to support the CCP openly.[39] Nonetheless, the key to understanding the eventual JCP–CCP breakup lies in the nature of the JCP's dissatisfaction with the all-countries formula. In the JCP's foreign policy line, the principle of self-reliance and independence was a logical derivative of a combination of domestic and international imperatives.

Domestically, the Miyamoto kenji JCP regime, which had barely survived a harsh intra-party conflict in the late 1950s and the early 1960s, found its ideological legitimacy in opposition to peaceful coexistence and support for struggle by a united front against imperialism.[40] Although these views resembled the Chinese position, a dilemma for Miyamoto was that siding openly with Beijing would undermine his commitment to a united front, unless he were to concede that the Soviet Union was as imperialistic as the United States. At this juncture, to preserve the legitimacy of his leadership and to cope with the intensifying Sino-Soviet rift, Miyamoto could do nothing but advocate a foreign policy of self-reliance and independence. Miyamoto used the term 'jishu dokuritsu' (meaning self-reliance and independence) for the first time in public in an interview with NHK broadcast on 23 September 1963.[41]

The issue, however, did not unfold in an international void. In retrospect, the ultimate cause of the Miyamoto regime, i.e., the principle of self-reliance and independence, paved the way for a rift with the communist parties of both China and the Soviet Union. The JCP broke up with the Soviet Union first, and then with the CCP.

[38] *Ibid.*, p. 206; *Akahata*, 4 August 1963.

[39] Horie Fukashi and Araki Yoshi, 'Nihon Kyosan-to no Gaiko-rosen: Jishu-Dokuritsu-rosen to Miyamoto-taisei no Kakuritsu Katei' [Foreign Policy Line of the Japan Communist Party: Process of the Establishment of the Self-Reliance and Independence Line and the Miyamoto Regime], in Horie Fukashi and Ikei Masaru (eds.), *Nihon no Seito to Gaiko Seisaku [Japanese Political Parties and Foreign Policy]* (Tokyo: Keio Tsushin, 1980), p. 167. A Japanese version of the Chinese government's statement is found in Oa Kyokai (ed.), *Chuso Ronso Shuyo Bunken-shu [Compilation of Major Sources of Sino-Soviet Dispute]* (Tokyo: Nikkan Rodo Tsushin-sha, 1965), pp. 581–4.

[40] For an analysis on the establishment of the Miyamoto regime, see Horie and Araki, 'Nihon Kyosan-to no Gaiko-rosen', pp. 153–66.

[41] Its text was published in *Akahata*, 27 September 1963.

The JCP already was directly involved in a bitter confrontation between the Soviet and Chinese representatives over the PTBT at the Ninth World Congress Against Atomic and Hydrogen Bombs in early August 1963. The JCP barely maintained its independent position and succeeded in adopting an appeal to the effect that 'the US nuclear war policy poses the greatest threat to world peace'.[42] A few weeks later, however, *Pravda* carried an article entitled 'Hiroshima's Voice' by Jucov, the Soviet representative to the Congress, in which he condemned the JCP by name for opposing the PTBT and for siding with China in the Congress. The JCP interpreted this as the first exertion of Soviet pressure aimed at forcing the JCP to support the PTBT.[43] After the exchange of a few letters, both parties met in Moscow for abortive talks in March 1964. In May, Shiga Yoshio, a standing committee member of the JCP, voted in the Diet for the ratification of the PTBT in defiance of the party decision and therefore was expelled from the party. In July, the Soviet Union voiced support for Shiga and his followers and unilaterally made public the letters which it had previously sent to the JCP. It was at this juncture that the two parties broke ties.[44]

Following their disassociation, the JCP denounced the Soviet Union as 'modern revisionists', but at the same time did not forget to spell out its call for the solidarity of international communist movements.[45] With respect to the US bombing of North Vietnam in 1965, the JCP reaffirmed its earlier adherence to the principle of international solidarity against imperialism, which was not to exclude the Soviet Union.[46]

In February and March of 1966, when the JCP and the CCP met in Beijing, they clashed over the alternative formulas of an 'international united front against US imperialism' versus a 'united front against the United States and the Soviet Union'. At one point during the course of the meetings, both sides came to an agreement to issue a joint communiqué which would have shelved the disagreements. At this point, Mao Zedong stepped in and voiced disagreement, insisting that the communiqué support a 'united front against the United States and the Soviet Union'. The JCP did not yield and the meeting broke up.[47] In October 1966, the Tenth Party Congress of the JCP revised the party rules to stipulate the self-reliant and independent line, and thus

---

[42] Asahi Shinbun-sha (ed.), *Nihon Kyosan-to*, p. 207.

[43] *Ibid.*, p. 209.

[44] For the development of these events, see *ibid.*, pp. 210–12. For a report by Hakamada who led the delegation to Moscow in March 1964, see *Nihon Kyosan-to Jiten [Encyclopedia of the Japan Communist Party]* (Tokyo: Zenbo-sha, 1978), pp. 792–806. For the central committee resolution to expel Shiga, see *Nihon Kyosan-to Jiten*, pp. 885–6.

[45] For example, see Miyamoto's report to the JCP Ninth Party Congress on 24 November 1964, in *Nihon Kyosan-to Jiten*, pp. 806–63.

[46] Horie and Araki, 'Nihon Kyosan-to no Gaiko-rosen', p. 173.

[47] See a report of the Miyamoto–Mao meeting by Oka Masayoshi, in *Nihon Kyosan-to Jiten*, pp. 1014–24. For a detailed analysis of this process, see Horie and Araki, 'Nihon Kyosan-to no Gaiko-rosen', pp. 174–9.

implicitly declared its independent position from both the Chinese and the Soviet communist parties.[48]

4.3.2. Impact on Friendship Trade

As the JCP–CCP rift intensified, China attempted to eliminate pro-JCP elements from Friendship Trade. This led to a drastic transformation in the Friendship Trade structure. The first step took place on 29 August 1966 in the meeting with the Japan Cooperation Council for the Chinese exhibitions to be held in October and November in Kitakyushu and Nagoya. In this meeting, Zhang Ziquan, general secretary of the Chinese delegation, criticized the uncooperative attitude of 'the JCTPA-controlled secretariat of the Cooperation Council' in three respects: (1) the secretariat's reluctance to sell Chinese arts and crafts beyond a limited amount, (2) its unwillingness to sell Chinese publications on Maoism, and (3) its reluctance toward advertisement and mobilization for the exhibitions.[49] The Chinese charged that the secretariat was controlled by the JCTPA, as indicated by the fact that three of the four members were from the JCTPA.[50] Kawase Kazutsura, chairman of the Cooperation Council, then turned the joint meeting on the spot into an emergency directors' meeting, which replaced Okamoto Saburo of the JCTPA with Hagiwara Teiji of the JAPIT as general secretary of the Cooperation Council's secretariat.[51] China next deprived the JCTPA of its privileges in Japan–China trade, such as its role as a shipping agent.

In response to this Chinese offensive, the friendly firms divided into four groupings. The first consisted of dummy firms of large trading corporations, such as Daiichi Tsusho (Mitsui), Wako Koeki (Marubeni-Iida), and Meiwa Sangyo (Mitsubishi), which played a central role in expelling JCP elements from Friendship Trade. The second group included medium-sized friendly firms, such as Nishinihon Boeki, Kyoei Shoji, and Dainihon Tsusho. They were not happy about the JCP elements in Friendship Trade and collaborated with the first group. About half of the firms belonged to the third group, which swam with the tide so as not to miss chances for business with China. This group generally acted with the first and the second groups. The pro-JCP group, therefore, became a minority and found the balance quite unfavourable to itself.[52]

---

[48] *Nihon Kyosan-to Jiten*, p. 1092.

[49] See a summary of the statement made at this meeting by Zhang Ziquan, who was in charge of Chinese overseas exhibitions in the CCPIT, in *Shin Chugoku Nenkan 1967*, pp. 79–80, and Takemoto Yasuo, 'Chugokuten Mondai to Nitchu Boeki Sokushin-kai' [The Question of Chinese Exhibitions and the JCTPA], *AKJ*, 659 (1966), pp. 2–4.

[50] *Shin Chugoku Nenkan 1967*, p. 78.

[51] *Nihon Keizai Shinbun*, 14 September 1966; *Shin Chugoku Nenkan 1967*, p. 80; Takemoto, 'Chugokuten Mondai', p. 4.

[52] 'Yuko Boeki no Saihensei' [Restructuring of the Friendship Trade], *Ekonomisuto*, 44 (1966), p. 37. See also 'Kaze ni Soyogu Nitchu Boeki', pp. 100–108.

Thus, due to their fear of losing trade opportunities with China, as well as dissatisfaction with the JCP's domination of the JCTPA, a majority of firms pressed for a reorganization to meet Chinese demands. Under pressure from both China and the dissatisfied member firms, the JCTPA held four consecutive executive meetings on 5, 12, 13, and 19 September 1966. In the meeting on 13 September, general secretary Seki Hiromoto was dismissed, and a resolution was passed recommending the resignation of two directors, Sumii Masanori and Okamoto Saburo. On 19 September, the dismissal of the two directors was voted, forty-eight to seven.[53]

Not coincidentally, on the previous day, the JAPIT and the CCPIT had signed the minutes of their talks in Beijing, which contained the following passage:

... Both sides reached an agreement that unmistakable and open anti-China movements destructive to friendship are increasing among some of the executives of the Japan–China Trade Promotion Association, and that it is impractical to expect that they will play an active role in future Japan–China economic exchanges. Both sides believe that the Japan Association for the Promotion of International Trade is to take increasingly important responsibilities in the future.[54]

Facing attacks from both inside and outside, the JCTPA was unable to elect substitutes to replace the expelled executives. On 26 October 1966, the general meeting of the JCTPA passed a resolution stating that the JCTPA no longer had friendship with China and had lost its *raison-d'être*.[55] Hence, the JCTPA ended its seventeen-year long history. This episode demonstrates how vulnerable Friendship Trade was to Chinese displeasure.

With the dispersion of the JCTPA, the JAPIT came to the fore in Friendship Trade. To become the vanguard of Friendship Trade, however, it still had to be blessed with the Chinese mandate. The nature and conditions of the JAPIT–China connection were spelled out clearly in the 'Protocol Concerning the Promotion of Friendship Trade between Peoples of Japan and China', and the 'Joint Communiqué', signed between a JAPIT delegation and the CCPIT on 27 February and 17 March 1967, respectively.[56] Both the protocol and the joint communiqué reaffirmed commitments to the three political principles, the three trade principles, and the principle of inseparability of politics and economics, and designated US imperialism, Japanese reactionaries, Soviet revisionism, and JCP revisionists as the 'four enemies' to friendly relations between Japan and China. Hereafter, in addition to the above-mentioned three sets of principles, struggles against the four enemies became a necessary condition for Japanese friendly firms to be allowed in China trade.

53 Takemoto, 'Chugoku Mondai to Nitchu Boeki Sokushin-kai', pp. 4–6; *Shin Chugoku Nenkan 1967*, p. 80.

54 *Kankei Shiryo*, p. 235; *Sengo Shiryo*, p. 439.

55 *Shin Chugoku Nenkan 1967*, p. 80. For the dissolution statement, see *AKJ*, 664 (1966), p. 23.

56 *Kankei Shiryo*, pp. 237–44; *Sengo Shiryo*, pp. 439–41, *Kihon Shiryo*, pp. 292–6.

The protocol, the joint communiqué, and a more than 100 page report compiled by the JAPIT delegation were all filled with unstinted praise of the Chinese Great Proletarian Cultural Revolution and the thoughts of Mao Zedong. The report, for example, said that, 'The Chinese Great Proletarian Cultural Revolution will without question win a decisive victory, and this guarantees a bright future of Japan–China trade.'[57] It further resolved unyielding struggle against the four enemies, and defined the thoughts of Mao Zedong not only as the decisive weapon to defeat the enemies, but also as the thoughts central to the movements to develop Japan–China friendship and trade.[58]

Considering the radical political atmosphere of the Cultural Revolution, the JAPIT could not have remained in charge of Friendship Trade without accommodating Chinese political assertiveness. To explain this attitude of the JAPIT, Kawase Kazutsura, who headed the delegation to China, brusquely stated, 'Because we are building up friendly relations with China, it is natural that we should accept Chinese demands.'[59] With the signing of the protocol and the joint communiqué, and with the latter defining the former as 'the platform of Friendship Trade', the leading role of the JAPIT was formally institutionalized.[60]

As a consequence of these developments, the JAPIT needed some organizational readjustments. First, with the JAPIT denouncing the JCP as one of the four enemies, most of its JCP-affiliated members seceded from the Party to remain in the JAPIT, while a few left the JAPIT to retain their loyalty to the JCP. In one case, the JAPIT even fired a JCP activist who was unwilling to leave its secretariat.[61] Thus, the JAPIT reorganized itself as a purely pro-China, anti-JCP organization.

Second, as a result of designating the Soviet Union as one of the four enemies, the Soviet Union on 27 April 1967 told the representatives of the JAPIT in Moscow that it would terminate its relations with the JAPIT; this was enforced on 12 May.[62] The JAPIT's trade dealings with the Soviet Union were not of great significance, however, and it had been prepared for this step when it signed the protocol. This was indicated by Hagiwara Teiji, managing

[57] Nihon Kokusai Boeki Sokushin Kyokai Hochu Yuko Daihyo-dan [JAPIT Friendship Trade Delegation to China], *Puroretaria Bunka Daikakumei to Nitchu Boeki no Tenbo: Hochu Hokoku [The Great Proletarian Cultural Revolution and the Prospects of Japan–China Trade: The Report of China Visit]* (1967), pp. 64–5.

[58] *Ibid.*, p. 68.

[59] *Nihon Keizai Shinbun*, 25 March 1967.

[60] Thus, the protocol came to be called 'the second protocol of Friendship Trade', the one signed in December 1962 being the first.

[61] Kawakatsu, *Yuko Ichiro*, p. 118.

[62] Tanaka Shujiro, 'Soren ga Kokusai Bosoku to Kankei Danzetsu Shita Shin no Riyu: Nisso Boeki Sokushin-shi Josetsu' [True Reason Why the Soviet Union Terminated Relations with the JAPIT: History of Japan–Soviet Trade Promotion], *Kokusai Boeki* (monthly), (July 1967), pp. 7–8.

director of the JAPIT, on his return from China as general secretary of the JAPIT delegation. He criticized 'the policy of socialist countries to contain China', and said that the JAPIT was prepared for a likely deterioration of trade relations with the Soviet Union.[63]

Thereafter, the JAPIT in Tokyo and the JAPIT-Kansai in Osaka became the two major organizations in Friendship Trade. Thus, the deterioration of the JCP–CCP relationship in 1966 precipitated the reordering of the Friendship Trade window organizations. Naturally, friendly firms suffered the same fate.

The total number of friendly firms amounted to some 320 when China began to assail the JCP elements in the end of August 1966, but by the end of the following year the number had declined to about 280. This decline itself may not seem substantial, but one-quarter of the 280 firms trading with China at the end of 1967 were established after October 1966.[64] Thus, only about 210 out of 320 survived the turbulent two months from the end of August to the end of October, when the pro-JCP JCTPA was forced to dissolve itself.

Among the more than 100 friendly firms that disappeared at this time were firms which were very active in Japan–China trade. The 'gosanke', the three most influential pro-JCP friendly firms, is illustrative. Only two days after China began to pressure the JCTPA representatives in the Japan Cooperation Council for Chinese exhibitions, Sanshin Koeki was unilaterally informed in Beijing that China would not deal with it any more. China also refused to renew visas for the other two, Haga Tsusho and Mutsumi Boeki, and the representatives of the gosanke resident in Beijing were obligated to leave China in early September 1966.[65] By the end of 1966, Sanshin Koeki had cut its employees by half to about ten and switched to trade with other communist countries. Mutsumi Boeki had reduced its employees from seventy to thirty, with its volume of trade transactions declining to 20 per cent of that before the summer. It also had switched its targets to other communist countries. Haga Tsusho's employees had decreased to nine compared with the previous level of thirty-three, and it engaged only in shipping products under contracts signed previously with China.[66]

With the disappearance of the pro-JCP firms from Friendship Trade, Chinese criteria for the rating of Japanese friendly firms also changed. Now China required political combativeness and radicalism from all types of friendly firms, based on the three sets of principles and the struggle against the four enemies as articulated in the protocol signed between the JAPIT and the CCPIT on 27 February 1967.

[63] *Nihon Keizai Shinbun*, 25 March 1967.
[64] Lee, *Japan Faces China*, p. 151.
[65] 'Kaze ni Soyogu Nitchu Boeki', p. 102.
[66] *Nihon Keizai Shinbun*, 30 December 1966.

The first testing ground for Japanese friendly firms was the Canton trade fair held in April–May 1967. At this fair, the Chinese rank-ordered the participating friendly firms on the basis of the extent to which they had cooperated in Chinese exhibitions held in Kitakyushu and Nagoya in 1966, and the extent to which they had fought against 'the JCP revisionists' in the Zenrin Kaikan incident in the spring of 1967.[67] Those firms which participated in these activities only in the hope of 'not missing the bus' were handicapped in negotiating contracts.[68]

At the Canton trade fair in the autumn of 1967, a touchstone for friendly firms was a struggle against Prime Minister Sato's visit to Taiwan in September. Almost all friendly firms from every corner of the country, or close to 300 firms, reportedly mobilized 1,500 people for political demonstrations in Tokyo in late August.[69] On 7 September, when Sato left for Taiwan, 700 friendly firms' employees were among the demonstrating crowd at the Haneda airport.[70]

In addition to these criteria, the attitude toward the thoughts of Mao Zedong became another yardstick for judging the sincerity of Japanese participants in Canton trade fairs. Indeed, during the Cultural Revolution, the first half of the one-month period of the fair was given to the study of 'Quotations from Chairman Mao Zedong'. Under these circumstances, an anecdote of a businessman concluding an advantageous contract by referring to 'Quotations from Mao' does not sound totally absurd.[71] Thus, the thoughts of Mao even became a tool for business; as a president of a trading corporation said, 'Reading "Quotations from Mao" is much more effective than entertaining buyers from the United States or the Soviet Union.'[72]

The Friendship Trade system thus survived the crises caused by disorders in the system itself and the strained relations between Japan and China, by unilaterally complying with Chinese radical political demands. The evidence of its survival is shown in Table 4.1 which reveals that both the number of participants and the total value of contracts made at the Canton trade fairs did not decline very much even during the Cultural Revolution, and in fact both increased throughout the 1960s.

Friendship Trade proved so resilient largely because of its predisposition to unilateral compliance with Chinese political assertiveness. This predisposition, amply indicated above, is also illustrated by the preface to every friendship contract concluded at the biannual Canton trade fair:

---

[67] The Zenrin Kaikan was an accommodation facility for pro-mainland overseas Chinese students studying in Japan. In March 1967, violent clashes took place there between those students and Japanese communists.

[68] *Nihon Keizai Shinbun*, 18 May 1967.

[69] *Japan Times*, 29 August 1967.

[70] 'Konransuru Nitchu Boeki-shosha no Uchimaku' [Inside Stories of Japan–China Trade Firms in Disarray], *Toyo Keizai*, 3366 (1967), p. 55.

[71] Ibid., p. 55.   [72] Ibid., p. 56.

TABLE 4.1. Japanese participants and contracts at Canton trade fairs

Year	Participants	Contracts[a]	Year	Participants	Contracts[a]
1961S	40	11	1966S	690	95
1961F	50	17	1966F	750	127
1962S	110	11	1967S	850	130
1962F	160	22	1967F	930	130
1963S	180	14	1968S	900	110
1963F	230	36	1968F	910	140
1964S	300	42	1969S	700	130
1964F	430	47	1969F	900	180
1965S	470	74			
1965F	600	130			

[a] $ million.

Source: Hagiwara Teiji, 'Chugoku no Keizai Kensetsu to Nitchu Boeki' [Chinese Economic Construction and Japan–China Trade], *Ajia Rebyu*, 1 (1970), p. 73.

In order to promote friendly relations and economic exchanges between the peoples of Japan and China, both sides had friendly business negotiations and agreed to sign this contract on the items below, on the basis of the three political principles of Japan–China relations, the three trade principles, and the principle of inseparability of politics and economics.[73]

All this was made possible by the fundamental mechanism of Friendship Trade, where the system could function on the basis of Japanese compliance with Chinese political demands as well as Chinese blessing. The structural factor which enabled such unilateral mechanism to function, in turn, derived from pluralism in Japanese organizations in charge of Friendship Trade.

As a result, Japan–China trade maintained its relative stability in trade volumes throughout the 1960s, when the political environment was the worst in the postwar years. As shown in Table 4.2, the decline in LT/MT Trade, caused by negative political trends, was offset by Friendship Trade transactions.

TABLE 4.2. Friendship trade and LT/MT trade

	1963	1964	1965	1966	1967	1968	1969
FT[a]	51	195	299	416	406	436	562
%	37	63	64	67	73	79	90
LT/MT[a]	86	115	171	205	152	114	63
%	63	37	36	33	27	21	10
Total[a]	137	310	470	621	558	550	625

[a] $ million.
% Share in total Japan–China trade.

Source: JCAET, *Nitchu Oboegaki no 11-nen*, p. 204.

73 Hirai Hakuji, *Nitchu Boeki no Kiso Chishiki [Basic Knowledge on Japan–China Trade]* (Tokyo: Tabata Shoten, 1971), p. 198.

5
LT/MT Trade

LT Trade between Japan and China started as a result of a trade memorandum signed by Liao Chengzhi and Takasaki Tatsunosuke on 9 November 1962. It was named LT Trade after the initials of the two signatories. As Chinese domestic politics made a radical turn during the Cultural Revolution, it was reorganized and renamed Memorandum Trade in 1968 (when referring to both of these trade forms as a set, they will be abbreviated to LT/MT Trade).

LT/MT Trade is often regarded as semi-governmental trade. The Japanese government was actually involved in the process. In the lead-up to the signing of the LT Trade agreement, several LDP politicians who maintained contact with the Japanese government played a significant role. When LT Trade began, the Japanese government decided to extend Export–Import Bank credit to a single case. Several bureaucrats were dispatched to the Japanese LT/MT liaison office in Beijing. These governmental connections have often been highlighted in the assessment of LT/MT Trade, as characterizing the trade as semi-governmental in nature.

Contrary to this prevailing view, this chapter contends that a closer look at the core elements of LT/MT Trade reveals its essentially non-governmental nature. After all, the margin for any significant involvement by the Japanese government was severely curtailed by its relations with the United States and Taiwan, as well as by domestic politics where the power of pro-Taiwan forces was not negligible. In this context, a draft plan for LT Trade was prepared by a Japanese businessman, Okazaki Kaheita. Also, as seen below in detail, the controversial decision to include light industrial plant facilities in the LT agreement was made by Takasaki Tatsunosuke during the negotiations in Beijing, in defiance of the government's instruction given to him before departing for Beijing. These facts, which have not been given due attention, represent the essential components of the LT agreement, possible only through dedicated initiatives by non-governmental Japanese actors. Moreover, from the time when LT Trade was reorganized into Memorandum Trade, it was predominantly non-governmental pro-China Japanese who sustained the trade channel despite all kinds of political difficulties.

The purpose of this chapter is to explicate the non-governmental nature of LT/MT Trade, and thus to unravel the roles of the Japanese government and the private sector in the overall context of the trade relationship. From this analysis, we expect to illuminate the first tier of the pluralist structure of Japan–China relations in the 1960s as pointed out in Chapter 3 (the government-private relationship). Also, if read with Chapter 4 on Friendship Trade, the second tier of structural pluralism (complexity within the private sector) will be brought into relief.

In addition, it is important to understand the non-governmental nature of LT/MT Trade in order to comprehend its continuity into the post-diplomatic normalization phase. Otherwise, one would be trapped into the interpretation that the trade channel simply developed into a governmental trade agreement after normalization. As seen below, however, the legacies of LT/MT Trade were manifest in Japan–China trade in the 1970s in a significant way, and were not necessarily absorbed by the government all together. To understand the importance of this continuity, the history of LT/MT Trade needs to be considered.

5.1. GENESIS

The foundation of the LT Trade agreement was laid by the so-called 'Okazaki plan', and a series of China visits paid by two senior LDP politicians, Matsumura Kenzo and Takasaki Tatsunosuke. Circumstantial evidence suggests that Chinese leaders had long wanted to establish a channel of communication with these pro-China LDP politicians.

5.1.1. The First Matsumura and Takasaki Missions

Matsumura's first important postwar encounter with China was his meeting with Guo Moruo, who visited Japan as president of the Academy of Sciences of China in December 1955. Matsumura was impressed particularly by Guo's remark that the Chinese Revolution was like the Meiji Restoration of Japan.[1] This apparently resonated with Matsumura's conviction that Chinese nationalism was a driving force behind the Chinese Revolution, and that Japan–China relations ought to be considered from the perspective that Japan and China are both Asian nations. In this meeting, Guo asked Matsumura to visit the new China sometime, and Matsumura replied favourably. Matsumura also met Liao Chengzhi in December of the following year in Tokyo, and Liao also invited Matsumura to China.[2] Although the Nagasaki flag incident of May 1958 delayed Matsumura's plans to visit China, the near total breakdown of the bilateral exchange of people and goods actually added new meaning to his forthcoming China visit. He hoped to establish a stable channel of communication between Japan and China.[3]

---

[1] Tagawa Seiichi, *Matsumura Kenzo to Chugoku [Matsumura Kenzo and China]* (Tokyo: Yomiuri Shinbun-sha, 1972), p. 76.

[2] Matsumura Kenzo and Kazami Akira, 'Chugoku wa Ikaga Deshitaka' [How was China?], *Chuo Koron*, 75 (1960).

[3] Tagawa, *Matsumura Kenzo to Chugoku*, p. 85.

Matsumura visited China in October–November 1959, leading a group of seventeen including seven media reporters and his son and daughter. This Matsumura mission had an important impact on the subsequent development of Japan–China relations in two respects.

First, the group contained several people who eventually came to play important roles in the bilateral relationship. In particular, it included two LDP politicians, Furui Yoshimi and Tagawa Seiichi, who played central roles in the LT/MT Trade arrangements throughout the 1960s. Furui was a political protégé of Matsumura, and Tagawa was then his secretary. For both, it was the first postwar visit to China, and before the normalization of diplomatic relations in September 1972, Furui visited China twelve times, and Tagawa, eleven times.[4] The mission also took Okubo Tadaharu as an interpreter. Okubo also continued to work in the LT/MT Trade negotiations, and in the post-normalization era became an executive director of the Japan–China Association of Economy and Trade, established in 1972 as an organization to take over LT/MT responsibilities (Chapter 7). Another LDP politician in the mission, Takeyama Yutaro of the Matsumura faction, became one of the few politicians involved in LT Trade, until he became governor of Shizuoka prefecture in 1967.

Second, the Matsumura mission built a political bridge for Takasaki Tatsunosuke to go to China. Before leaving for China, Matsumura had told Takasaki, who had also been wishing to visit China, half frankly and half in jest, 'It is too early for you to visit China now. What is written in my face is politics, but what is written in your face is trade. So I will go first.'[5] When Zhou Enlai asked about Takasaki, Matsumura disclosed this little conversation with Takasaki. Zhou then said, 'When Mr. Murata Shozo was alive, we had true communication,' to which Matsumura replied, 'The person who can succeed Murata today, who has deep understanding both in politics and economics, is Takasaki.'[6] Zhou gave Matsumura a letter addressed to Takasaki, which formally invited him to China.

Takasaki visited China in October 1960, for the first time after he had returned from Manchuria in November 1947 as the former president of Manchu Heavy Industry (established as a corporate body under the auspices of *Manchukuo* in 1937). This was not, however, his first encounter with Zhou Enlai. They had met in April 1955 as representatives of Japan and China at the Bandung Conference. One morning, they had a secret talk, and Zhou extended a *de facto* invitation to Takasaki by saying, 'The heavy industry of north east China is now a foundation for Chinese industry. Don't you want to see your grown-up child?'[7] Zhou was apparently referring to Takasaki's

4 Furui, *Nitchu 18-nen*; Tagawa, *Nitchu Kosho Hiroku*.
5 Matsumura Kenzo, 'Nitchu Kankei wo Do Dakai Suruka' [How to Break the Deadlock in Japan–China Relations], *Asahi Janaru*, 2 (1960), p. 10.
6 Ibid., pp. 10–11.
7 Takasaki Tatsunosuke, 'Shu Onrai to Kaidan-shite' [Meeting with Zhou Enlai], *Chuo Koron*, 76 (1961), p. 274.

remark in his memoir about the Manchurian days published in 1953 (Chapter 1). Since Takasaki was a member of the Hatoyama and Kishi cabinets, he had not been able to visit China for some time afterwards. But now Matsumura brought back a formal invitation from Zhou.

The Takasaki group included fourteen economic and business experts from various manufacturers. A major mission of the delegation was an inspection trip to north east China. Takasaki and Zhou had frank talks on issues ranging from the Japan–US Security Treaty to Chinese economic conditions.[8]

Although these missions by Matsumura and Takasaki did not produce any direct results in the bilateral relationship, they established a precedent of a division of labour between Matsumura and Takasaki. In the subsequent materialization of the LT Trade agreement, the former was in charge of cementing the political framework, and the latter signed the trade agreement. The fact that these missions were so well received by China indicates that channels were now open between the Chinese leaders, on the one hand, and Japanese LDP politicians, albeit not part of the mainstream or the government, on the other. This led to further Matsumura and Takasaki missions in 1962. Before examining them, let us take a brief look at the Okazaki plan, which provided a blueprint for the LT Trade agreement.

5.1.2. The Okazaki Plan

At the time, Okazaki Kaheita was chairman of Ikegai Tekko, becoming president of All Japan Airways in 1961. Okazaki had joined the Japan Association for the Promotion of International Trade (JAPIT) in 1954, but left it in 1957 because of his uneasiness about the JAPIT turning into a political pressure group. Okazaki was also deeply concerned about the character of Friendship Trade, which was subject to Chinese manipulation. He thus felt a strong need to establish a normal trade channel with China, with which Matsumura concurred.[9]

Just as Okazaki and Matsumura were searching for a way to break the deadlock in bilateral relations, in the spring of 1962, Prime Minister Ikeda Hayato asked Okazaki if a more sensible form of China trade than the Friendship Trade scheme would be possible.[10] Okazaki wrote a plan including the following points: direct participation by manufacturers, or associations of manufacturers; a long-term (3–5 years) barter agreement; creation of overall coordinating institutions; availability of deferred payment; and nomination of guarantees in order to consolidate the foundation of a new

[8] Ibid.; Takasaki Tatsunosuke, 'Watashi no Mita Chugoku'.

[9] Okazaki Kaheita, 'Chugoku no Genjo to Nitchu no Shorai' [The Present Situation in China and the Future of Japan–China], *AKJ*, 529 (1963), pp. 10–12; Inside Document of a Japan–China trade organization designated as 'secret' (hereafter cited as *Inside Document*).

[10] JCAET, *Nitchu Oboegaki no 11-nen*, p. 39; *Inside Document*.

scheme.[11] This Okazaki plan was presented to Ikeda through the Kochi-kai, the Ikeda faction, in July 1962. At the end of the month, Okazaki was informed by Chief Cabinet Secretary Kurogane Yasuyoshi that his plan was still under examination but that there would be no major problems. At the end of August, Kurogane contacted Okazaki again and told him to go ahead with the plan.[12]

By this time, Okazaki had already transmitted the plan to the Chinese side. In July 1962, a Chinese chess delegation visited Japan. Joining the delegation as deputy head was a high-ranked Japan specialist, Sun Pinghua (director of the Chinese People's Institute of Foreign Affairs), who had also been a member of the delegation dispatched to Japan in July 1960, the first since the Nagasaki flag incident. Before leaving for Japan, Sun was instructed by Zhou Enlai to make contact with Matsumura and Takasaki.[13] Okazaki met Sun one evening at a Japanese restaurant to explain his plan, and Sun expressed his support.[14] In early September, Matsumura told Okazaki that he would visit China and discuss the plan with the Chinese side.[15]

There is a widely held misperception that the opening of the LT Trade channel was due to Chinese initiative, but the reverse is true. Also, its driving force came from outside the government. Governmental involvement was not insignificant, as revealed by the fact that the Okazaki plan was presented to the Ikeda faction, but this was because the Okazaki plan included measures which would require governmental approval, such as deferred payment, which reflected the intention on the part of Okazaki to draw the Japanese government into China trade to the fullest extent possible. In order to understand the real momentum behind the LT Trade framework, it is important to observe that the government did no more than decide on concrete measures within the broader framework laid out in the Okazaki plan. This plan was developed and negotiated with the Chinese side by pro-China businessmen and politicians who were not formally associated with the ruling government.

5.1.3. The Second Matsumura Mission

The political groundwork for the realization of the Okazaki plan was laid by the second Matsumura mission in September 1962. Upon hearing a report of Sun Pinghua's trip to Japan, Premier Zhou Enlai and Vice-Premier Chen Yi jointly sent an invitation to Matsumura on 4 September 1962. Matsumura left for China in a private capacity on 12 September, arriving in Beijing on the 14th. During his seven-day stay (from 14 to 20 September) in Beijing, Matsumura met Zhou Enlai on five occasions, including two receptions. They had

[11] JCAET, *Nitchu Oboegaki no 11-nen*, p. 40.
[12] *Ibid.*
[13] Sun Pinghua, 'Zhong-Ri Youhao Suixiang-lu (12)' [Recollections on China–Japan Friendship], *Shijie Zhishi*, 20 (1985), p. 20.
[14] *Inside Document.*
[15] *Ibid.* The date is according to Okazaki's recollection.

extensive discussions on 16 September for three hours, on the 17th for four hours, and on the 19th for three hours. The Matsumura–Zhou meeting on the 16th was devoted exclusively to political issues.[16]

The second Matsumura–Zhou meeting also began with political discussions, including the Taiwan issue. Matsumura presented a plan to exchange media reporters to fill the gap in mutual understanding, which eventually materialized in 1964. After spending about two hours on political discussions, they went onto the main object of the Matsumura mission, new trade arrangements. This discussion proceeded without major problems because of the groundwork laid by the Okazaki–Sun meeting in the summer. Agreements were reached on expanding Japan–China trade, establishing liaison offices in both countries, nominating guarantees from both countries, creating associations of manufacturers per trade item, and the composition of trading goods. It was also agreed that the details of trade arrangements would be decided when Takasaki visited China.[17]

By the third meeting on 19 September, a joint memorandum of the Matsumura–Zhou talks had been prepared. In this connection, Zhou reaffirmed and further elaborated on the Chinese position as to the three political principles, the three trade principles, and the principle of inseparability of politics and economics, but he did not force the Japanese side to adhere to these principles. The joint announcement issued after the meeting read as follows:

> Premier Zhou Enlai and Vice Premier Chen Yi had friendly and frank discussions with LDP advisor Matsumura Kenzo for three days of 16, 17, and 19 [September].
>
> The Chinese side expressed its continuous adherence to the three political principles, the three trade principles and the principle of inseparability of politics and economics, and affirmed that these principles are as valid as ever.
>
> Both sides expressed their desire to promote and develop bilateral trade further.
>
> Both sides agreed that they should adopt a gradual and cumulative method, and strive for normalization of bilateral relations including both political and economic fronts.[18]

This statement was read to the press on 19 September as a 'joint announcement'. This reflected a Chinese concession to Matsumura's request that the statement should not be taken for a joint communiqué, and should be as brief as possible. It referred only to the Chinese adherence to the three sets of principles in Japan–China relations, and not to that of Japan. The Chinese side had originally prepared a longer draft of the statement, which declared that 'politics and economics are inseparable', thus seeking to give the impression that the Japanese side had given in to Chinese political demands. To the surprise of Tagawa who wrote the Japanese draft, they nonetheless accepted the Japanese revision very easily.[19]

---

[16] Tagawa, *Nitchu Kosho Hiroku*, pp. 37–50.   [17] *Ibid.*, pp. 40, 46.
[18] *Kankei Shiryo*, p. 125; *Sengo Shiryo*, p. 269; *Kihon Shiryo*, p. 214.
[19] Tagawa, *Nitchu Kosho Hiroku*, pp. 41–4.

On the day the joint announcement was read, Chen Yi went so far as to state to the Japanese press accompanying the Matsumura mission that 'China understands the current situation of Japan. Mr. Matsumura's explanation made it clear to us that Japan is now in a difficult position to cut its relations with Taiwan. The real issue is the US conspiracy to create "two Chinas", and we should strictly distinguish [our] relations with Japan [from those with the United States].'[20] Prior to the release of the joint announcement, Zhou closed the third Matsumura–Zhou meeting by saying, 'It is quite natural that we should disagree on several points, for I am a leader of the CCP and Mr. Matsumura is a leader of the LDP. We agreed, however, that we should promote friendly relations and coexist peacefully on the basis of these differences.'[21]

All this indicates an unusual Chinese flexibility and understanding toward Matsumura and the role he played in the promotion of Japan–China relations. This demonstrated Chinese realism, which formed a clear contrast with the case of Friendship Trade. This difference in the Chinese stance certainly cannot be attributed to any change in Chinese policy, since it was after the LT arrangements had been formally agreed upon that the Friendship Trade system was consolidated by the signing of the protocol. The Chinese apparently pursued both policies simultaneously. Furui recalls that Matsumura thought that the Friendship Trade system should be abolished, so that all trade could be incorporated into a single, comprehensive trade channel, but Zhou did not agree.[22]

5.1.4. The Second Takasaki Mission and the Signing of the LT Agreement

Matsumura came back to Japan on 25 September and conferred with Takasaki on the following day. Matsumura had laid the political groundwork and set forth a general framework for the new trade scheme, and Takasaki's role now was to negotiate its details. In the meantime, he sought to obtain governmental endorsement for the scheme of long-term trade by deferred payment, and to arrange participation in his mission by prominent industrial leaders. As to the possible products to be traded, Matsumura and Zhou had already reached a broad consensus. Japan would export chemical fertilizers, agricultural chemicals, steel, chemical fibre plants, and agricultural machinery, in exchange for Chinese coal, salt, iron ore, soya beans, corn, and traditional Chinese medicines.[23] The materialization of the trade plan therefore required cooperation by the steel, fertilizer, and machinery industries. Takasaki had originally intended to depart for China on 18 October, but decided on the 13th to postpone his departure because of delays in decisions by

---

[20] *Sengo Shiryo*, p. 269.   [21] *Ibid.*, p. 48.
[22] Furui, *Nitchu 18-nen*, p. 77.   [23] Tagawa, *Nitchu Kosho Hiroku*, p. 46.

the government and the ammonium sulphate and steel industries. Takasaki also aspired to solicit governmental approval for a deferred payment method in China trade, in order to secure a stable basis for a long-term trade agreement.

By the middle of 1962, the Ikeda cabinet had reached a general decision to approve deferred payments for Japan–China trade. A major point of dispute between Takasaki and the government was over its conditions. The government's position was relatively clear-cut from the start. The Japanese government could not allow more favourable conditions than (1) the ones provided for China by western countries, and (2) the ones Japan provided for a third country (most importantly Taiwan).

The governmental consensus was formed through Administrative Vice-Ministers' conferences on 13 and 15 October, including the MITI, the Ministry of Foreign Affairs, the Ministry of Finance, and the Economic Planning Agency. These were followed by consultations among the four Ministers, Fukuda Hajime, Ohira Masayoshi, Tanaka Kakuei, and Miyazawa Kiichi, on 16 October. The decision was conveyed to Takasaki by Fukuda on 17 October, which included the following. (1) The term of a trade agreement should be limited to five years or less, and exports and imports should be balanced during that period of time. (2) Conditions of deferred payment should not exceed those provided by western countries for China or those extended by Japan to a third country. The government would approve of deferred payment of one year for compound fertilizer and one and a half years for steel and agricultural machinery. Deferred payments for ammonium sulphate and urea would not be authorized. (3) Plant exports should be treated separately from an overall, long-term trade plan.[24]

The government did not allow deferred payment for ammonium sulphate because it had not offered it even to Taiwan or South Korea. Takasaki apparently was unhappy with this decision, because ammonium sulphate, seen as important to the Chinese agricultural development plan, was a central item in the new trade plan. Nonetheless, MITI Minister Fukuda stated that this was the most the government could do, and Minister of Foreign Affairs Ohira said that it was difficult to have second thoughts on this governmental decision.[25]

Two industries which took a cautious approach to the Takasaki mission, although for different reasons, were the steel and the ammonium sulphate industries. The negative posture of the steel industry can be explained by its close ties with *zaikai* (the big business community) and the United States. The United States had been the leading importer of Japan's steel since 1958, absorbing 25.5 per cent and 28.1 per cent of Japan's total steel exports in 1961

24 *Nihon Keizai Shinbun*, 13 October 1962 (evening), 14 October 1962, 16 October 1962, 16 October 1962 (evening), 18 October 1962.
25 *Nihon Keizai Shinbun*, 18 October 1962.

and 1962, respectively.[26] Moreover, the steel industry was a central component of *zaikai*, and Nagano Shigeo, president of Fuji Iron and Steel Co. and a
leader of the steel industry, was called one of the 'four emperors' reigning
over the business community. As strong supporters of the LDP regime and of
close Japan–US relations, big business was quite wary of US reactions to the
expansion of Japan–China trade. Thus, they were quick to react to the statement by Assistant Secretary of State Averell Harriman on 26 September
1962, which pointed out the political dangers involved in the expansion of
Japan–China trade. On 28 September, Ishizaka Taizo, president of Keidanren
(Japan Federation of Economic Organizations) repeated Harriman's concern by saying that Japan–China trade was a matter of politics, and he even
stated that Keidanren would not press any requests on the Takasaki mission
but might apply a brake.[27]

On 27 September, Takasaki met Nagano and Inayama Yoshihiro (president
of Yawata Iron and Steel Co.), two giants of the steel industry, and asked them
to dispatch an influential steel figure to China. They did not give an immedi-
ate reply. Instead, Inayama stated that the steel industry would have to take
Japan–US relations into full consideration, but that, within such limits, it
would cooperate with the long-term barter trade scheme. To be concrete,
Inayama expressed his readiness to purchase Chinese coal for his company in
exchange for Japan's fertilizer and agricultural machinery. He did not forget
to add, however, that Japan–China trade would not expand very much even
under this new trade scheme.[28] By early October, the steel industry had come
to the decision that it would not dispatch a prominent leader this time.
Nagano said on 9 October that the steel industry representatives would be of
managing director or chief of purchasing department rank.[29] As it turned
out, a managing director and a purchasing department chief from two steel
companies (Toyo Kokan and Amagasaki Seitetsu) participated in the
Takasaki mission.

The ammonium sulphate industry was reluctant for different reasons. Its
trade with Taiwan occupied 34.0 per cent and 31.6 per cent of its total exports
in 1960 and 1961, respectively.[30] The impact of the Taiwan factor on the ammonium sulphate industry was more direct than that of the steel industry's
US connection, for Taiwan threatened to cancel contracts for fertilizer imports from Japan if the industry sent a representative to Beijing.

Before Taiwan applied this pressure, Shibata Shukichi, president of the
Ammonium Sulphate Industry Association, had said that, even though the

---

[26] Calculated on the basis of data from *Nihon Tekko Yushutsu Kumiai 20-nen-shi [Twenty-Year History of the Japan Steel Export Association]* (Tokyo: Nihon Tekko Yushutsu Kumiai, 1974), p. 716.

[27] *Nihon Keizai Shinbun*, 29 September 1962.

[28] *Asahi Shinbun*, 28 September 1962; *Nihon Keizai Shinbun*, 28 September 1962.

[29] *Nihon Keizai Shinbun*, 3 October 1962, 10 October 1962.

[30] Calculated on the basis of data from *Nihon Ryuan Kogyo-shi [History of Japan Ammonium Sulphate Industry]* (Tokyo: Nihon Ryuan Kogyo Kyokai, 1968), p. 778.

government would not allow deferred payments, he would send an appropriate person if only to investigate the Chinese situation.[31] On 15 October, however, Taiwan gave notice to the representatives of the Mitsui, Mitsubishi, and Sumitomo trading corporations in Taipei that it would cancel fertilizer contracts if the industry decided to dispatch a representative.[32] Shibata, obviously disturbed by this Taiwanese reaction, changed his previous attitude and told Takasaki on 19 October that the chances against his industry sending any representatives would be 80 to 90 per cent.[33]

By the night of 21 October, Takasaki had met Shibata several times to persuade him to change his mind, but to no avail. On 22 October, Takasaki announced that he would postpone his 24 October departure because the mission would be meaningless without participation by the ammonium sulphate industry.[34] That same evening, Okazaki Kaheita met Prime Minister Ikeda and asked him to reconsider the government's stand against providing export credits for ammonium sulphate.[35]

Ikeda could not provide any measures to protect the industry from the Taiwanese retaliation, nor did he reconsider its previous policy against any deferred payments for ammonium sulphate and urea. After a regular cabinet meeting on 23 October, however, he discussed the issue with Minister of Finance Tanaka Kakuei, MITI Minister Fukuda Hajime, Minister of Construction Kono Ichiro, and Minister without Portfolio Kawashima Shojiro. They agreed that ammonium sulphate should be on the list of goods for export and the industry should send a representative.[36] On the basis of this agreement, Minister of Agriculture and Forestry Shigemasa called in Shibata and attempted to persuade him to reconsider the industry's posture.

As it turned out, it was Takasaki who took the lead in negotiations with China to include ammonium sulphate in the LT Trade agreement. This initiative by Takasaki proved to be very important to the subsequent development of Japan–China trade, because China eventually took the place of Taiwan as the leading purchaser of Japanese fertilizer. In retrospect, therefore, it was very significant that Shibata, still concerned about Taiwan, compromised by requesting Suekuni Takeichiro, a special appointee of the Japan Chemical Fertilizer Export Promotion Association, to join the Takasaki mission. Shibata, however, did not intend to allow Suekuni to officially represent the ammonium sulphate industry.[37] In the end, it was Takasaki's initiative in Beijing that counted; this became a turning point for the industry in switching its major market from Taiwan to China, as seen below.

[31] *Nihon Keizai Shinbun*, 10 October 1962.
[32] *Asahi Shinbun*, 18 October 1962.
[33] *Asahi Shinbun*, 20 October 1962.
[34] *Nihon Keizai Shinbun*, 22 October 1962 (evening).
[35] *Asahi Shinbun*, 23 October 1962 (evening).
[36] *Nihon Keizai Shinbun*, 23 October 1962 (evening).
[37] *Asahi Shinbun*, 24 October 1962.

The members of the Takasaki mission held final consultations on 24 October, and formally decided to leave for China on 26 October. The mission had thirty-three members, including twenty-three representatives of related industries, with Takasaki as head, and Okazaki as deputy head and consultant. The other core members included three LDP Dietmen, Takeyama Yutaro, Matsumoto Shunichi, and Noda Takeo. Tabayashi Masakichi, Kawai Ryoichi (executive director of Komatsu Manufacturing Co.), Okubo Tadaharu, Inoue Genzo (secretary to Takasaki), and Hirahara Fusako (Takasaki's daughter) also joined the mission.[38]

Discussions in Beijing centred almost exclusively on economic and technical matters for the new trade arrangements. Takasaki and Okazaki, on the Japanese side, and Liao Chengzhi and Ye Jizhuang (Minister of Foreign Trade), on the Chinese side, discussed general developments, while Okazaki, Takeyama, and Tabayashi, assisted by the industry representatives, were the Japanese negotiators on the concrete terms of the agreement, with Lu Xuzhang (Vice-Minister of Foreign Trade) and others.

The negotiations went quite smoothly. The Japanese side was particularly impressed by the resoluteness and strong leadership displayed by Zhou Enlai during the process. Matsumoto and Noda came back to Japan on 3 November in the middle of the negotiations, to inform Ikeda of developments. They reported that Zhou himself had often been involved, and gave the highest priority to the conclusion of a long-term agreement rather than such particulars as the size of trade in the first year.[39] Okazaki remembered that Zhou had stated clearly to Takasaki that he would be directly responsible for the negotiations, and designated Liao Chengzhi as the person in charge on his behalf.[40]

The memorandum on Japan–China trade signed by Liao and Takasaki on 9 November 1962 reaffirmed the political basis established by Matsumura and Zhou six weeks earlier. The preface stated:

Mr. Liao Chengzhi and Mr. Takasaki Tatsunosuke, in accordance with the tenor of the talks on the expansion of Japan–China trade held between Premier Zhou Enlai and Mr. Matsumura Kenzo in September this year, and to further develop private trade between the two countries on the basis of equality and reciprocity and by a gradual and cumulative method, exchanged the following memorandum.[41]

In the memorandum, the two sides agreed to promote long-term, overall trade with 1963–1968 as the initial five-year period, during which the average annual total of transactions would reach about 36 million pounds sterling (about $100 million). They also agreed that the Chinese side would export

---

[38] For a complete list of the mission, see *Nihon Keizai Shinbun*, 25 October 1962, and *Asahi Shinbun*, 26 October 1962.

[39] *Nihon Keizai Shinbun*, 3 November 1962.

[40] *Inside Document*; Okazaki, 'Chugoku no Genjo to Nitchu no Shorai', p. 15.

[41] For the full text, see *Kankei Shiryo*, pp. 212–13, *Sengo Shiryo*, p. 358, *Kihon Shiryo*, pp. 215–16.

coal, iron ore, soya beans, corn, miscellaneous beans, salt, tin, and other products, and the Japanese side would export steel, chemical fertilizers, agricultural chemicals, agricultural machinery, farming equipment, industrial plant, and other items.

Details of the trade plan for 1963 were settled in a separate agreement signed simultaneously with the memorandum.[42] It stipulated that Japan would export 50,000 tons of ammonium sulphate in 1963. However, the type of ammonium sulphate was of low quality, and had not been exported to Taiwan. Moreover, the volume was limited to 50,000 tons, whereas the agreed amounts of compound fertilizer and urea were 200,000 tons each.

Takasaki took a strong lead, however, in inserting a stipulation that the Japanese side agreed to export ammonium sulphate of better quality, the kind exported to Taiwan, starting from 1964. Takasaki indeed took advantage of the fact that Shibata was not authorized to represent the industry. Later, Taiwan put its words into action and cancelled its contract with the Japanese counterparts. The loss was compensated by aggressive Chinese purchase. In 1963, China purchased 200,000 tons of ammonium sulphate from Japan, despite the fact that the agreed amount was just 50,000 tons. In 1964, China became the leading importer of Japanese ammonium sulphate.

Takasaki also made an important decision about exporting plant facilities, defying the earlier decision by the Japanese government. The trade agreement for 1963 specified an annual amount of about $1 million in plant for the years 1963 to 1965. Okazaki later recalled that the Chinese side had informed him of its intention to import chemical fibre plant facilities from the Kurashiki Rayon Company, and that on hearing of this Takasaki had immediately decided to include plant exports in the agreement.[43] The MITI later expressed dissatisfaction in a document dated 28 November 1962 submitted to the Prime Minister. It stated that the agreement on plant was contrary to the governmental decision and therefore could not be approved.[44] As it turned out, however, the MITI changed its stand the following year, and approved plant export by deferred payments. This eventually brought about a political controversy over the 'Yoshida letter (1964)', which is a telling proof that Takasaki's decisions were highly political ones. This will be further discussed below.

Thus, the core components of the LT Trade agreement were the results of Takasaki's initiatives in Beijing. Ikeda was certainly willing to expand Japan–China trade beyond the level of Friendship Trade, but his freedom of action was severely curtailed by the international environment. In this context, non-governmental initiatives made an important breakthrough. This was well demonstrated by the fact that the Ikeda government first decided against including plant exports in the new trade scheme. Takasaki also made an important decision on exporting ammonium sulphate, which was also contrary to

---

[42] *Kankei Shiryo*, pp. 213–14; *Sengo Shiryo*, pp. 358–9.
[43] *Inside Document.*   [44] *Ibid.*

the government's decision. As seen below, the limitations of governmental involvement would surface again over the issue of Export–Import Bank credits in 1963 and 1964.

Thus, Japanese non-governmental actors ushered in a new decade in postwar Japan–China relations.

5.2. ORGANIZATIONS

5.2.1. The Takasaki Office

The subsequent developments of LT Trade were organizationally sustained by the Japan–China Overall Trade Liaison Council (JCOTLC). Its headquarters was called the Takasaki office, and its counterpart in China, the Liao office. A Beijing liaison office was later established in January 1965.

One week after the signing of the LT agreement, the members of the Takasaki mission gathered in Tokyo and decided to set up the JCOTLC with Takasaki as its chairman.[45] This was a formal role, and Okazaki was the man in charge from the start, taking responsibility for handling trade business. Thus, Okazaki naturally was selected chairman of the JCOTLC when Takasaki died in February 1964.[46] In order to assure coordination among related Japanese firms and a strong bargaining position against their Chinese counterparts, the membership was restricted to concerned industry associations—not individual firms—including the Japan Iron and Steel Exporters' Council, the Japan–China Machinery Exporters' Association, the Japan Soda Industry Association, the Japan Ammonium Chloride Fertilizer Association, the Japan Urea and Ammonium Sulphate Industry Association, the Japan–China Association of Agricultural Chemical Exporters, and others.

The JCOTLC was administered by several pro-China individuals. When it reorganized itself into a 'juridical foundation' (*zaidan hojin*) in September 1967, with Okazaki as chief director, such important figures as Matsumoto Shunichi, Watanabe Yaeji, Kawai Ryoichi, Munakata Yoshitoshi, and Okubo Tadaharu shared responsibilities as directors, and Murakami Kimitaka was the auditor.[47] Matsumoto was a career diplomat from the prewar period; he was Vice-Minister of Foreign Affairs from 1942 to 1944 and again in 1945. From 1952 to 1954, he served as ambassador to Great Britain, and in 1955 was elected to the Lower House of the Diet. The highlight of his diplomatic career came in June 1955, when he was appointed by Prime Minister Hatoyama as the Japanese plenipotentiary to negotiate a communiqué to establish diplomatic relations with the Soviet Union (signed jointly by him, Hatoyama, and Kono Ichiro in October 1956). Okazaki was a close friend of

---

45 *Nihon Keizai Shinbun*, 17 November 1962.
46 *Nihon Keizai Shinbun*, 29 February 1964.
47 JCAET, *Nitchu Oboegaki*, p. 86.

Matsumoto's, and asked him to take part in the second Takasaki mission of November 1962, so that someone with connections to the Foreign Ministry would be involved in the new Japan–China trade.[48]

Watanabe, Kawai, and Murakami had been together at both the University of Tokyo and the MITI (before 1949, the Ministry of Commerce and Industry). Murakami became acquainted with Okazaki while serving at the Japanese embassy office in Shanghai during the war, when Okazaki was a councilor. Murakami left the MITI and became a director of the Japan External Trade Organization (JETRO) in 1962. From that time, he worked closely with Okazaki on Chinese affairs. He was promoted to deputy chief director of JETRO in 1966, and remained in that position until his death in 1972. Watanabe recalls that Murakami influenced him and Kawai to 'form a scrum' to assist Okazaki in developing China trade.[49]

Of course, Watanabe and Kawai had their own reasons. Intellectually, Watanabe shared Okazaki's long-term view on Japan–China relations; he believed that the bilateral relationship ought to be seen from a perspective ranging over hundreds and thousands of years. In order to study how to get along with communism, communist China among others, he volunteered in 1956 to be dispatched to the Japanese embassy in Moscow, where he served as a councillor from 1957 to 1960. Watanabe decided to leave the MITI in April 1966 at the age of forty-nine, when he was Bureau Chief of International Trade. He made this decision, according to his own explanation, because his status in the Japanese administration precluded his going to China.[50]

Kawai Ryoichi left the MITI as early as 1954 in order to take part in the management of Komatsu Manufacturing Co., of which his father was president. He was promoted to managing director in 1960, to vice-president in 1963, and to president in 1964. His interest in Chinese affairs can be seen as derived partly from his background as a MITI bureaucrat, and partly from his role as a businessman. In fact, Komatsu Manufacturing Co. was a leading manufacturer of agricultural machinery, which China badly needed from Japan. It was therefore quite understandable that his father, Kawai Ryosei, had him join the second Takasaki mission. Kawai Ryosei himself was enthusiastic about China, due to both his belief in 'an objective economic principle' and more subjective feelings. He believed in 'the perpetual law that trade is inversely proportional to distance', and also strongly held mixed sentiments

48 *Inside Document.*
49 Watanabe Yaeji, 'Nitchu Kankei no Ayumi to Hoko' [Past and Future of Japan–China Relations], *Boeki Seisaku*, 177 (1974), pp. 5–6.
50 Ibid., p. 6; Interview with Watanabe Yaeji, the Watanabe Law Office, Tokyo, 24 September 1986 (hereafter cited as Watanabe Interview); 'Watanabe Yaeji Shi' [Mr. Watanabe Yaeji], in Tsusho Sangyo Chosa-kai (ed.), *Sangyo Seisaku-shi Kaiso-roku, Dai-36-bunsatsu [Recollections on Industrial Policies, Vol. 36]* (Tokyo: Sangyo Chosa-kai, 1986), pp. 75–6, 85; Watanabe Yaeji, 'Chugoku no Kindaika to Wagakuni no Kyoryoku' [Chinese Modernization and Japanese Cooperation], *Boeki Seisaku*, 251 (1980), pp. 6, 9.

typical of Japanese attitudes toward China: admiration as a source of Japanese culture and guilt consciousness with regard to the war. These views undoubtedly influenced his son.[51]

The JCOTLC was also supported by several pro-China LDP politicians, led by Matsumura Kenzo. In fact it functioned as a secretariat office for Matsumura, whom Zhou Enlai had recognized as a 'general liaison' between Japan and China.[52] Consequently, the JCOTLC also maintained close contacts with LDP politicians who were closely associated with Matsumura, such as Furui Yoshimi, Tagawa Seiichi, and Takeyama Yutaro, who participated in subsequent annual LT missions to China.

5.2.2. The Beijing Liaison Office

The exchange of liaison offices in both capitals resulted from the third Matsumura mission of April 1964, which included two LDP politicians, Takeyama Yutaro and Furui Yoshimi. The Takasaki office (the name had been retained despite Takasaki's passing in February 1964) joined the mission, and was represented by Okazaki Kaheita and Okubo Tadaharu. On 18 April, the delegation concluded two important memoranda with the Liao office: 'Memorandum of Talks between the Takasaki Tatsunosuke Office and the Liao Chengzhi Office Concerning Mutual Establishment of Liaison Offices and Mutual Exchange of Representatives', and 'Memorandum of Talks between the Takasaki Tatsunosuke Office and the Liao Chengzhi Office Concerning Exchange of News Reporters of Japan and China'.[53] They stipulated that Japan and China would exchange three representatives and two staff members for the liaison offices, and up to eight news reporters; the length of stay would be limited to a year or less; and the Takasaki office and the Liao office would take responsibility for the security of trade representatives and reporters.[54]

Thus, five members of the Tokyo liaison office of the Liao office, headed by Sun Pinghua as chief representative, arrived in Tokyo on 13 August 1964, and three Japanese representatives left Japan on 25 January 1965 for their posts in the Beijing liaison office. The Takasaki office appointed Soma Tsunetoshi as chief representative, and Owada Yuji of the JCIEA and Tanaka Sosuke of the Bank of Tokyo as representatives.[55] Although Soma assumed the Beijing post in a private capacity as an advisor to the JCIEA, the MITI connection was

[51] Kawai Ryosei, 'Nitchu Kankei wo Kataru' [Talking About Japan–China Relations], *Sekai*, 231 (1965); Kawai Ryosei, 'Nitchu Hukko no Toki' [The Time of Japan–China Normalization], *Chuo Koron*, 76 (1961).

[52] Tagawa, *Nitchu Kosho Hiroku*, p. 44.

[53] *Kankei Shiryo*, pp. 222–3; *Sengo Shiryo*, pp. 364–5; *Kihon Shiryo*, pp. 232–4.

[54] For an accessible but informative description concerning the exchange of news reporters between Japan and China, see Yamada Reizo, 'Shiren ni Tatsu Nitchu Kisha Kokan' [Japan–China Exchange of Reporters in an Ordeal], *Chugoku*, 75 (1970).

[55] *Asahi Shinbun*, 12 January 1965.

clear. Soma was a career MITI bureaucrat known as an expert on communist trade since he had started to handle China and Soviet trade as deputy chief of the export section of the international trade bureau in 1957.[56]

Indeed, the MITI was quite serious about the Beijing liaison office. In January 1965, what later came to be called the 'China Academy' was created in the MITI under the strong leadership of Watanabe Yaeji. The Academy trained as many as fifty MITI bureaucrats in Chinese language and affairs: twenty-one from January to July 1965, fifteen from July to December 1965, two from January to March 1966, and four in each of the remaining three quarters in 1966.[57] These bureaucrats were freed from their regular ministerial duties to concentrate on the classes offered by the Academy. The program apparently went beyond the extent that even the MITI could condone, and met with strong opposition inside the MITI, thus having to be terminated after two years. Nonetheless, the intensive training in Chinese language and affairs produced as many as fifty China hands in the MITI. It was these officials who constituted the core of the trade representatives dispatched to the Beijing liaison office.[58]

Out of eighteen bureaucrats who were sent to this liaison office before diplomatic normalization in September 1972, eleven were from the MITI. The others included five from the Ministry of Foreign Affairs, one from the Ministry of Finance, and one from the Ministry of Agriculture and Forestry.[59] However, only one of the Ministry of Foreign Affairs officials went to Beijing before the Nixon shock. In this case, exceptionally, Takuma Toshitada resigned from the Ministry before leaving for Beijing, joining the Beijing liaison office in May 1966. The Ministry of Foreign Affairs issued an unusual statement that Takuma had 'simply changed his occupation'.[60]

The major responsibilities of the Beijing office were the annual negotiations of Japan–China trade under the LT/MT arrangements, and taking care of the annual delegation from the Takasaki office and the Japanese press corps.[61]

5.3. TRANSFORMATION TO MEMORANDUM TRADE

5.3.1. Two Plant Facilities Contracts

Although LT Trade made a very promising start, prospects for its further development gradually darkened. This transformation in the general tone of LT

---

[56] Soma Tsunetoshi, 'Nitchu Boeki ni Seii wo' [Sincerity to Japan–China Trade], *Ekonomisuto*, 46 (1968), p. 54.

[57] 'Watanabe Yaeji Shi', pp. 86–9.

[58] Ibid., pp. 72–3; Watanabe, 'Chugoku no Kindaika to Wagakuni no Kyoryoku', p. 8.

[59] JCAET, *Nitchu Oboegaki no 11-nen*, p. 84.

[60] *Asahi Shinbun*, 15 May 1966.

[61] Interview with Shimakura Tamio, the Institute of Developing Economy, Tokyo, 30 May 1985. Shimakura was dispatched to the Beijing liaison office from the Ministry of Agriculture and Forestry, where he stayed from 1969 to 1972.

Trade was most typically seen in the case of the governmental decision on export credits for the export of plant facilities.

On 14 July 1963, a contract was signed to export Kurashiki Rayon's chemical fibre plant facilities, on condition that export credits would be provided by the Export–Import Bank of Japan. The Chinese chemical industry delegation to Japan had originally expressed a desire to import a Kurashiki plant in January 1958. This did not develop into full-scale negotiations, however, because of the Nagasaki flag incident in May 1958. After circumstances became more favourable to the reopening of Japan–China trade, China revived the plan in the spring of 1962. Thus, the Kurashiki Rayon Co. sent its first mission to China in September 1962. In November, its second mission joined the Takasaki mission. The Kurashiki representative signed a protocol with full support from Takasaki, meaning that Takasaki would be responsible for persuading the Japanese government to permit Export–Import Bank credits.[62] This was the first plant export contract with China under LT Trade, and indeed in the history of postwar Japan–China trade.

This was followed by a contract to export a Nichibo chemical fibre plant, which was initialled in May 1964 and formally signed on 20 September 1964. The Chinese side had inquired about importing Nichibo's plant at about the same time as the case of Kurashiki, and Nichibo also sent representatives to China with the second Takasaki mission of November 1962. According to Okazaki, however, the Chinese side wanted to start off with the smaller-scale Kurashiki plant.[63] Hara Kichihei, then president of Nichibo, recalls that Takasaki called him in when export credits were extended to Kurashiki, and said that it was difficult to approve both contracts at the same time, but that the Kurashiki decision would break the impasse.[64]

5.3.2. Ikeda and Export Credits

As mentioned earlier, a consensus had been reached in the Ikeda administration by the middle of 1962 to allow deferred payments in Japan–China trade. But, the core issue in this case was the granting of export credits by the Export–Import Bank. The MITI took the lead, and Watanabe Yaeji was again a central actor as he had been in creating the China Academy in the MITI. In the spring of 1963, Watanabe, through the intermediary of Kawai Ryoichi, secretly met Sun Pinghua and Wang Xiaoyun, who were visiting Japan with an orchid delegation. Sun also met MITI Trade Section Chief Yashiki Hiroshi at the house of Utsunomiya Tokuma. After these secret meetings with the Chinese officials, Watanabe took it on himself to force approval of deferred payments for the export of the Kurashiki plant. At the time, the approval of

[62] Ohara, 'Tai-Chugoku Puranto Yushutsu ni Tsuite'.

[63] *Inside Document.*

[64] Hara Kichihei, 'Nichibo Puranto Shodan Tenmatsu-ki' [A Story of Nichibo's Plant Negotiations], in Kawakatsu, *Yuko Ichiro*, pp. 128–35.

Export–Import Bank credits for exports was a bureau-level responsibility, and Watanabe, as Vice-Minister for Administration, successfully persuaded International Trade Bureau Chief Matsumura Keiichi as well as Trade Section Chief Yashiki Hiroshi. Watanabe was prepared to take responsibility for this decision, which later caused friction with MITI Minister Fukuda Hajime but eventually was upheld by the government.[65]

The government's next concern over the Kurashiki case had to do with the interest rate of the deferred payment, which was set at 4.5 per cent in the original contract, although the average for textile machinery exports to other countries was from 5.75 to 6 per cent. In a meeting between Takasaki Tatsunosuke and MITI Minister Fukuda Hajime on 19 August 1963, however, a compromise was reached that the rate would be increased to 5–6 per cent, but the increase in China's burden would be compensated by cutting the total sale price from 7.4 to 7.2 billion yen. On the following day, the Ministers of MITI, Foreign Affairs, and Finance (Fukuda, Ohira, and Tanaka) agreed that the Kurashiki plant export would be permitted on condition that the interest rate would be 6 per cent rather than 4.5 per cent. This agreement was formally endorsed by the cabinet on 23 August.[66] The report presented to the cabinet by the MITI on 23 August stated two specific criteria for allowing this plant export: (1) conditions should not be more favourable than those given to plant exports to free-world countries; and (2) this export should not bring about a sharp increase in the portion of Export–Import Bank's credits provided for trade with the communist bloc versus other areas. Kurashiki's contract did not pose a problem with regard to the second condition, and with the interest rate raised to 6 per cent, the report confirmed that the first condition was also satisfied.[67]

The Taiwan government strongly protested against this decision by the Japanese government. It regarded export credits by the Export–Import Bank of Japan as governmental economic aid to mainland China, and thus as contradictory to the basic principles of postwar Japan–Taiwan relations. This protest was conveyed to Foreign Minister Ohira by the Taiwan ambassador to Japan on 22 August 1963, and on the same day Chiang Kai-shek elaborated the point in a telegram to Yoshida Shigeru. Yoshida not only was the Japanese signatory of the Japan–Taiwan Peace Treaty in 1952, but also was seen in Taiwan as the man who had raised Ikeda to the prime ministership.[68] Taiwan

[65] Watanabe Interview; Interview with Sun Pinghua, President of China–Japan Friendship Association, Beijing, 21 June 1986 (hereafter cited as Sun Interview); Sun Pinghua, 'Zhong-Ri Youhao Suixiang-lu (14),' *Shijie Zhishi*, 22 (1985), p. 18; 'Watanabe Yaeji Shi', pp. 71–2; Watanabe, 'Chugoku no Kindaika to Wagakuni no Kyoryoku', p. 7.

[66] *Nihon Keizai Shinbun*, 20 August 1963, 20 August 1963 (evening); *Asahi Shinbun*, 20 August 1963 (evening), 23 August 1963 (evening).

[67] MITI, 'Biniron Puranto no Chugoku-muke Yushutsu ni Tsuite: Kakugi Hokoku' [On the Chemical Fiber Plant Export to China: A Report to the Cabinet] (1963).

[68] *Asahi Shinbun*, 23 August 1963; Chang, *Nikka*, pp. 205–6.

also activated the route of the Japan–China (Taiwan) Cooperation Commit-tee to approach the LDP Taiwan lobby, such as Kishi Nobusuke and Ono Banboku. When these pressures turned out to be ineffective, Taipei decided to recall its ambassador to Japan, Chang Lisheng, who returned to Taipei on 21 September 1963.[69]

A completely unrelated event complicated the issue further. On 7 October 1963, Zhou Hengqing, a Chinese interpreter accompanying a hydraulic ma-chinery industry mission to Japan, ran into the Soviet embassy to seek refuge. When he was transferred to the Japanese police, he changed his desired des-tination, first to Taiwan, and then to Japan. On 24 October, Zhou changed his mind again and insisted that he wanted to go back home.

The Japanese government decided on 26 October to send him back to China. This incident fuelled Taipei's suspicions about the intentions of the Ikeda government, which had already been aroused by the LT agreement and the extension of export credits to the Kurashiki Rayon plant. On 31 Decem-ber, the Taiwan government called back its chargé d'affaires (who had taken the place of the ambassador recalled in September), two councillors, and a first secretary, who left Japan on 2 January 1964. On 10 January, it further re-taliated by suspending governmental procurement of Japanese goods, which was about 40 per cent of Japanese exports to Taiwan.[70]

According to the memoir by Chang Chun, Chiang Kai-shek's Chief Sec-retary, Yoshida Shigeru told the Taiwanese chargé d'affaires in Tokyo, who visited Yoshida on 30 December 1963, that he would attempt to persuade Ikeda to pay a visit to Taiwan, and that if he refused Yoshida himself would visit on behalf of Ikeda.[71] Kurogane Yasuyoshi, Cabinet Secretary of the Ikeda administration, recollects that Ishii Mitsujiro, a leading member of Taiwan lobby, visited Ikeda on 7 January 1964, and formally raised, for the first time, the issue of Yoshida's visit to Taiwan.[72] The Ikeda government also felt a need to soothe Taipei, and responded on the following day. Foreign Minister Ohira said that the government would welcome a Yoshida visit to Taiwan, provided that his talks with Taiwan leaders would be limited to talks at the 'higher level' without going into concrete 'negotiations' on such issues as the defection of Zhou Hengqing. Ikeda met Yoshida on 8 February to per-sonally convey this government policy.[73]

Thus, Yoshida visited Taiwan in a private capacity on 23 February 1964 to ameliorate the strains which had developed since the Japanese government's decision to extend Export–Import Bank credits. Chiang Kai-shek expressed to Yoshida Taipei's official stance on Japan–China trade: it would be con-doned if the trade remained purely private, but by no means could Taipei

[69] *Ibid.*, p. 190.
[70] *Asahi Shinbun*, 25 October 1963, 3 January 1964, 12 January 1964.
[71] Chang, *Nikka*, p. 207.
[72] *Inside Document.*   [73] *Asahi Shinbun*, 8 January 1964 (evening); *Inside Document.*

tolerate an implication of economic aid. In order to normalize the deteriorating relationship, Yoshida and Chiang confirmed their shared view (that is, they did not issue a formal agreement on the basis of the Japanese government's policy) that Japan should send an important government official (tacitly indicating Foreign Minister Ohira) in the near future.[74] Subsequently, Ohira visited Taiwan in July. By that time, however, Taipei had already softened its attitude toward Tokyo, and it did not take issue with Ohira on such particulars as the plant question. This was due to the so-called Yoshida letter, dated 7 May 1964.

This Yoshida letter (1964) was sent as a private letter, and even the fact that it had been sent was not made public at the time. But according to a report in the *Mainichi Shinbun* on 5 August 1965, Yoshida made two promises to Taipei concerning Japan's plant exports to China:

(1) Concerning the matter of restricting the financing of plant exports to communist China to a purely private basis, study will be made so as to reflect your (nationalist government's) intention.
(2) Within this year (Showa 39 [1964]), Nichibo's chemical fiber plant export to communist China through the Export–Import Bank shall not be approved.

Kurogane's recollections confirm these two points. According to him, Kitazawa Naokichi, an LDP parliamentarian and a protégé of Yoshida, visited Ikeda sometime in early May 1964 with a typewritten sheet of paper, which included the above two points.[75] The fact that Ikeda saw the letter but did not oppose it meant that Ikeda approved of the two points. In fact, Cabinet Secretary Kurogane announced on 9 May that the government would study the possibility of private financing in place of Export–Import Bank financing for plant exports to China; that such measures were now under study in the Ministry of Finance, MITI, the Ministry of Foreign Affairs, and the Economic Planning Agency; and that Nichibo's plant export would not be approved until some conclusion about the financing matter was reached.[76] This announcement was nothing other than a governmental reiteration of the Yoshida letter (1964), suggesting that Taiwan's influence had prevailed over Ikeda. Okazaki Kaheita, too, recollects that he was called in by Ikeda at the end of May 1964 and was informed of the existence of the Yoshida letter (1964). Ikeda told Okazaki that he was unable to let Export–Import Bank credits be used during that year.[77]

All this may appear to give an impression that Ikeda complied with Taiwanese pressure. But the Yoshida letter itself contained an element of compromise, in that the letter promised to refrain from providing Export–Import Bank credits to Nichibo's plant export during the year of Showa 39 (which was understood as the government's fiscal year, extending into March 1965), but did

74 *Asahi Shinbun*, 26 February 1964, 27 February 1964.   75 *Inside Document.*
76 *Asahi Shinbun*, 9 May 1964 (evening).   77 *Inside Document.*

not make any binding reference to specific measures for the years ahead, except to promise further study of alternatives. In fact, Ikeda regarded the Yoshida letter as an opportunity to let Taipei cool off, and intended to approve Export–Import Bank credits in the following year. According to Okazaki, Ikeda told him in May 1964 that he would save Taiwan's face that year but would allow the credit the following year.[78] Hara Kichihei, president of Nichibo, also remembers that Ikeda told him that Export–Import Bank credits would be extended in 1965.[79]

But before the cooling-off period was over, Ikeda had fallen ill and the question of the Yoshida letter (1964) was placed in the hands of Sato Eisaku, who formed his first cabinet on 9 November 1964.

5.3.3. Sato and the Yoshida Letter (1964)

The new Sato administration approved the export of Nichibo's plant in January 1965, but denied the provision of Export–Import Bank funds. On 8 February 1965, Sato pronounced before a Lower House committee that his government would be constrained by the Yoshida letter (1964). Sato even widened its application beyond plant exports. On 11 February, the Sato government approved, but denied the use of Export–Import Bank credits for, the export of a freighter from the Hitachi Shipbuilding Co. This Hitachi case was in a sense a testing ground for Sato's China policy, for he could have ignored the Yoshida letter in this decision, on the grounds that it was limited only to plant exports. The Hitachi contract, which had been signed on 16 November 1964, stipulated that the Japanese government would have to approve Export–Import Bank financing by 15 February 1965.

After the Sato government's decision on 11 February, the Chinese side decided to take a wait-and-see posture by extending the deadline to 31 March. Liao Chengzhi announced on 24 March, 'Our attitude toward Japan is that of wait-and-see. Japan–China relations in the future will depend on the Japanese government's posture toward the Yoshida letter. As long as the Sato government is constrained by it, the expansion of LT Trade cannot be expected. The Japanese government can either deny the validity of the Yoshida letter, or show in deed that it is not constrained by it.'[80] The Japanese government announced on 30 March, however, that the Hitachi contract ought to be carried out immediately and that the matter of export credits was to be considered separately.

The contract for the Hitachi freighter expired on 31 March 1965, and that for the Nichibo plant on 30 April. The Chinese side also cancelled plans to import about forty other plant and related facilities, currently being negotiated,[81]

[78] *Ibid.*   [79] Hara, 'Nichibo Puranto Shodan Tenmatsu-ki', p. 129.
[80] *Nihon Keizai Shinbun*, 25 March 1965.
[81] For their listing, see Hirai, *Nitchu Boeki no Kiso Chishiki*, p. 132.

which were small and did not necessarily require export credits. Japanese plant were totally excluded from the Chinese third five-year plan, starting from 1966, and were compensated with European plant.[82] Thus, the Chinese side acted on the words of Chen Yi, stated in February 1965, that the real issue was not a matter of financing but the fact that the Japanese government allowed Taiwan to intervene in Japan–China relations, and thus took sides in the plot to create 'two Chinas'.[83]

As a consequence of these developments in 1964 and 1965, Japan–China relations shifted into a new phase. It is particularly important to note that the bilateral relationship had already deteriorated at this time—that is, before the dawn of the Chinese Cultural Revolution. This series of events exemplified the limitation of the Japanese government's involvement in China trade, which could even be detrimental to the maintenance of the political base of realism constructed by Matsumura Kenzo.

5.3.4. Memorandum Trade

Thus, a virtual transformation of LT Trade had already taken shape by late 1965, when a delegation from the Takasaki office visited China to negotiate the 1966 trade agreement. Liao Chengzhi told this delegation that so long as the Yoshida letter (1964) remained effective there would be no negotiations about plant and freighters.[84] Therefore, the 1966 trade agreement, signed on 18 September 1965, recorded an increase of only $34 million from the previous year's level. However, total Japan–China trade in 1966 actually increased by $150 million. Consequently, the share of LT Trade in total Japan–China trade declined from 36 per cent to 33 per cent in 1966. The following years continued the decline in LT Trade transactions, whereas Friendship Trade increased every year except 1967 (see Table 4.2 on page 78).

Worried about the future of the LT agreement, Matsumura Kenzo decided to visit China to arrange an extension of LT Trade beyond the initial five-year period, which would expire in 1967. He paid his fourth postwar visit to China in May 1966, accompanied by Takeyama Yutaro and Matsumoto Shunichi. Matsumura conferred with Foreign Minister Chen Yi for three hours on 14 May, and with Premier Zhou Enlai for over four hours on 17 May. As had been the pattern with past Matsumura missions, details of trade were not raised in these meetings. Instead, Matsumura and Zhou agreed in principle that the LT agreement would be extended in the forthcoming annual negotiations in 1967.[85]

[82] For their listing, see *ibid.*, pp. 141–2.

[83] *Asahi Shinbun*, 4 February 1965 (evening).

[84] *Nihon Keizai Shinbun*, 7 September 1965 (evening).

[85] Matsumura Kenzo *et al.*, 'Nitchu Kankei eno Teigen: "Dai-4-ji Matsumura Hochu" wo Megutte' [Suggestions for Japan–China Relations: Concerning the 'Fourth Matsumura China Visit'], *Sekai*, 249 (1966).

The fact that Matsumura had to go such lengths to obtain this assurance from Zhou, more than a year before the expiration of the initial period, clearly indicated that the LT Trade system had already changed fundamentally. Prime Minister Sato's trip to Taiwan in September 1967 further aggravated the situation. Originally, Sato had planned to stop in Taiwan as part of his tours to the Pacific and South East Asian countries; a first round was planned for September, and a second round, including a Taiwan visit, scheduled for October. But Sato changed his mind in July, deciding to visit Taiwan independently of his Asian-Pacific tour, in response to a strong request from the Taiwan government.[86]

In response to Sato's decision, the Chinese side took further steps to apply pressure on the LT Trade system itself. On 4 September 1967, Wang Xiaoyun, representing the Liao office, issued a warning to the Takasaki office that it was not good for the Takasaki office to take Sato's Taiwan trip lightly. This was the first time that China had criticized the attitude of the Takasaki office toward Japanese governmental China policy. A Chinese diplomatic source in Beijing raised the level of this warning on 8 September. He said that China could not help concluding that the Japanese side did not have the will to protect LT Trade, so long as the Takasaki office and related industries remained hesitant in taking a combative attitude against Sato's anti-Chinese behaviour, and that the possibility had emerged that the LT Trade negotiations would not be held.[87] The Chinese side here revealed its intention to use LT Trade as an instrument to pressure the Japanese government, which it had refrained from doing ever since the system had started on the basis of the Matsumura–Zhou announcement on 19 September 1962. This tendency persisted into the subsequent phase of the transformation of the LT Trade system.

With the expiration of the 1962 LT memorandum in sight, the Takasaki office, in mid-October 1967, proposed to the Liao office through its liaison office in Beijing that formal negotiations on a new agreement should commence. This was followed by a letter dated 14 October to Liao Chengzhi from Matsumura Kenzo, which requested the early opening of a new round of negotiations. As it later turned out, Liao Chengzhi, who had been the highest person next to Zhou responsible for Japanese affairs, was being pushed behind the scenes when Matsumura attempted to contact him. The Chinese response did not come until the morning of 7 November, when the Liao office notified the Takasaki office that a telegram had been sent by Sun Pinghua to Matsumura the previous night. This telegram proposed that a delegation of a small number of representatives from the Takasaki office should visit China by 10 November. The Takasaki office notified the Chinese side on the following day that it could by no means dispatch a delegation before 20 November. The Chinese side notified the Takasaki office on 10 November that the matter

[86] Kusuda (ed.), *Sato Seiken 2792-nichi (Jo)*, p. 213.
[87] *Nihon Keizai Shinbun*, 5 September 1967 (evening), 9 September 1967.

might well be relegated to a different occasion for reconsideration.[88] Subsequently, the term of the LT Trade agreement expired, and no Japanese delegation was sent to China in 1967.

However, Zhou had not given up the LT Trade channel connecting China with Japan. On 18 January 1968, Zhou entrusted a JSP parliamentarian, Ishino Hisao, with a message to Matsumura that China would contact a Japanese delegation if it consisted of a small number of people.[89] This message by Zhou marked an important turning point in several respects. First, it was indeed a welcome statement to the Japanese side, which had become more and more apprehensive about the future of the LT arrangements since the end of 1967. Its significance was underscored by the fact that it was the first reference to LT Trade made by Zhou since May 1966.

Second, however, Zhou's statement was undoubtedly indicative of a qualitative transformation in the LT relationship. For one thing, Zhou for the first time broke the past pattern of transmitting Chinese LT Trade policy through the formal LT route. Also, Zhou deliberately chose to say that the Chinese side was ready to 'contact' the Japanese counterpart, not to 'negotiate'. This was interpreted by a reporter for the *Nihon Keizai Shinbun* in Beijing, as suggesting that the Chinese intended to give priority to contacts concerning political pre-conditions over negotiations on trade terms. This Chinese intention was underscored by the fact that an official of the Chinese People's Institute of Foreign Affairs, which was hosting Ishino in China, visited him at his hotel that evening to make sure that the Japanese translation of Zhou's wording was correct.[90]

The Japanese side interpreted this message correctly. A week before the departure of its delegation, the JCOTLC called an emergency general meeting and passed a resolution calling for the continuation and expansion of LT Trade and the elimination of political obstacles to the bilateral relationship, such as the Yoshida letter (1964).[91] This was the first political statement issued by the LT Trade office against the government of Japan. As a group of pro-China people committed to China trade, the LT organization ascribed the deterioration of the relationship to the Sato government, and thus proved its pro-China stance.

On 29 January 1968, China approved the admission of a Japanese delegation composed of Furui Yoshimi, Tagawa Seiichi, and Okazaki Kaheita as representatives, plus two staff members from the Takasaki office. The delegation left for China on 1 February. At the reception ceremony on 4 February, Liu Xiwen (assistant to the Minister of Foreign Trade) denounced the Sato government bitterly and insisted that LT Trade ought to be developed on the

88 JCAET, *Nitchu Oboegaki no 11-nen*, pp. 98–9.
89 *Ibid.*, p. 100.
90 *Nihon Keizai Shinbun*, 19 January 1968 (evening).
91 JCAET, *Nitchu Oboegaki*, pp. 100, 128.

basis of the political principles which were applied to Friendship Trade.[92] Thus, the treatment of the three political principles and the principle of the inseparability of politics from economics became the central issue during the following negotiations.

By the time the first trade talks were finally held, five rounds of political talks and six informal contacts had taken place between 8 and 19 February 1968. On 21 February, the trade talks started, and they continued until 4 March. While the details of a new trade plan were under discussion by the staff members of the liaison office, Tagawa and Furui had four rounds of talks, between 27 February and 1 March, on the revision of the 1964 agreement to exchange news reporters. It was decided that the number of exchanged reporters should be decreased from eight to five. The final formal meeting was held on 5 March and the communiqué of the political talks and the Memorandum Trade agreement were signed on the following day. The Japanese delegation met Zhou that evening.[93]

The communiqué of talks designated 'US imperialism and the Japanese authority' as the cause for obstacles in the relationship between Japan and China. The communiqué also stated:

...The Chinese side emphasized that it will uphold the three political principles and the principle of inseparability of politics and economics. The Japanese side concurred....

Both sides agreed and confirmed that the three political principles and the principle of inseparability of politics and economics are the principles which should be abided by in Japan–China relations, and are the political foundations of the relationship between us; and expressed a determination to make further endeavours for attaining these political foundations.[94]

Thus, for the first time in the history of LT Trade, political conditions were stipulated as a basis for further developments of trade relations. Previously, these had been carefully avoided by both Japan and China in line with the 1962 Matsumura–Zhou announcement. Actually, the communiqué indicated that the old LT Trade mechanism was no longer functioning. This transformation of the LT Trade system into what came to be labelled Memorandum Trade was shown by several important results of the negotiations which preceded the signing of the two documents on 6 March 1968.

First, the period of the agreement was reduced to one year. The Japanese side wanted to renew the original five-year agreement, but the Chinese side disagreed on the grounds that the Sato government's anti-Chinese policies had eroded the basis for a long-term agreement. The Chinese side eventually compromised so that the new agreement would be based on (1) the tenor of

92 Tagawa, *Nitchu Kosho Hiroku*, p. 76.
93 *Ibid.*, pp. 78–93, 99–104.
94 *Kankei Shiryo*, p. 270; *Kihon Shiryo*, p. 304.

the Zhou–Matsumura talks of 1962, (2) the communiqué of political talks
which was about to be issued, and (3) the principle of the LT agreement
which remained valid until 1967. The Japanese side interpreted this as congruent with the old LT agreement in principle, and accepted the Chinese
proposal.[95]

The Chinese were apparently very wary about giving an impression that
the new form of Japan–China trade was different from the older pattern. One
suspects that those who were in charge of Japanese affairs had found themselves in a difficult political position in the midst of the Cultural Revolution.
The importance of such factors was underscored by the third Chinese proposal pertaining to the transformation of the LT system. They requested on
27 February that the names of the Liao office and the Takasaki office be
changed to 'the China–Japan Memorandum Trade Office', and 'the Japan–
China Memorandum Trade Office', respectively. The Japanese side agreed to
this proposal on the grounds that Takasaki had already passed away and that
Liao Chengzhi himself, who did not show up at all during the negotiations,
appeared to be in a difficult position.[96] Indeed, Liao was under severe attack
by radicals, who saw the Liao office as a private office owned by Liao himself.[97]

Thus, a new form of Japan–China trade started as Memorandum Trade.
The new trade agreement was signed on 6 March 1968 together with the
communiqué of political talks. The preface stated:

The representatives of the [Japanese] Japan–China Memorandum Trade Office and
the [Chinese] China–Japan Memorandum Trade Office, on the basis of the communiqué of talks issued on 6 March 1968, and the memorandum exchanged by both sides
on 9 November 1962, consulted about the 1968 Memorandum Trade and reached an
agreement as follows.

The same portion of the 1966 agreement, the last of the annual LT agreement, read:

On the basis of the memorandum exchanged between Mr. Takasaki Tatsunosuke and
Mr. Liao Chengzhi on 9 November 1962, Mr. Okazaki Kaheita and Mr. Liu Xiwen
consulted about the fifth year (1967) trade, and reached an agreement as follows.

Two important changes from LT to MT are shown here. First, no personal
names were referred to in the new version of the trade agreement, and second, the political talks which preceded the trade talks were defined as a basis
of the new trade agreement. The new trade agreement of 1968 also included
two highly political stipulations which had been absent from the previous
year's version:

Concerning plants that were to be exported to China, the Japanese side said that it
would continue to endeavour to eliminate the obstacle of the 'Yoshida letter' installed
by the Japanese government.

95 Tagawa, *Nitchu Kosho Hiroku*, pp. 94–5.
96 *Ibid.*, p. 99.   97 Sun Interview.

Both concerned parties will negotiate and sign trade contracts on the basis of this trade agreement and the three political principles and the principle of inseparability of politics and economics as confirmed by the communiqué of political talks.

These phrases in both prefaces and these two political stipulations were repeated in the trade agreements of 1969 and 1970.[98]

Thus, LT Trade, which had started on the basis of political relativism, transformed itself into the highly political Memorandum Trade. In this process, the dedication of Japanese pro-China actors who persevered in the very strained process of political negotiations with the Chinese radicals was outstanding. The survival of the LT/MT Trade channel owed much to these Japanese. As seen below, after diplomatic normalization, the Memorandum Trade channel was absorbed by a new channel represented by the Japan–China Association on Economy and Trade.

Under Ikeda and Sato, the Japanese government neither conspired with the pro-China actors nor did it block their activities. Between the government and the private sector, there basically remained a mechanism of 'division of labour' based on the principle of separation of politics from economics. Within this overall system, Japanese non-governmental actors moved according to their own motivations and goals. As a result, Japan–China trade relations in the 1960s developed a pluralist structure equipped with its own dynamism to overcome the deterioration of the political environment.

[98] *Inside Document.*

6
Diplomatic Normalization and Trade

The previous four chapters illuminated the structure and process of Japan–China trade as they evolved during the 1950s and the 1960s in the absence of formal governmental relations. This trade relationship cannot be explained fully by a perspective which emphasizes the supremacy of strategic concerns in international relations. This is not to say, however, that incentives for trade exchanges outweighed strategic concerns between the two countries. Rather, it shows that Japan's overall behaviour toward China was conditioned by both general political considerations and particular objectives to trade with China, and that Japan's pursuit of China trade has to be explained primarily by factors which evolved independently of dominant strategic considerations. This 'two-track' mechanism is brought home, albeit in a reverse way, by the fact that normalization of diplomatic relations between Japan and China can be ascribed almost exclusively to the transformation of the strategic environment in East Asia, which evolved around the *rapprochement* between the United States and China in 1971–1972.

This chapter, therefore, begins with an overview of the predominant political factors and process of Japan–China diplomatic normalization. The analysis then illuminates the roles and functions of the established Japan–China trade organizations and individuals during this transitional process of diplomatic normalization, and examines how Friendship Trade and Memorandum Trade made a transition into the post-normalization era. Although pre-normalization trade factors were not the central cause for diplomatic normalization, they nonetheless played a significant role during the normalization process and continued to be relevant actors in the post-normalization phase of Japan–China relations.

The two key elements of the transition were, first, a new set of four conditions enunciated by Zhou Enlai in April 1970 and Japanese firms' reactions to them; and, second, China visits by Japanese top business leaders in 1971. In both of these developments, Friendship Trade and Memorandum Trade elements played active, though sometimes covert, roles. These old trade networks gave the business community the opportunity to become the front-runner in Japan's movement toward diplomatic normalization. In effect, movements within the business community anticipated and facilitated the emergence of a domestic atmosphere favourable toward closer ties with China, an atmosphere within which the government could move if it decided to do so. This is symbolized by what Prime Minister Tanaka Kakuei reportedly told a

Mitsubishi delegation bound for Beijing in August 1972: 'It would make things easier for me if you go first.'[1]

6.1. DIPLOMATIC NORMALIZATION: AN OVERVIEW

6.1.1. *Sino-American Rapprochement and Japan*

The single most important factor behind the Japan–China diplomatic normalization in September 1972 was the Sino-American *rapprochement* achieved under Richard Nixon, who became US President in January 1969. The Nixon administration pursued three major diplomatic agendas: the withdrawal from Vietnam, construction of *détente* relations with the Soviet Union, and *rapprochement* with China. A blueprint synthesizing these ambitious goals into a coherent strategy was drawn up by Nixon's national security advisor Henry Kissinger. In short, Nixon and Kissinger aspired to create a new international environment that would allow them to reduce excessive US overseas commitment. They thought that they would be able to withdraw from Vietnam in a 'credible' fashion only if they succeeded in the creation of a 'structure for peace', sustained by stable relations with both of the two Communist giants.

Rapprochement with China was to provide a breakthrough in this ambitious plan. The crucial turning point was the military clash between China and the Soviet Union along the border in March 1969. Kissinger recalls that Nixon and Kissinger did not fully appreciate its strategic implications straight after the incident. Hypersensitive reactions by the Soviet Union and North Vietnam, however, aroused them to its significance: on 11 March, to Kissinger's remark that the incident was a Sino-Soviet problem, the Russian ambassador to the United States, Anatoly Dobrynin, 'insisted passionately that China was everybody's problem', and on 22 March, in negotiations with North Vietnam in Paris, Xuan Thuy 'volunteered the surprising outburst that the United States had nothing to gain by seeking to take advantage of the divisions between the Soviet Union and China'.[2] After this, China, the Soviet Union, and Vietnam began to link with each other in a broader strategic picture.

The greatest asset for such US diplomacy was the intensifying Sino-Soviet rift. This placed North Vietnam in a difficult position between China and the Soviet Union, and served as a significant impetus for China and the Soviet Union to give priority to improving relations with the United States over Vietnam. China needed the United States to cope with the Soviet threat; so did the Soviet Union in order to reconstruct its trouble-ridden diplomacy that

---

[1] *Asahi Shinbun*, 24 August 1972.
[2] Henry Kissinger, *White House Years* (Boston: Little, Brown, 1979), pp. 172–3.

was further aggravated by the intensifying conflict with China.[3] The American design toward NorthVietnam was to isolate Hanoi, and to draw its belligerent leadership into a settlement of theVietnamWar through negotiations.

In August 1969, Nixon made an important initiative by conveying a message to China through the Pakistani channel to the effect that the United States would not isolate China in the intensifying Sino-Soviet confrontation.[4] By the spring of 1971, China accepted the American linkage between Sino-American *rapprochement* and the US withdrawal from Vietnam; in March 1971, Zhou Enlai visited Hanoi and conveyed the US intention to the North Vietnamese leaders.[5] In April, China made a dramatic move to invite the US national table tennis team that was in Japan to participate in the world table tennis contest, signalling that China was now ready to move forward.

Thus, Kissinger secretly visited China on 9–11 July, and finalized an arrangement for Nixon to go to China. On 15 July, Nixon disclosed Kissinger's secret trip and announced that he would visit China before May 1972. North Vietnamese Premier PhanVan Dong visited China in November 1971 and requested the cancellation of Nixon's China visit, but Mao Zedong flatly rejected the plea, advising him instead to accept a negotiated settlement of the VietnamWar with the SouthVietnamese government kept intact.[6] Nixon visited China in February 1972, and signed the Shanghai Communiqué declaring historic Sino-American *rapprochement*.

Upon hearing Nixon's announcement on 15 July, the Soviet Union urged Nixon to visit Moscow before his China trip, and began to exhibit apparent eagerness to conclude the ongoing Strategic Arms Limitation Talks before the US–Soviet summit meeting. Washington declined this request, and, frustrated, Moscow requested Nixon's official visit in May or June, soon after his planned trip to China.[7] Moscow also declined Hanoi's request to cancel Nixon's trip to Moscow, and instead pushed for a solution of theVietnamWar through negotiations with the United States. Nixon visited Moscow in May, and signed the SALT and the ABM treaties that came to symbolize *détente* relations between the two superpowers in the 1970s. Isolated, North Vietnam signed the Paris Peace Agreement in January 1973.

Thus, a new international structure emerged in the Asia-Pacific which in effect amounted to the reconstruction of Pax Americana under new circumstances. The core concept of the new US diplomacy was reflected in the Nixon Doctrine, initially expressed as an 'unofficial' remark by Nixon in July 1969 in Guam and eventually formulated into a three-point policy in Nixon's

---

3 Raymond L. Garthoff, *Détente and Confrontation: American–Soviet Relations from Nixon to Reagan* (Washington, DC:The Brookings Institution, 1985).

4 Kissinger, *White HouseYears*, pp. 180–81.

5 Garthoff, *Détente and Confrontation*, p. 255.

6 Seymour M. Hersh, *The Price of Power: Kissinger in the Nixon White House* (New York: Summit Books, 1983), p. 442.

7 Kissinger, *White HouseYears*, pp. 833–7.

speech in the Congress in November 1969 and in his first foreign policy report to the Congress in February 1970.[8] The first and the second points assured US commitment to the treaty obligations and a nuclear umbrella for the allied countries, while the third asked the allies to assume primary responsibilities for their own defence.

Accordingly, Japan was expected to strengthen its own defence efforts and to assume some responsibility for regional security. The Sato–Nixon joint communiqué announced in November 1969 included important stipulations from this point of view; the so-called 'Korea clause' and the 'Taiwan clause' said, respectively, that 'The Prime Minister . . . stated that the security of the Republic of Korea was essential to Japan's own security,' and that 'The Prime Minister also said that the maintenance of peace and security in the Taiwan area was also a most important factor for the security of Japan.' By the same token, the United States began to push for Japan's increased defence efforts under the slogan of 'burden sharing' in the 1970s.

The Sato administration, however, was not prepared to see the implications of these strategic developments from the dominant international point of view. The most telling case was the reversion of Okinawa which was promised in the 1969 Sato–Nixon joint communiqué. From an American perspective, the reversion of Okinawa, an essential military base for the execution of the Vietnam War, was acceptable only along the lines of the Nixon Doctrine. It was natural, therefore, that the reversion would bring about Japan's larger responsibility for the maintenance of regional stability as symbolized by the Korean clause and the Taiwan clause of the Sato–Nixon joint communiqué. Knowing that these clauses would cause an uproar in the Japanese Diet and mass media, however, Sato took them as 'concessions' to the United States for returning Okinawa. The primary consideration on the part of Sato was to regain the administrative right of Okinawa as an achievement of his 'autonomous diplomacy', a diplomacy showing that Japan was not always blindly following the United States.

After all, the massive reorganization of the international environment since the late 1960s was perceived by most Japanese primarily as an opportunity to diversify its diplomatic horizon in the name of autonomous diplomacy. Thus occurred a 'China boom' in Japanese society, in which both the business community and the government moved quickly and decisively to normalize diplomatic relations with Beijing.

6.1.2. Normalization as Autonomous Diplomacy

The Japanese Ambassador to Washington, Ushiba Nobuhiko, was informed of Nixon's announcement on 15 July less than an hour before it was made.

[8] Richard M. Nixon, *US Foreign Policy for the 1970s: A New Strategy for Peace* (Washington, DC: US Government Printing Office, 1970).

Prime Minister Sato is said to have learned of the announcement only several minutes prior to it (on 16 July, Japan time). This came as a great shock to Sato, since it had been agreed that both governments would remain in close consultation on the China question. Among Japanese policy-makers, there arose a strong feeling that they had been betrayed by the United States. A Foreign Ministry official who played a key role in normalization stated, 'there was resentment over the fact that the United States had gone ahead of Japan in opening up contact with China. Unless Japan got ahead of the United States in the actual normalization, the people would not accept such a verdict.'[9] For the Tanaka cabinet which succeeded the Sato administration, 'it was a matter of survival in domestic politics to achieve normalization before the United States did'.[10]

Sato attempted to contact China by various means, but was met with a firm Chinese denial. In Japan, too, the dominant mood was that Sato had been around for too long and that he should step down with the reversion of Okinawa. Thus, after the return of Okinawa on 15 May 1972, Sato announced his resignation on 17 June. In the LDP presidential election in July, Tanaka Kakuei defeated Fukuda Takeo who had received Sato's full support. One of the important causes was a policy agreement by Tanaka, Ohira Masayoshi, and Miki Takeo in the middle of the LDP presidential election, to the effect that they would oppose Fukuda on condition that any of them would pursue diplomatic normalization with China if elected. On 7 July, after the first cabinet meeting, Tanaka declared that he would hasten diplomatic normalization with China, to which Zhou Enlai responded positively two days later.

Thus, with the establishment of the Tanaka administration, diplomatic normalization was already a foregone conclusion. Tanaka was determined, and more importantly, the Chinese leadership was equally determined to grab the momentum of Sino-American *rapprochement* and achieve normalization as quickly as possible. It was well anticipated that if the process was prolonged domestic opposition in both countries would gain influence. Despite the presence of several complicated issues, the actual negotiation process was surprisingly short, with the joint communiqué to establish diplomatic normalization signed on 29 September 1972, less than three months after the inauguration of the Tanaka cabinet. Chinese concessions to Japanese claims were the key to the speed.

The Japanese negotiators concentrated their main efforts on the question of compatibility between the Japan–Taiwan peace treaty signed in 1952 and the legal issues in the joint communiqué. The Japanese side insisted, for instance, that the termination of 'the state of war' had already been declared with Taipei, which Japan had recognized at the time as the sole legitimate government representing China, and therefore the same words could not be

9 Ogata, *Normalization with China*, p. 37.   10 *Ibid.*, p. 50.

repeated again. The Chinese compromised with the wording of the termination of 'the abnormal state of affairs', in Article 1 of the joint communiqué. Another legal issue was the Chinese renouncement of the right to demand war reparation, which had also been stated in the Japan–Taiwan peace treaty. The Chinese compromise was to drop the term 'right', with the agreed Article 5 stating that the Chinese government 'renounces its demand for war reparation from Japan'.

The question of Taiwan was more complicated. The Chinese position had been conveyed to the Japanese side in the form of 'the three principles for the restoration of relations', which said: (1) PRC is the sole legitimate government representing China, (2) Taiwan is a province of China and an inalienable part of the Chinese territories, and (3) the Japan–Taiwan treaty is unlawful and should be abolished. The first point posed no problem, and Article 2 of the joint communiqué declared: 'The Government of Japan recognizes the Government of the People's Republic of China as the sole legal Government of China.'

Regarding the second and third points, the joint communiqué made only an indirect reference. While declaring in the preamble that, 'the Japanese side reaffirms its position that it intends to realize the normalization of relations between the two countries from the stand of fully understanding "the three principles for the restoration of relations" put forward by the Government of the People's Republic of China', Article 3 stated that 'the Government of Japan fully understands and respects' the stand of the PRC Government that 'Taiwan is an inalienable part of the territory of the People's Republic of China', and that the Japanese government 'firmly maintains its stand under Article 8 of the Potsdam Proclamation'. Article 8 of the Potsdam Proclamation declared that the Cairo Declaration should be fully implemented, which in turn had stipulated that Japan should return all the territories taken from China. By this stipulation, Japan assumed a stand (which was basically directed against the domestic audience) that Japan was in no position to speak about Taiwan. As regards the Japan–Taiwan peace treaty, there was no direct reference in the joint communiqué, and instead Foreign Minister Ohira Masayoshi stated in a press conference that 'the Japanese government's stand is that as a result of normalization with China the treaty ceased to be significant and came to an end', implying that it had been in existence before then.

These concessions over critical issues concerning the Taiwan question, a matter of principle for Chinese diplomacy, were a clear indication that they were eager to establish normalization without much delay. Domestically, the Chinese leaders were concerned about political opposition gaining strength. Externally, strategic considerations prevailed over legal details. This was demonstrated by Article 7 of the joint communiqué which said: 'The normalization of relations between Japan and China is not directed against any third country. Neither of the two countries should seek hegemony in the Asia-Pacific region and each is opposed to efforts by any other country or group of countries to establish such hegemony.' Despite the inclusion of the so-called 'third country clause', its anti-Soviet implications were obvious for the Chinese leaders.

The Japanese side took the 'anti-hegemony' clause as quid pro quo for the Chinese concessions.[11] It is not necessarily fair, however, to interpret these differences between China and Japan as showing that China was driven by strategic considerations while Japan was simply concerned about legal details. Behind Japan's preoccupation with legal details were political considerations toward influential pro-Taiwan forces within the LDP. The Japanese government also understood the anti-Soviet nature of the anti-hegemony clause, which was indicated by its insistence on the third country clause. After all, what stood out in the Japanese response was a lack of preparedness to view Japan's position in the international dynamism evolving around the Sino-Soviet rift, Sino-American *rapprochement*, US–Soviet *détente*, and the anticipated American withdrawal from Vietnam.

Prime Minister Tanaka later summarized his views toward Japan–China diplomatic normalization in three points. First, the China issue was 'a domestic issue rather than a diplomatic issue', and 'the settlement of the China issue removes two-thirds of domestic problems'. Second, the combined population of the two nations 'comprises one-fourth of the world's population. Without the settlement of such relations, there would be no stability of Japan.' Third, 'Japan should establish friendly relations with China alongside with [maintaining] Japan–US security treaty. With the formation of the triangular relationship among Japan, the United States and China, peace in the Far East is secured.'[12] These remarks reveal that Japan–China diplomatic normalization was, first of all, a domestic problem for Tanaka. Then comes Tanaka's fantasy of a special relationship with China. Regional security considerations form the last point.

The third point is by no means a comparable vision to that pursued by the United States or China, but reveals that Tanaka was excited about the fact that the Japan–US security relationship and Japan–China diplomatic normalization finally became compatible. Not only for Tanaka but for many in charge of policy-making, this was the most conspicuous change in postwar Japanese diplomacy. For one thing, its importance lay in domestic politics, because 'two incompatible objectives that had divided Japanese domestic politics for more than two decades' were now reconciled.[13] On the external front, Japan–China diplomatic normalization was considered to be a lead-off event of autonomous diplomacy in the 1970s, which aimed at constructing

[11] *Ibid.*, p. 56.
[12] Yanagida Kunio, *Nihon wa Moete-iruka [Is Japan Burning?]* (Tokyo: Kodan-sha, 1983), p. 266.
[13] Ogata, *Normalization with China*, p. 51.

diversified relations with Asia in a compatible fashion with the basic diplomatic stance of collaboration with the United States.

A major goal of this diplomacy was to expand the margin of autonomy within the basic framework of Japan–US cooperation. In diplomatic normalization with China, therefore, the Japanese government considered normalization itself as a goal. In this, the government was not that different from the Japanese business community and non-governmental pro-China actors, to whose analysis we will now turn.[14]

6.2. ZHOU'S FOUR CONDITIONS AND JAPANESE FIRMS

On 19 April 1970, in a meeting with a Memorandum Trade group led by Matsumura Kenzo, Zhou Enlai enunciated a new set of four conditions applicable to all Japanese firms conducting China trade. By this time, the United States and China had already begun groping for a high-level meeting. On 2 May, Wu Shudong, deputy chief secretary of the Canton trade fair, reiterated what came to be known as 'Zhou's four conditions' to the Japanese firms participating in the trade fair.[15] These conditions stated that China would not have trade exchanges with (1) trading firms and manufacturers supporting aggression by Taiwan and South Korea, (2) trading firms and manufacturers with large investments in Taiwan and South Korea, (3) enterprises supplying arms and ammunition to US imperialism for aggression against Vietnam, Laos, and Cambodia, and (4) US–Japan joint enterprises and subsidiaries of US firms in Japan. Zhou's four conditions proved to be an effective tool to induce a China tilt among Japanese firms, and thus to generate a favourable atmosphere for diplomatic normalization.

The majority of friendly firms did not face major problems because they had not done anything contrary to the conditions. Aside from these, there were three distinct groups of firms, which reacted differently to Zhou's four conditions: (1) firms which depended heavily on China trade and thus had a strong incentive to accept the conditions, (2) an in-between group, and (3)

---

[14] For a careful study on this theme, see Ogata Sadako, 'The Business Community and Japanese Foreign Policy: Normalization of Relations with the People's Republic of China,' in Robert A. Scalapino (ed.), *The Foreign Policy of Modern Japan* (Berkeley: University of California Press, 1977). For the Japanese version which expands the analysis by including a case study on Japanese capital liberalization and thus introduces a comparative perspective, see Ogata Sadako, 'Nihon no Taigai-seisaku Kettei-katei to Zaikai: Shihon Jiyuka, Nitchu Kokko Seijoka Katei wo Chushin ni' [Japanese Foreign Policy Making Process and the Business Community: Cases of Capital Liberalization and Japan–China Diplomatic Normalization], in Hosoya Chihiro and Watanuki Joji (eds.), *Taigai-seisaku Kettei-katei no Nichibei Hikaku [Comparative Study of Foreign Policy Making Process between Japan and the United States]* (Tokyo: Tokyo-daigaku Shuppan-kai, 1977). My analysis in this chapter is greatly indebted to these articles by Prof. Ogata, as well as her kind suggestions and criticism.

[15] Tagawa, *Nitchu Koshyo Hiroki*, pp. 260–61; *Kankei Shiryo*, pp. 286–7.

firms which had a large trade with Taiwan, and thus were reluctant to accept Zhou's four conditions.

The first type included firms in the steel and fertilizer industries. The steel industry had exported a total of 1,260,000 tons of steel to China in 1969, second only to the United States, compared with 570,000 tons to Taiwan. The four leading firms in China trade were Sumitomo Metal Industries, Nippon Kokan K.K., Kawasaki Steel Corporation, and Nippon Steel Corporation. All but Nippon Steel Corporation quickly accepted Zhou's four conditions; Sumitomo Metal Industries on 9 May, Kawasaki Steel Corporation on 11 May, and Nippon Kokan K.K. on 12 May.[16]

The case of Nippon Steel Corporation was more complicated because its chairman, Nagano Shigeo, was an influential pro-Taiwan business leader, and was chairman of the Japan Chamber of Commerce and Industry. On 14 May, Nagano announced that according to his firm's interpretation it had never contravened the conditions and thus would accept them. This response, however, elicited a further Chinese request for a commitment not to participate in the Japan–China (Taiwan) Cooperation Committee. Speculation at the time was that there was an intra-company conflict between chairman Nagano and president Inayama who favoured a flexible approach. On 26 May, Nippon Steel Corporation decided to withdraw from the ongoing Canton trade fair, and on 8 June it agreed to attend the Japan–China (Taiwan) Cooperation Committee meeting scheduled for the following month. Apparently, Nagano's position as a business leader had prevailed over Inayama's pro-China stance.[17]

The dependence of the fertilizer industry on the China market was still more conspicuous. In 1969, 76 per cent of its exports went to China.[18] It had no reason to hesitate, and on 11 May, the heads of the six major fertilizer firms (Sumitomo Chemical Co., Mitsui Toatsu Chemicals, Mitsubishi Chemical Industries, Ube Industries, Showa Denko K.K., and Nissan Chemical Industries) gathered and decided jointly to accept Zhou's four conditions.[19]

The middle group had various responses. First, among the top ten trading corporations, Nissho-Iwai Corporation, Sumitomo Corporation, Ataka Sangyo, and Nichimen Corporation accepted Zhou's four conditions one after another in May 1970. These companies except Nichimen had not conducted China trade on their own; after accepting Zhou's four conditions, they were only allowed to deal with China through their respective dummy firms, namely, Daiho, Daika Boeki, and Toshima Shokai. Nothing really changed

---

[16] *Toyo Keizai*, 3534 (1970), p. 78. Incidentally, these were the top four steel producing firms in Japan in 1969 and 1970. See Tekko Shinbun-sha (ed.), *Tekko Nenkan, Showa 46-nendo-ban [SteelYearbook, 1971]* (Tokyo: Tekko Shinbun-sha, 1971), pp. 23–34.

[17] *Chugoku*, 80 (1970), p. 68; Okamoto, *Nitchu Boeki Ron*, pp. 241–2.

[18] *Nitchu Keiho*, 27 (1974), p. 251.

[19] Fujita Isao, 'Beichu Shinjidai-ka no Nihon Zaikai' [Japanese Big Business in the New Era of US–China Relations], *Keiei Mondai*, 10 (1972), p. 240.

for these corporations except that their loyalty to China was reconfirmed. At this time, the Chinese still accepted trade through dummies, rather than pushing for the direct involvement of big trading corporations. In other words, as of May 1970, the Chinese were not yet ready to transform the trade relationship. The smaller trading corporations which accepted the conditions in May included Chori Co., Nomura Boeki, and Itoman & Co.[20]

Second, three manufacturers accepted Zhou's four conditions in May in the hope of not missing out on the China market: Hino Motor Co., Isuzu Motors, and Komatsu Manufacturing Co.[21] These firms, like the trading companies mentioned above, had dealt with China since the 1960s, and more or less leaned to the China market due to economic considerations.

Things were different, however, for firms that did not want to 'miss the bus' for economic reasons but which had substantial stakes in Taiwan and South Korea. For these firms, the old Japan–China trade routes were important as intermediaries. The case of the Toyota group illustrates this point.

Toyota Jihan, a marketing firm within the Toyota Motor group, had taken the lead in the group's move into the China market. It was said that Toyota Jihan told the Chinese side that it would accept Zhou's four conditions in the autumn of 1970. This offer was not approved by the Chinese side, however, because Toyota had been trading with Taiwan and South Korea, and indeed was providing technology. Toyota Jihan reportedly then approached Okazaki Kaheita of the Memorandum Trade office for assistance.[22]

About six months later, the Chinese side made a move. On 9 April 1971, Wang Xiaoyun visited the Toyota factory and conferred with Kato Masayuki, vice-president of Toyota Jihan.[23] Wang was then visiting nearby Nagoya as deputy head of the Chinese national team at the 31st World table tennis contest, which received world-wide attention because of the 'ping-pong diplomacy' between China and the United States. Two weeks later, it was announced that Toyota Jihan had sent a document to China through the JAPIT-Kansai, suggesting the involvement of its managing director Kimura Ichizo (see below). The message was that Toyota would continue to deal with Taiwan and South Korea on a commercial basis, but would neither invest nor expand its business beyond the current level.[24] China accepted this offer, and Toyota Jihan was able to send representatives to the spring Canton trade fair of 1971.

By this time, China had apparently relaxed the conditions so that maintaining a current level of involvement in Taiwan and South Korea could be interpreted as acceptable. China was now pursuing an active and flexible strategy of getting Japanese firms to switch sides. It might be noted that Wang Xiaoyun's meeting with Toyota leaders, as well as with other business leaders in both Kansai and Tokyo (see below), coincided with the Chinese invitation

[20] Okamoto, *Nitchu Boeki Ron*, p. 241; *Mainichi Shinbun*, 15 June 1972.
[21] *Ibid.*, p. 241.   [22] *Zaikai*, 15 December 1971, p. 99.
[23] *Toyo Keizai*, 3595 (1971), p. 68.   [24] *Asahi Shinbun*, 23 April 1971.

for a US ping-pong team to visit China. This coincidence indicates that the flexible approach to Japanese business was linked to changes in its policy toward the United States. By this time, Zhou Enlai had already issued an invitation to the White House welcoming a China visit by either Secretary of State, Kissinger, or the President himself (dated 21 April and delivered to the White House by the Pakistani Ambassador on 27 April 1971).[25] These more relaxed criteria opened the door for the big four trading corporations, the third and most interesting group of firms, to go into China trade.

Mitsubishi Corporation, Mitsui & Co., Marubeni-Iida Corporation, and C. Itoh & Co. (Ito-Chu) had all been too involved with Taiwan during the 1960s to participate in China trade on their own. At the time, for example, these big four trading corporations alone handled 40 per cent of Japan–Taiwan trade. They therefore had set up dummy firms to trade with China. China, however, stopped dealing with these dummies after Zhou's four conditions were announced. On 9 May 1970, these four dummy firms were told at the Canton trade fair that they were no longer welcome because their parent firms were members of the Japan–China (Taiwan) Cooperation Committee.[26]

In response, the dummy firms chose to cut their financial and personnel relations with the parent corporations in order to maintain loyalty to China. Keimei Koeki (Mitsui) reshuffled its top management at the end of May, while Wako Koeki (Marubeni-Iida) dismissed the executives who had been dispatched from the parent company, and left the office building it shared with Marubeni-Iida in June. Shinnihon Tsusho (Ito-Chu) cut off its financial and personnel relations with Ito-Chu, reducing its capital from 100 million to 40 million yen and its staff by half. Consequently, Wako Koeki was allowed to return to China trade in July, and Shinnihon Tsusho in September. Meiwa Sangyo (Mitsubishi), on the other hand, was the largest dummy firm, and it continued to cooperate with its parent corporation in other areas than China trade. It therefore was not able to make a comeback until 1 September 1972, after its parent corporation had been designated a friendly firm.[27]

These developments in 1970 clearly show that China was now attempting to force the four major trading corporations to decide their attitude toward Zhou's four conditions. Among them, Ito-Chu was the first to return to the China trade. In January 1971 its president Echigo Masakazu decided to go into China trade, and soon after began to make unofficial contact with China through an anonymous person.[28] This person was Kimura Ichizo, managing director of the JAPIT-Kansai. Kimura had conferred with Zhou Enlai at the

[25] Kissinger, *White House Years*, pp. 713–14.
[26] *Zaikai*, 15 June 1970, p. 13.
[27] *Chugoku*, 81 (1970), p. 77; 82 (1970), p. 88; 84 (1970), p. 71.
[28] Interview with an anonymous source of Ito-Chu, Tokyo, 3 June 1985 (hereafter cited as Ito-Chu Interview).

beginning of 1971, and Zhou responded favourably to Kimura's suggestion that he would endeavour to send Japanese business leaders to China.[29] Plans for China visits by business leaders from Kansai and Tokyo indeed started to take shape soon after this meeting. It was in this context that Ito-Chu accepted Zhou's four conditions on 14 December 1971, and conveyed its willingness to visit China through the JAPIT-Kansai.[30] Ito-Chu executives eventually visited China on 5 March 1972, and it was designated a friendly firm, the first among the big four trading corporations.

This attracted widespread attention because, to the surprise of the delegation, China did not ask that a dummy firm be used.[31] China's relaxed criteria for Zhou's four conditions, allowing the current level of involvement in Taiwan and South Korea, had opened the way for a Japanese trading firm to engage in both China and Taiwan trades directly. This event, a first in the history of postwar Japan–China trade, marked the end of the dummy system. It is also quite significant that China accepted Ito-Chu, one of the big four, before Sumitomo Corporation and Nissho-Iwai Corporation. These companies accepted Zhou's four conditions soon after they had been announced in May 1970, but yet were denied direct contacts until April and July 1972, respectively.[32]

Next came Marubeni-Iida Corporation. It disclosed on 3 March 1972 that it had already expressed its willingness to go into China trade through the JAPIT-Kansai. It officially accepted Zhou's four conditions on 5 April, and sent a mission to China in June. By this time, Ito-Chu had already been accepted as a friendly firm, and therefore, Marubeni-Iida visited China with the intention that it would also establish a channel of direct contact with China; and the Chinese side was prepared to respond.[33]

The cases of Mitsubishi and Mitsui formed an interesting contrast. They simultaneously announced their acceptance of Zhou's four conditions on 14 June 1972. It was reported that managing directors of both corporations had met to consult about the matter the day before.[34] Nonetheless, it was not until 29 September—after diplomatic normalization—that Mitsui received an invitation to China, and it waited until 10 October to be designated a friendly firm.[35] In contrast, Mitsubishi received an invitation on 31 July and was granted friendly firm status on 18 August.[36]

---

[29] Kimura Interview; *Zaikai*, 1 June 1972, p. 15.
[30] *Asahi Shinbun*, 4 March 1972.
[31] Ito-Chu Interview; *Asahi Shinbun*, 14 March 1972 (evening).
[32] Incidentally, Sumitomo was allowed to deal directly with China on 3 April 1972, and Nissho-Iwai on 22 July. *Asahi Shinbun*, 3 April 1972 (evening); 23 July 1972.
[33] Interview with Hoshi Hiroto, General Manager, China Section, Marubeni Corporation, Tokyo, 3 October 1986; *Asahi Shinbun*, 4 March 1972.
[34] *Asahi Shinbun*, 15 June 1972.
[35] *Asahi Shinbun*, 11 October 1972 (evening).
[36] *Asahi Shinbun*, 19 August 1972.

This difference derives, as was the case with Ito-Chu, from a JAPIT connection with Mitsubishi. By this time, Kimura Ichizo was reaching the culmination of his endeavours as an intermediary to send business delegations to China. Delegations from Kansai and Tokyo business circles had already visited China. Kimura thought that a delegation of the Mitsubishi group, composed of Mitsubishi Corporation, Mitsubishi Heavy Industry, and Mitsubishi Bank, would symbolize the last stage in creating a business environment favourable to diplomatic normalization. The logic here is that the group was close to the government, especially through Mitsubishi Heavy Industry (which is the largest producer of weaponry in Japan), and that the group had a close relationship with Taiwan.[37]

Earlier, on 11 November 1971, just one day before the Tokyo business leaders' delegation left for China, Makita Yoichiro, president of Mitsubishi Heavy Industry, disclosed that heads of the Mitsubishi group had been discussing a plan to visit China.[38] On 7 June 1972, Fujino Chujiro, president of Mitsubishi Corporation, made it public that the Mitsubishi group started to approach China right after China was admitted into the United Nations, inquiring about the possibility of their sending a mission.[39]

A related source disclosed on 11 July 1972 that documents confirming the acceptance of Zhou's four conditions by the group were sent to the CCPIT at the end of June together with a request for an invitation to China.[40] This source was again Kimura Ichizo. Kimura stated in an interview that he once had a secret meeting with three heads of these companies and had them sign a memorandum declaring that they would accept Zhou's four conditions. China responded to it quickly, extending an invitation to the group on 31 July, and the mission left for China on 17 August. This was taken in Japan as an exceptionally quick reaction by the Chinese, since it usually took about three months before the Japanese side got a response of this kind.[41]

In fact, the president of Mitsui, apparently aware of Kimura working closely with Mitsubishi, stated on 14 July that Mitsui was going to contact China on a formal basis without using 'a webfoot of a duck', referring to someone with important China connections moving 'underwater' as a broker.[42] Mitsui instead approached the Chinese Memorandum Trade liaison office in Tokyo through Okazaki Kaheita, a central figure in the LT/MT Trade arrangements, and visited China after diplomatic normalization in October 1972.[43]

These moves by Japanese firms were further reinforced by the developments in *zaikai*,[44] the big business community, thus advancing the China tilt in the Japanese business community toward diplomatic normalization.

37 Kimura Interview.

38 *Asahi Shinbun*, 12 November 1971.

39 *Asahi Shinbun*, 8 June 1972.

40 *Asahi Shinbun*, 12 July 1972.

41 *Asahi Shinbun*, 24 August 1972.

42 *Asahi Shinbun*, 15 June 1972.

43 *Asahi Shinbun*, 12 July 1972.

44 *Zaikai* is used here as indicating a loose grouping of major industrial and financial leaders who devote considerable time to the interests of the business community as a whole.

6.3. DEVELOPMENTS IN THE *ZAIKAI* COMMUNITY

6.3.1. A Delegation of Kansai Business Leaders

It was at the beginning of 1971 that plans to send business leaders from Kansai and Tokyo started to materialize through mediation by the old Japan–China trade channels. Minenaga Ryosaku, who was at the time secretary general of Kansai keizai Doyukai (the Kansai Committee for Economic Development), echoed Kimura in saying that the Kansai business circle started to plan for a delegation to China after Kimura's report of his meeting with Zhou Enlai in January 1971. Kansai business leaders were to lead off because they were politically less attached to the central government and many of them had kept traditional business interests in the China market. The dispatch of a Kansai business leaders' delegation was decided as a core 1971 project of the JAPIT-Kansai. Matsubara Yosomatsu (chairman of the JAPIT-Kansai; president of Hitachi Shipbuilding Co.) was instrumental in transmitting the plan to Kansai *zaikai* leaders.[45]

The JAPIT-Kansai's first major step was to arrange a meeting on 13 April of several business leaders with Wang Xiaoyun who was in Japan as deputy head of the Chinese national table tennis team. As revealed five days later by the *Asahi Shinbun*, Wang conferred with leaders of the Kansai-based Sumitomo group, including Hyuga Hosai (president of Sumitomo Metal Industries), Hasegawa Norishige (president of Sumitomo Chemical), Yamamoto Hiromu (president of Sumitomo Trust & Banking), and Tsuda Hisashi (president of Sumitomo Corporation). In the afternoon, Wang also conferred with old Japan–China people, including Matsubara Yosomatsu, Morii Shonai (acting chairman of the JAPIT-Kansai), Kawakatsu Den (vice-chairman of the JAPIT-Kansai; president of Nippon Spindle Mfg.), and Kimura Ichizo. Wang said that China looked forward to welcoming their visit at any time. Kansai Doyukai responded by establishing a 'China Problem Discussion Group' on 19 April.[46]

These activities led the heads of Kansai's major business organizations to gather at the JAPIT-Kansai on 6 May 1971. They agreed to form a delegation among top leaders of Kansai *zaikai* and to visit China in September or October.[47] The trip was realized virtually as scheduled, a fact which supports the claim of Minenaga, the delegation's secretary general, that the Kansai delegation would have gone even if the 'Nixon shock' had not occurred.[48] For China, however, the Nixon shock was a foregone conclusion by this time.

The delegation, which left for China on 16 September 1971, included six business leaders from five major economic organizations in Kansai: Saeki

---

45 Minenaga Interview; *Zaikai*, 15 September 1971, p. 88.
46 *Asahi Shinbun*, 18 April 1971; *Toyo Keizai*, 3595 (1971), p. 68.
47 *Asahi Shinbun*, 7 May 1971.   48 Minenaga Interview.

Isamu (chairman of the Osaka Chamber of Commerce and Industry; president of Kinki Nippon Railway), Nakatsukasa Kiyoshi (vice-chairman of the Kansai Economic Federation; president of Kanegahuchi Chemical Industry), Hyuga Hosai (vice-chairman of the Kansai Economic Federation; president of Sumitomo Metal Industries), Yamamoto Hiromu (chairman of the Kansai Committee for Economic Development; president of Sumitomo Trust & Banking), Saji Keizo (chairman of the Kansai Committee for Economic Development; president of Suntory), Nagata Takao (chairman of the Osaka Industrial Association; president of Shikijima Textile); plus Kawakatsu Den. Kimura Ichizo, who had arranged the visit with the CCPIT, joined the delegation as advisor.[49]

The single most important purpose of the delegation was to lay the groundwork for diplomatic normalization. This was indeed the original intention shared by Kimura and Zhou in early 1971, and was successfully transmitted to the Kansai business community, as indicated by its statements during the China visit. On the day of its departure from Osaka, the delegation declared that, on the basis of recognizing one China, it would respect the five peaceful conditions and the three political principles.[50] While Zhou's four conditions were directed toward private firms and corporations, the five peaceful conditions and the three political principles were tools to solicit the China tilt by the *zaikai* community. As seen below, this point was clearly stated to the Tokyo business leaders by Wang Xiaoyun in May and by Wang Guoqun in August.

While in China, the delegation expressed its unanimous view that Beijing represents the legitimate government of China, that Taiwan is part of China, and that diplomatic normalization is a pre-condition for expansion of economic exchanges. When the Chinese side asked for concrete actions proving their recognition of one China, the delegation responded that its China visit was one such action, and promised to cooperate with Tokyo business leaders to promote diplomatic normalization. Zhou Enlai indeed asked them to encourage Tokyo *zaikai* members to visit China, and the delegation issued a statement on returning to Osaka airport that it would call for action by various groups in Japan.[51]

In contrast to this enthusiasm in Kansai, Tokyo business leaders were more cautious. When the delegation members upgraded the Kansai Doyukai's China Problem Discussion Group into a national forum for *zaikai* leaders in November 1971, Tokyo business leaders declined to join.[52] The Kansai

49 Yoshimura Toshio, 'Kansai Zaikai Hochu Misshon Doko-ki' [Travel Records of the Kansai Big Business Mission to China], *Zaikai*, 1 November 1971.

50 *Asahi Shinbun*, 16 September 1971.

51 Yoshimura, 'Kansai Zaikai Hochu Misshon Doko-ki,' pp. 119–21; Saeki Isamu, 'Nitchu Seijo-ka to Zaikai no Yakuwari' [Japan–China Normalization and the Role of Big Business], *Ekonomisuto*, 49 (1971), pp. 53–4.

52 Shimizu Chojiro, 'Tenkan-suru Kokusai-seiji to Zaikai' [World Politics in Transition and Big Business], *Sekai*, 318 (1972), p. 123.

leaders' forward posture was underscored by the fact that they endorsed China's two sets of principles even before China was admitted into the United Nations, which was a surprise for the Tokyo business leaders.[53]

6.3.2. A Delegation of Tokyo Business Leaders

A plan for a delegation of Tokyo business leaders had been under way in par-allel with the Kansai initiative since early 1971.[54] Kikawada Kazutaka, chair-man of Keizai Doyukai (the Japan Committee for Economic Development), was a central and enthusiastic promoter of this plan. He had met Nan Hanchen, chairman of the CCPIT, in Tokyo in 1964, and in fact almost went to China.[55] The Doyukai grouping again took the lead in 1971. On 14 January 1971, its annual statement called for measures to draw China into the inter-national community.[56] One measure was a Tokyo *zaikai* delegation.

In the Kansai case, the JAPIT-Kansai was the single pipeline to China. But in the Tokyo case, both the Friendship Trade and Memorandum Trade routes were activated. As we have seen, Kimura Ichizo had approached both com-munities in early 1971. Indeed, Kimura's role as intermediary was also con-spicuous in this case, which again suggests an exceptional degree of Chinese confidence in his role.

The JAPIT in Tokyo, as the local organization, was involved in this process and was eager to play a central role. In fact, a managing director of the JAPIT in Tokyo reportedly told the Chinese in the summer of 1971 that it would be responsible for arranging a Tokyo *zaikai* delegation.[57] Its role remained nom-inal, however, because Doyukai preferred the Memorandum Trade office for two practical reasons. First, Kawai Ryoichi, president of Komatsu Manu-facturing Co., was a vice-chairman of Doyukai and also had been active in LT/MT Trade since the early 1960s as a director of the Memorandum Trade office. Second, Doyukai placed the 'highest trust' in Okazaki Kaheita, the representative of the Memorandum Trade office, who had tried to arrange a Doyukai delegation in 1964.[58] Besides these pragmatic reasons, Doyukai, as one of the four business mainstream organizations, naturally felt at ease with the Memorandum Trade route, which was located closer to the Japanese 'establishment' than Friendship Trade.

The plan for the Tokyo *zaikai* delegation gained momentum in a series of meetings in Tokyo between *zaikai* leaders and two Chinese high officials,

53 Fujita, 'Beichu Shinjidai-ka no Nihon Zaikai', p. 249.
54 Minenaga Interview; *Asahi Shinbun*, 21 April 1971, 13 October 1971 (evening).
55 Yamashita Seiichi, 'Asu wo Mitooshita Kikawada Kazutaka Shi' [Mr. Kikawada Kazutaka Who Foresaw the Future], *Nitchu Keizai Kyokai Kaiho* (hereafter cited as *NKKK*), 48 (1977), pp. 17–20.
56 *Asahi Shinbun*, 15 January 1971.
57 Fujita, 'Beichu Shinjidai-ka no Nihon Zaikai', p. 250.
58 *Toyo Keizai*, 3574 (1971), p. 26.

Wang Xiaoyun and Wang Guoquan. As noted above, Wang Xiaoyun, who was leading the Chinese national table tennis team to Nagoya, had met Kansai business leaders on 13 April 1971. While Wang was in Nagoya, Kimura Ichizo arranged a secret meeting with Imazato Hiroki (chairman of Nikkeiren, the Japan Federation of Employers' Organizations; president of Nippon Seiko K.K.). Imazato then arranged a meeting with Tokyo business leaders.[59]

On 19 April 1971, a week after his talks in Kansai, Wang Xiaoyun conferred with a group of Tokyo business leaders in Tokyo. This group included Kikawada Kazutaka (chairman of Keizai Doyukai, the Japan Committee for Economic Development; president of Tokyo Electric Power Company), Iwasa Yoshizane (vice-chairman of Keidanren, the Japan Federation of Economic Organizations; president of Fuji Bank), Nakayama Sohei (permanent director of Doyukai; advisor to Industrial Bank of Japan), Kawai Ryoichi (vice-chairman of Doyukai; president of Komatsu Manufacturing Co.), Suzuki Haruo (former vice-president of Doyukai; president of Showa Denko K.K.), Yamashita Seiichi (managing director of Doyukai), and Imazato Hiroki, who hosted the meeting. Kimura Ichizo was also present.[60] Although the majority of participants were from Doyukai, leaders of three out of the four major economic organizations were present.

In this meeting, Wang Xiaoyun made it clear that the three political principles and the five peaceful principles were a set of conditions for normalization of relations between Japan and China.[61] These points were later repeated by Wang Guoquan, vice-president of the China–Japan Friendship Association, who visited Japan on 15 August 1971 to attend the funeral of Matsumura Kenzo. On 30 August, Wang Guoquan conferred with Kikawada, Iwasa, Nakayama, and Yamashita who had attended the meeting with Wang Xiaoyun in April, plus Nagano Shigeo (president of Nissho, the Japan Chamber of Commerce and Industry; chairman of Nippon Steel Corporation). In this meeting, which was held at the Tokyo liaison office of the Chinese Memorandum Trade office, Kikawada expressed his 'full support' for the five peaceful principles, and indirectly expressed an understanding toward the three political principles by saying that Japanese opinion was being consolidated in a favourable direction.[62]

Nagano's presence was important in the Tokyo business community's China tilt in several respects. First, it meant that at least one leader from all four major economic organizations was now involved with China. Second, on the same day as this meeting, Nippon Steel Corporation announced that it was now ready to accept Zhou's four conditions. Nippon Steel Corporation

59 Shirai Hisaya, *Kiki no Naka no Zaikai* [Big Business in Crisis] (Tokyo: The Saimaru Press, 1973), p. 92.
60 *Toyo Keizai*, 3595 (1971), p. 69.
61 *Asahi Shinbun*, 25 April 1971; Tanaka Hiroshi, 'Chugoku Sekkin wo Mosaku-suru Zaikai' [Big Business in Search of Access to China], *Ekonomisuto*, 49 (1971), p. 77.
62 *Asahi Shinbun*, 30 August 1971 (evening).

had been the sole holdout among the five major steel corporations trading heavily with China. Three days later, Nagano himself announced he would abide by Zhou's four conditions, and also decided to participate in a delegation to China.[63]

There can be no doubt that the entire climate of opinion in the business community had been greatly affected by the Nixon shock on 16 July. But it is also worthy of note that Nagano had decided to comply with Zhou's four conditions on 11 July, five days before the Nixon shock (Japan time).[64] On the following day, he agreed with Inayama Yoshihiro, president of Nippon Steel Corporation, that their firm would no longer participate in the Japan–China (Taiwan) Cooperation Committee and the Japan–Korea Cooperation Committee. This decision was immediately cabled by Kimura Ichizo to Beijing. Inayama therefore could announce, immediately on hearing the news from Washington on 16 July (Japan time), that his firm would not attend the two Cooperation Committees. The fact that Nagano, one of Japan's top business leaders, had changed his strategy toward China even before the Nixon shock was greatly appreciated in Beijing, and explains why Wang Guoquan met Nagano on 30 August.[65]

On 2 September, Nagano met three Friendship Trade leaders—Hagiwara Teiji (managing director of the JAPIT-Tokyo), Kawase Kazutsura (president of Toko Bussan), and Yamada Kojiro (managing director of Nishinihon Boeki)—to express officially his acceptance of Zhou's four conditions. That evening, he told Imazato Hiroki, who was in charge of the composition of the delegation, that he would participate.[66] The news that China was likely to accept Nagano was brought back by Kimura Ichizo on 7 September.[67]

From then on, the planning for a Tokyo delegation gained momentum, but several twists and turns indicated the complexity of the issue for the Tokyo *zaikai*, in contrast with the case of the Kansai delegation. First, Kikawada, the Doyukai president, attempted to downplay every possible political implication of his China visit. In an interview by the *Asahi Shinbun*, when asked about the issue of 'one China', he said that he just wanted to pay a casual visit without thinking about such delicate matters. Kikawada was determined to avoid any occasion which might force him to clarify his position on political issues, precisely because he knew the political importance of his action. In the *Asahi* interview, he had denied that his visiting China would have any implications for the China policy of the Sato government. Presumably, Kikawada's position as a *zaikai* leader, who had traditionally been in close touch with the government, was the factor behind his cautiousness.[68]

---

[63] *Asahi Shinbun*, 3 September 1971.
[64] *Ibid.*, Shirai, *Kiki no Naka no Zaikai*, p. 98.
[65] Shirai, *Kiki no Naka no Zaikai*, p. 98; *Zaikai*, 15 October 1971, p. 41.
[66] *Asahi Shinbun*, 3 September 1971.   [67] *Asahi Shinbun*, 8 September 1971.
[68] *Asahi Shinbun*, 10 September 1971.

In his attempts to detach himself from politics, Kikawada tried to take advantage of a letter from Guo Moruo, honorary chairman of the China–Japan Friendship Association, which Kimura Ichizo brought back from China on 7 September 1971 and delivered to Kikawada on the following day. The letter expressed condolence over the passing of Matsunaga Yasuemon, Kikawada's mentor in the electric power industry and a prewar acquaintance of Guo's. It also included words inviting Kikawada to China.

Kikawada took this opportunity and met Nakayama Sohei and Imazato Hiroki on 9 September, to request that two separate groups should visit China. They decided that Kikawada, Imazato, and Yamashita should go in the middle of October, and another group of nine business leaders at the beginning of November. Kikawada thought that his visit would be just a return of courtesies to Guo Moruo, thereby freeing him from any political responsibilities.[69]

This decision was transmitted to China through the Memorandum Trade office. The Chinese side, however, responded in early October that it wanted a united delegation. Kikawada finally complied, but he still refused to lead the delegation; he and Nagano agreed on 7 October that they would join the delegation as advisors.[70]

On the other hand, Imazato was outspoken in stating in an interview that Taiwan is part of China and Beijing represents the only legitimate government of China.[71] Nagano had already accepted Zhou's four conditions as president of Nippon Steel Corporation, and reportedly told Hagiwara Teiji, managing director of the JAPIT-Tokyo, that he would stand by 'one China'.[72] Shoji Takeo, who eventually accepted the leadership of the delegation also stated candidly in an interview that Beijing represents China.[73]

Lacking a consensus, the delegation had to de-emphasize its political tone. First, all the members joined the delegation in a private capacity, rather than as representatives of business organizations or firms, and the delegation was called a 'delegation of Tokyo business people'. Second, to downgrade its prominence, Shoji Takeo, a relatively minor figure, was selected as head of the delegation. He was a former president of Japan Aviation Manufacturing Co. but had no current position in any business organizations or firms. Third, on 10 November, two days before departing for China, the delegation members agreed that they would not take a joint position on any political issues.[74] All these points sharply contrasted with the case of the Kansai delegation: its members represented their business organizations; Saeki, who headed the

69 *Ibid.*
70 *Asahi Shinbun*, 8 October 1971.
71 *Asahi Shinbun*, 2 September 1971.
72 *Asahi Shinbun*, 10 September 1971 (evening).
73 *Asahi Shinbun*, 14 October 1971.
74 *Asahi Shinbun*, 13 October 1971 (evening), 14 October 1971, 15 October 1971, 11 November 1971.

delegation, was a leader of the Kansai *zaikai*; and the delegation expressed unanimous support for the three Chinese political principles.

The nine core members of the Tokyo delegation, who left for China on 12 November 1971, were Shoji, Kikawada, Nagano, Imazato, Iwasa, Kawai, Nakajima Masaki (vice-chairman of Doyukai; president of Mitsubishi Steel Mfg.), Minato Moriatu (vice-chairman of Doyukai; president of Nikko Research Center), and Yamashita.[75] In Beijing, they met Chinese leaders including Guo Moruo, Wang Guoquan, Liu Xiwen (chairman of the CCPIT), Bai Xianguo (Minister of Foreign Trade), Li Xiannian (Vice Premier), and Zhou Enlai.

The delegation was not pressed to declare a political stance in any of the meetings. Apparently, the Chinese leaders saw sufficient value in the visit itself. To draw Tokyo business leaders, who gave priority to the Japan–US relationship from an overall economic perspective, into Chinese hands, highly political demands were counterproductive. It was more effective to emphasize the compatibility between Japan–US relations and Japan–China normalization, particularly at a time when Sino-American *rapprochement* was becoming open. It was indeed in this strategic consideration that Zhou Enlai told Iwasa that, 'It is good and important for China, too, to see good relations between Japan and the United States. I beg your further efforts to maintain good and deeper Japan–US relations.'[76]

Thus, the China visit by the Tokyo business leaders was a highly political act, in that it made the China tilt by the Japanese business community decisive. Shoji Takeo's oral report to the press on 22 November declared that Japan should exert itself to prepare conditions for diplomatic normalization as soon as possible.[77] Given that the Chinese were determined not to negotiate with the Sato government under any circumstances, this flat statement on behalf of the Tokyo business delegation in effect left the Sato government no room to manoeuvre in China policy. This new climate of opinion was reinforced by the 1972 developments noted above, when big trading corporations accepted Zhou's four conditions for trade. These decisions themselves were affected by the Tokyo delegation's favourable impression of their visit to China, including the favourable and flexible treatment it was given by Chinese leaders.[78]

Thus, Japan–China diplomatic normalization was achieved in the midst of a China boom in Japanese society reinforced by the China tilt of the business community.

---

[75] *Asahi Shinbun*, 12 November 1971.
[76] Iwasa Saneatsu, *Kaiso 80-nen: Gurobarisuto no Me [Recollections of 80 years: An Eye of a Globalist]* (Tokyo: Nihon Hosei-gakkai, 1990), p. 183.
[77] *Asahi Shinbun*, 23 November 1971.
[78] See a discussion by the delegation members in *Asahi Shinbun*, 20 November 1971.

6.4. TRANSFORMATION OF FRIENDSHIP TRADE

6.4.1. Termination of the System

The event that had the greatest impact on the system of Friendship Trade in the early 1970s was the announcement of Zhou Enlai's four conditions. This caused the reorganization of the dummy system, and the involvement of big firms and trading corporations in Japan–China trade.

There were two patterns in this reorganization. First, facing Chinese resolution to cut business partnerships between parent firms and their dummies, some dummy firms chose to cut off their relations with their parent corporations. This move was facilitated by the desire of the parent firms to withdraw capital and staff, upon learning that the possibility of resuming trade with China was rather remote.[79] Thus, some dummies became independent of their parents, including Wako Koeki (Marubeni-Iida), Shinnihon Tsusho (Ito-Chu), and Meiwa Sangyo (Mitsubishi). The second pattern was represented by Daiho and Daika Boeki, dummy firms of Nissho-Iwai Corporation and Sumitomo Corporation, respectively. These firms depended on the parent companies much more heavily than the dummies of the big four corporations, and therefore chose to be absorbed by their parent corporations when the parents went into China trade on their own.[80]

Through this process, as seen above, all of the major trading corporations had accepted Zhou Enlai's four conditions concerning Japan–China trade by the time of diplomatic normalization. Once the big trading corporations were designated as friendly firms, virtually all Japanese firms were allowed into the China market and the significance of the friendly firms designation was lost.

Hoping to adjust to this new reality, the Japan Association for the Promotion of International Trade (JAPIT) sent a delegation to Beijing from 9 February to 4 March 1973. It met from 12 to 20 February with the China Committee for the Promotion of International Trade (CCPIT), Minister of Foreign Trade Bai Xianguo, and Vice-Premier Li Xiannian, and learned that China was no longer interested in designating friendly firms. This marked the end of the Friendship Trade system.[81] JAPIT managing director Hagiwara Teiji reported on the visit to the board of directors on 7 March. He said that the agreement reached in China confirmed that the inseparability of politics and economics, the three political principles, and Zhou's four conditions were all incorporated into the Japan–China joint communiqué of 29 September 1972, and therefore all firms could now take part in Japan–China trade if they supported the Joint Statement.[82]

---

79 Ito-Chu Interview.
80 *Asahi Shinbun*, 25 July 1972, 8 August 1972.
81 *Kokusai Boeki*, 20 February 1973, 27 February 1973.
82 *Kokusai Boeki*, 13 March 1973; *Nihon Keizai Shinbun*, 8 March 1973.

6.4.2. Friendly Firms and the JAPIT

This new development, coupled with the creation of the Japan–China Association on Economy and Trade (JCAET) aroused great concern among the firms and individuals who had been active in the old Friendship Trade. They foresaw a decline of their role in Japan–China trade in the post-normalization era. In fact, the share of the Canton trade fair in total Japan–China trade, which had been the central arena for Friendship Trade, declined sharply in the 1970s, as shown in Table 6.1.

Nonetheless, China continued to declare on every possible occasion that it would continue to deal with both big and small firms and with both new and old friends. Zhou Enlai stated on 16 July 1972 to Sasaki Kozo of the JSP that China welcomed new firms but would also continue to deepen its relations with old friendly firms even after diplomatic normalization. Sun Pinghua attended the friendly firm division meeting of the JAPIT-Kansai on 26 July 1972, and stressed that China would continuously strengthen friendship with old friendly firms. Zhou Enlai also assured Hagiwara on 30 August 1972 that China would walk on 'two legs', indicating the new and the old of Japan–China trade.[83]

In fact, most of the friendly firms remained active in Japan–China trade in the 1970s, owing in part to concrete measures taken by China. For example, the Chinese side advised many small friendly firms to specialize in a single commodity, so that they could serve as specialized intermediaries between Japanese big trading corporations and their Chinese counterparts. Newcomers were told not to intervene in such traditional transactions, but rather to develop new areas of trade.[84]

A typical case was the chemical fertilizer trade. The contract was a lump sum agreement signed by a delegation of Japan's chemical fertilizer industry and the Chinese National Chemicals Import and Export Corporation. After diplomatic normalization, the Chinese side continued to assign a sizable portion of the contract to old friendly firms according to their transactions under the old Friendship Trade system. Thus, in 1974, old friendly firms were assigned 65 per cent of urea, 49 per cent of ammonium chloride, and 33 per cent of ammonium sulphate.[85]

TABLE 6.1. *Canton trade fair and Japan–China trade, 1972–1981*

Year	1972	1973	1974	1975	1976	1977	1978	1979	1980	1981
Contract[a]	370	540	350	450	430	720	800	770	370	510
%	33.6	26.9	10.6	11.9	14.2	20.6	15.7	11.6	3.9	4.9

[a] $ million
% Share in the total Japan–China trade.

Source: JCAET, *Shiryo Nitchu Keizai*; Chugoku Kenkyu-jo, *Shin Chugoku Nenkan*, respective issues.

[83] *Asahi Shinbun*, 17 July 1972; *Kokusai Boeki*, 8 August 1972, 5 September 1972.
[84] *Asahi Shinbun*, 25 July 1972.   [85] *Nitchu Keiho*, 43 (1975), p. 231.

Two more examples are illustrative. First, when the LongTermTradeAgreement (LTTA) came into effect in 1978, the LTTA Committee of Japan proposed about twenty trading firms to handle coal imports from China. The Chinese side, however, asked for about twenty more old friendly firms to be added to the list, and the Japanese side had to accept them.[86] Second, according to a businessman from one of the big four trading corporations, when a Japanese trading corporation negotiates over exports of steel, several old friendly firms are customarily present at the negotiation table, and they take a certain share of the agreed transaction.

The JAPIT has also maintained a privileged position in Japan–China trade in the post-normalization era. A turning point for the JAPIT was its June 1973 delegation, which was the largest Japanese economic delegation to China after normalization. This delegation was closely watched because, according to a managing director of Sumitomo Corporation, the attitudes of large corporations toward the JAPIT would depend on how it was treated by Chinese leaders after normalization.[87] The delegation was well received by leaders of the Ministry of Foreign Trade, the CCPIT, and the China–Japan Friendship Association, as well as Zhou Enlai. This was 'more than expected', and thus assured the continuous importance of the JAPIT.[88]

Indeed, its 'face' or name-value in China, which is the product of its solid experience in Japan–China trade since the 1950s, is a great asset to the JAPIT. Its overall impact on Japan–China trade has diminished, because Japanese firms no longer need its clearance to be designated by the CCPIT as friendly firms. The JAPIT, however, had long cultivated reliable channels of communication not only with the CCPIT and the Chinese Ministry of Foreign Trade, but also with the Ministries of Machine-Building, Machinery, and Industry.[89] Tokyo's JAPIT claims to have contacts with 1,400 different Chinese organizations and firms, including about 300 at the centre. These channels of communication are valuable to many Japanese firms. Services which the JAPIT provides for its member firms include: presenting proposals and suggestions and finding solutions to problems in the development of Japan–China trade; helping to plan trade exchanges; mediating transactions and dealing with complaints; dispatching and accepting economic and trade missions; technical exchanges; holding mutual trade fairs; and research and publication. In other words, the channels of communication, information, knowledge, and skills developed over the two decades before normalization are still a source of influence and a reason for the survival of the JAPIT in the post-normalization era.

[86] Interview with Ichikawa Emon, deputy secretary-general of the LTTA Committee of Japan, Tokyo, 18 October 1985.

[87] *Nihon Keizai Shinbun*, 16 June 1973 (evening).

[88] *Nihon Keizai Shinbun*, 24 June 1973; *Asahi Shinbun*, 26 June 1973.

[89] Interview with Machiba Hiromichi, managing director of the Japan–China Economic Relations and Trade Center (former JAPIT-Kansai), Osaka, 26 April 1985.

Nonetheless, if the the old Friendship Trade mechanisms were completely at the mercy of free economic competition, it would have been overpowered by the newcomers in the post-normalization era. Something more than economic utility was at work. Most importantly, the Friendship Trade actors remained allies of China in its diplomacy with Japan. The Chinese certainly remember how useful friendly organizations and firms were to them both politically and economically during the 1960s. For example, they were frequently manipulated by the Chinese government into participating in anti-governmental demonstrations. Economically, too, Friendship Trade proved very useful to China in sustaining bilateral trade transactions in times of political difficulties between the two countries. In the early 1970s, the Friendship Trade elements were quite helpful in transmitting Chinese political intentions to the Japanese business community in the process leading to diplomatic normalization. In essence, the Friendship Trade remnants have remained an asset to Chinese diplomacy with Japan.

6.5. TRANSFORMATION OF MEMORANDUM TRADE

On 29 October 1972, just one month after diplomatic normalization, the final Memorandum Trade agreement was signed in Beijing. A month later, the Japan–China Association on Economy and Trade (JCAET) was established. When the JCAET and the MITI dispatched a joint delegation to China in January 1973, the JCAET was recognized by China as a new Japanese organization, taking the place of the Memorandum Trade office. Thus the promoters of LT/MT Trade in the 1960s made a transition into the JCAET in the post-normalization phase.

6.5.1. China–Asia Trade Structure Research Center

The origins of the JCAET date back to May 1971, when Inayama Yoshihiro (vice-chairman of Keidanren; president of Nippon Steel Corporation) and Tanaka Shujiro (managing director of the JAPIT) established the China–Asia Trade Structure Research Center. This idea originally occurred to Tanaka in the autumn of 1970. Tanaka first intended to create a study group within the JAPIT to include academic China specialists and business leaders. Because his goal was diplomatic normalization, he concentrated on business mainstream people. Tanaka first approached Inayama, and with his help expanded his contacts in the business community. Kimura Ichizo also served as an intermediary between Tanaka and business people in the initial months.[90]

This initiative by Tanaka encountered strong opposition within the JAPIT. At the time, many big firms had not accepted Zhou's four conditions and

[90] Tanaka Interview; *Zaikai*, 15 July 1971, p. 112.

continued to participate in the Japan–China (Taiwan) Cooperation Committee. The majority of JAPIT executives were against working with these business mainstream firms and individuals. Tanaka therefore decided to leave the JAPIT, and this was 'approved' by the board of directors of the JAPIT on 27 May 1971.[91] Before his formal resignation, however, Tanaka had already left and established the Research Center on 17 May 1971. Subsequently, a weekly newspaper of the JAPIT carried an article entitled 'The Research Center Has Nothing To Do With The JAPIT'.[92] From the outset, therefore, movements to establish the Research Center, which eventually led to the creation of the JCAET, took a separate course from the transformation of the Friendship Trade system.

The Research Center's official purpose was to examine Japan–China economic relations in the post-normalization era, but the character of the participants suggested more than that. Inayama was the chief director, and the board of directors included Iwasa Yoshizane (president of Fuji Bank), Anzai Masao (chairman of Showa Denko K.K.), and Hotta Shozo (chairman of Sumitomo Bank). These firms provided the necessary funds. Several business leaders who later in the year took part in the Kansai and Tokyo business delegations to China, such as Hyuga Hosai, Imazato Hiroki, and Kawai Ryoichi, also participated in the Research Center. These top business leaders believed that the Research Center would eventually evolve into a new window for Japan–China trade, embracing the Japanese business mainstream. Strengthening this impression was the fact that Okazaki Kaheita and Watanabe Yaeji of the Memorandum Trade office also joined the Research Center.[93]

The Research Center's role as a new window of Japan–China economic exchanges was initiated by an economic mission headed by Inayama in August 1972, aimed at beginning post-normalization economic cooperation. At this time, even before diplomatic normalization, the mission proposed a long-term agreement exchanging natural resources for plant and other industrial goods—the genesis of the 1978 Long Term Trade Agreement.[94]

6.5.2. Establishment of the JCAET

By this time, the Memorandum Trade group was also planning for the new post-normalization structure of Japan–China trade organizations. Okazaki Kaheita, Watanabe Yaeji, and Kawai Ryoichi, the core members of the Memorandum Trade office, thought that post-normalization Japan–China trade could not be left to the JAPIT, and therefore some new organizational arrangements would be necessary. Since they were close to the business

[91] *Kokusai Boeki*, 8 June 1971.
[92] *Kokusai Boeki*, 27 July 1971.
[93] *Zaikai*, 15 July 1971, p. 113; Fujita, 'Beichu Shinjidai-ka no Nihon Zaikai', p. 250.
[94] *Asahi Shinbun*, 26 July 1972, 12 August 1972, 3 September 1972.

mainstream, and one of their central aims during the 1960s had been diplomatic normalization, they more than welcomed the MITI's involvement in new arrangements. It was therefore a success for them when their idea of 'an institution which would be to China trade what JETRO is to Japan's overall trade' was picked up by the MITI.[95]

Tanaka Shujiro recalls that after the Inayama mission to China in August 1972, he was called in by MITI Trade Bureau Chief Komatsu Yugoro, and was asked to cooperate in the establishment of a 'Japan–China Economic Center'. The core members of the Research Center subsequently decided that they would transform the Research Center into this new organization, eventually named the JCAET.[96]

Thus the JCAET arose out of the combination of the Memorandum Trade remnants and the forces behind the Research Center, with the MITI playing an overt intermediary role. The JCAET was jointly financed by the MITI and big business, with each contributing 300 million yen. Inayama Yoshihiro assumed the presidency, Kawai Ryoichi became chief director, and Okazaki Kaheita became standing advisor. Okubo Tadaharu, a core member of the LT/MT Trade system from the very beginning, and Tanaka Shujiro became two of the four full-time managing directors. Other LT/MT Trade people such as Watanabe Yaeji and Matsumoto Shunichi became directors, together with the top business leaders who had been 'pioneers' in the business community's China tilt, such as Imazato Hiroki, Iwasa Yoshizane, Hyuga Hosai, Suzuki Haruo, and so on. Kikawada Kazutaka, Saeki Isamu, Nagano Shigeo, and Uemura Kogoro (president of Keidanren) were listed as advisors.[97]

The JCAET took over the daily business of the Memorandum Trade office. In January 1974, after the Memorandum Trade liaison office in Beijing closed on 31 December 1973, the Beijing office of the JCAET was set up. Appointed as its representatives were two members of the old liaison office, Taira Kimiaki of JETRO and Osedo Shigeki of the Japan Export–Import Bank. At the same time, the JCAET established a trade division and in 1974 started to take over the trade duties of the Memorandum Trade office.[98]

As the magnitude of Japan–China trade increased during the 1970s, the JCAET began to assume broad responsibilities, which include the following.[99]

1. Economic and personnel exchange
   (i) Exchange of opinions between the Japanese government and business leaders, on the one hand, and leaders in Chinese economic and trade fronts, on the other

---

95 Watanabe Interview.   96 Tanaka Interview.
97 For the list of the JCAET's executives at the time of its establishment, see JCAET, *Showa 47-nendo Jigyo Hokoku-sho [1972 Annual Business Report]*, pp. 1–4.
98 JCAET, *Showa 48-nendo Jigyo Hokoku-sho*, p. 7; JCAET, *Showa 49-nendo Jigyo Hokoku-sho*, p. 24.
99 Listed from a business guide of the JCAET and its annual business reports.

(ii) Dispatch of regular missions of the JCAET
(iii) Cooperation in regional development in China
(iv) Economic exchanges among medium and small firms
2. Technical exchange
(i) Mutual exchange of delegations in the areas of energy, natural resource development, civil engineering, commerce, agriculture and fisheries, finance, light industry, and other fields
(ii) Dispatch of technical experts and reception of Chinese trainees
3. Promotion of trade transactions
(i) Service and advice for individual transactions
(ii) Promoting of exports of goods for the construction of the Chinese economy and imports of agricultural goods and natural resources
(iii) Cooperating with the LTTA Committee for stable imports of energy resources and for promoting plant exports
(iv) Guarantees for Chinese trade representatives in Japan
4. Research and information service.

The LT/MT Trade system thus made an organizational transformation into the JCAET. Matsumura Kenzo and Takasaki Tatsunosuke passed away before diplomatic normalization. Some LDP politicians such as Tagawa Seiichi and Furui Yoshimi, who had participated in the annual LT/MT delegations to China, now saw their mission as accomplished with normalization, and turned to other matters in the 1970s. Tagawa said in an interview that he had not been involved at all in these organizational affairs.[100] Bureaucrats who had served at the LT/MT liaison office in Beijing formed an alumni group called *Kakuyu-kai* (Club of Friends of Memorandum Trade), but their careers in the 1970s basically followed normal Japanese bureaucratic practice of rotating them as generalists, although several were assigned to the Embassy in Beijing as part of the regular rotation.

All the core members, who had been responsible for the management of the LT/MT Trade office during the 1960s, moved into the JCAET and occupied key posts throughout the 1970s. Okazaki Kaheita was a standing advisor until he passed away in 1989 at the age of 92. Watanabe Yaeji started as a director and served as chief director from 1976 to 1980. He then started a law office specializing in business relations with China, on the same floor as the JCAET office. Kawai Ryoichi was the first chief director, was elected vice-chairman in 1976, and succeeded Doko Toshio (who had succeeded Inayama in 1980) as chairman in 1986. Okubo Tadaharu was a managing director for fourteen years until 1986, when he established a consultant company specializing in Japan–China machinery trade.

The fact that some of these old China trade people started a second post-normalization career in the 1980s signifies that a 'new economic diplomacy'

<hr />

[100] Tagawa Interview.

had begun to characterize the bilateral economic relationship at the turn of the 1980s.[101] But during the 1970s at least, there is ample evidence that the legacy of the pre-normalization decades strongly conditioned the new trade arrangements between Japan and China. We will further elaborate on this point in the next chapter.

[101] Lee, *China and Japan*. Incidentally, Tanaka Shujiro also left the JCAET in 1984 and created the Japan–China North East China Development Association, located on the same floor as the JCAET.

7

Japanese Diplomacy with China in the 1970s

The normalization of governmental relations in 1972 ushered in a new era in postwar Japan–China relations. A long-standing political obstacle which had hindered Japan–China relations from developing into a full-scale relationship was removed. During the previous two decades, the scope of Japanese governmental involvement in the relationship had been severely limited by international strategic factors, and big business, curtailed by its close relationship with both the Japanese government and the Taiwan and US markets, was not much interested in China except as a potential future market. As a result, Japanese society had been deeply divided over the China issue, both politically and economically, between the pro-US camp and the pro-China group challenging the logic of the Cold War and Pax Americana. With Japan–China diplomatic normalization, however, the ideological cleavage over the China issue was considerably ameliorated in Japan. Also from the Chinese point of view, its political demands claimed in the three political principles were now satisfied: the government of Japan abandoned its 'anti-Chinese' attitudes, it recognized only 'one China', and diplomatic relations were normalized.

The normalization of diplomatic relations, however, did not give rise to totally new Japan–China trade. As argued in the introductory chapter, while from 1967 to 1971 the average yearly share of Japan–China trade in Japan's overall trade with North East Asian countries was 18.4 per cent, from 1972 to 1976 it increased by only 2 per cent to 20.4 per cent. Moreover, not until 1980 did Japan's trade with China 'recover' to the level of the 26 per cent share recorded in 1966. Given the most dramatic change in the political environments in the postwar years, this aspect of continuity, albeit only in trade volumes in monetary terms, is noteworthy. Just as the political framework of Japan–China relations had not fully determined the evolution of the trade relationship during the 1960s, the 1971/72 shift in the political environment did not dramatically change all aspects of post-normalization Japan–China trade. This chapter reveals that the trade relationship in the 1970s, at least before the introduction of China's new open-door policy at the end of the decade, still continued to have a logic of its own, where the legacies of the pre-normalization decades were still actively engaged.

In the 1970s, the construction of an overall friendly relationship with China became a dominant diplomatic issue for the Japanese government. Such a diplomatic goal came to be defined from a peculiar Japanese logic, refusing to be entangled in the US–China–Soviet triangular relationship. As such, Japanese diplomacy toward China continued to be motivated by a sense of autonomous diplomacy. Now that the conflict between collaboration diplomacy and autonomous diplomacy had seized to be a source of domestic political cleavage, the aspects of the latter came to stand out as representing an overall orientation of Japanese diplomacy in the 1970s.

Paradoxically, however, precisely because the dynamism of the US–China–Soviet strategic relationship was so dominant, the Japanese government became bogged down in its desperate attempt to conduct China diplomacy independent of strategic imperatives. The promotion of China trade, on the other hand, did not require such political energy, or to be more precise, was regarded by most Japanese as resonating Japan's overall diplomatic orientation to seek a friendly relationship with China. Under these circumstances, the legacies of the pre-normalization trade institutions and individuals continued to remain effective in the new trade relationship. Thus, this chapter will first give an overview of the political environment surrounding Japan–China relations and of Japan's diplomatic response therein, which will be followed by an examination of the actual mechanisms and processes of the trade relationship in the 1970s.

7.1. POLITICAL ENVIRONMENT: AN OVERVIEW

7.1.1. International Developments

In the new international environment since the US–China *rapprochement* and the US–Soviet *détente*, the US government attempted to avoid aligning with either China or the Soviet Union against the other, and to encourage both China and the Soviet Union to see the United States as leverage with which to gain political advantage over the other. Toward the end of the 1970s, however, the American wish to gain a 'swing' position was gradually eroded due to Soviet adventurism in the Third World, and the increasing sense of frustration and doubt about the effectiveness of the *détente* scheme. As the United States set out to normalize diplomatic relations with China under the Carter administration, the US priority shifted to alignment with China in confrontation with the Soviet Union. In this process, Washington turned its back on Hanoi, which had sought to establish diplomatic relations, thus interjecting the elements of the US–China–Soviet triangular relationship in South East Asia.[1] As seen below, negotiations over a peace and friendship treaty between Japan and China, as well as an important diplomatic overture by the

---

[1] Garthoff, *Détente and Confrontation.* The following account on the international developments draws heavily on this, unless otherwise noted.

Japanese government toward Indo-China, particularly Vietnam, were conducted in this changing international environment.

Under the Nixon and Ford administrations, when Henry Kissinger was a principal architect of US strategy, the US official stance to keep the 'swing' position was persistent despite some emerging domestic pressures for the use of a China card against the Soviet Union embarking on intervention in Angola in 1975/76. When China became increasingly critical about the Ford administration in 1975, which continued to improve relations with the Soviet Union by means of SALT II negotiations, grain sales, technology transfer, and the Helsinki accords in the summer of 1975, Kissinger visited China in October and President Gerald Ford himself visited in December. In the same month, the Ford administration approved the British sale to China of Rolls-Royce Spey jet engines and a Spey factory to build engines in China.[2] This decision, however, was reflective of the policy of diplomatic balancing rather than a China tilt, as demonstrated by another decision in October 1976 to approve the sale of Cyber-172 computer systems to both China and the Soviet Union.[3]

Not much development was seen in 1976 due to the demise of Zhou Enlai and Mao Zedong in January and September and the political turmoil in China (including the rise of the Gang of Four, the purge of Deng Xiaoping, the ascendance of Hua Guofeng to the top leadership, and the arrest of the Gang of Four), and the presidential elections in the United States. With the advent of the Carter administration in January 1977 and the return of Deng Xiaoping to power in July, however, US–China relations, as well as the US–China–Soviet triangle relationship, went into a distinct post-Nixon/Kissinger phase.

By mid-1977, the new Carter administration agreed that it would pursue diplomatic normalization with China by accepting the Chinese demand to put an end to US diplomatic relations with Taiwan.[4] The Carter administration, however, simultaneously continued to seek improved relations with the Soviet Union, particularly over the SALT negotiations. It was in this spirit of not playing the China card that Secretary of State Cyrus Vance, a strong proponent of *détente* relations with the Soviet Union, was sent to China in August 1977.[5] Because of Chinese resistance to the US position, the trip proved unsuccessful.

In the meantime, the Soviet–Cuban intervention in the Ethiopia–Somalia conflict in the Horn of Africa in January 1978 began to affect the strategic thinking of the Carter administration, which shifted toward playing the China

---

[2] Ogata, *Normalization with China*, p. 58.
[3] Garthoff, *Détente and Confrontation*, p. 561.
[4] Michel Oksenberg, 'A Decade of Sino-American Relations', *Foreign Affairs*, 61 (1982), pp. 181–3.
[5] Cyrus Vance, *Hard Choices: Critical Years in America's Foreign Policy* (New York: Simon and Schuster, 1983), pp. 78–83.

card against the Soviet Union. The turning point was President Carter's decision to send his national security advisor Zbigniew Brzezinski to China in May. At this juncture, Carter apparently opted for the use of the China card to show a tougher stance toward the Soviet Union, but was still hopeful of an early conclusion of a SALT II agreement. This was demonstrated by his decision in mid-March to send Vance to Moscow and Brzezinski to Beijing.[6] But both China and the Soviet Union (as well as Brzezinski himself) took the Brzezinski China trip differently. China was happy about Brzezinski's emphasis on common strategic interests *vis-à-vis* the Soviet Union,[7] and the Soviet Union saw the visit as the turning point in the policy of the Carter administration 'from a relatively considered and evenhanded "triangular diplomacy" to a single-minded pro-Peking and anti-Soviet orientation'.[8] Subsequently, a US–China joint communiqué was signed in mid-December, announcing the establishment of diplomatic relations in January 1979.

In the course of these developments, East Asian international relations were in a state of flux, particularly in Indo-China. In the beginning, the Carter administration had probed diplomatic normalization with Vietnam. As a first step in this direction, it had lifted restrictions on travel by Americans to Vietnam on 9 March 1977, and began talks with Vietnam on improving relations in Paris in May. Since Brzezinski's China visit in May 1978, however, the United States began to think that normalizing relations with Vietnam would antagonize China. Then, in October 1978, in order to complete the China transaction, Carter formally decided to suspend negotiations of diplomatic normalization with Vietnam.[9]

By the same token, the highly volatile strategic rivalry between China and the Soviet Union clouded the Indo-Chinese situation toward the end of 1978. China stood firmly behind the Khmer Rouge Cambodian government, which had severed diplomatic relations with Hanoi in December 1977. In the spring of 1978, Sino-Vietnamese relations further worsened over the Vietnamese treatment of Chinese residents, and in July China decided to suspend all aid to Vietnam. Undoubtedly, the new development in US–China relations along the anti-Soviet line encouraged China's tough stance toward its southern neighbour.

In the middle of the uncertain developments in US–China–Soviet strategic relations, Vietnam, in its desperate efforts to reconstruct a war-devastated country, had sought to cultivate a neutral stance between China and the Soviet

[6] Jimmy Carter, *Keeping Faith: Memoirs of a President* (New York: Bantam Books, 1982), pp. 193–4.

[7] For Brzezinski's account of his meetings with Chinese leaders, see Zbigniew Brzezinski, *Power and Principle: Memoirs of the National Security Advisor, 1977–1981* (New York: Farrar, Strause and Giroux, 1983), pp. 211–15.

[8] Garthoff, *Détente and Confrontation*, p. 711.

[9] Oksenberg, 'A Decade of Sino-American Relations', p. 186. Ogata, *Normalization with China*, pp. 66–71.

Union, simultaneously seeking diplomatic normalization with the United States. But the new developments in the strategic triangular relationship since May 1978 crushed Vietnam's diplomatic hopes. On 29 June, shortly before the suspension of Chinese aid, Vietnam joined COMECON, and on 3 November, it signed a treaty of friendship and cooperation with the Soviet Union.

This was followed by the Vietnamese invasion of Cambodia in December 1978, and the Chinese invasion of Vietnam in February 1979. Vietnam of course had Soviet backing, whereas China played the America card: when Deng Xiaoping visited the United States in January 1979, he stated that the Chinese 'consider it necessary to put a restraint on the wild ambitions of the Vietnamese and to give them an appropriate limited lesson', and asked the United States to provide 'moral support'.[10]

It was in the middle of this strategically turbulent decade that Japan tackled two of the most important diplomatic issues in the postwar years: a Japan–China Peace and Friendship Treaty and a new diplomatic overture toward South East Asia with Indo-China as a primary focus.

7.1.2. Japan's Diplomatic Response (1): Fukuda Doctrine

In essence, the basic stance of Japanese diplomacy toward China and South East Asia in the 1970s was to retain its diplomatic autonomy free from the logic of strategic rivalries among the United States, China, and the Soviet Union. Such a diplomatic propensity was a peculiar creation of postwar international politics and Japan's domestic politics, which made Japan's direct involvement in highly political dimensions of international relations an extraordinarily controversial issue in Japan's domestic politics as well as in Asia, often paralysing Japan's policy-making process. In this context, the pursuit of autonomous diplomacy was not equal to a quest for any independent strategic role, but rather was reflective of a hope to remain independent of international relations that were a function of military-strategic considerations. Given the fundamental policy of collaboration with the United States, maintaining a balance between Japan's autonomous diplomacy and US strategic interests was the basic necessity. To the extent that such diplomatic motives were derivative of Japan's peculiar conditions and its wishful thinking, not only were other countries often puzzled or frustrated by Japanese motives but Japanese policy-makers themselves were often frustrated by the tenacity of dominant strategic trends in regional politics.

An illustrative case in Japan's South East Asian policy was the announcement of the Fukuda Doctrine in August 1977.[11] The Fukuda Doctrine refers

[10] Ogata, *Normalization with China*, p. 53.

[11] For more, see Soeya Yoshihide 'Vietnam in Japan's Regional Policy', in James Morley and Nishihara Masashi (eds), *Vietnam Joins the World* (New York: M. E. Sharpe, 1997).

to a policy statement made by Prime Minister Fukuda Takeo in August 1977, clarifying the central policy of Japan toward South East Asia. The major thrust of this policy, as its drafters recall, was to bring about greater stability in South East Asia by encouraging peaceful coexistence between ASEAN and Indo-China, with Japan serving as a bridge between the two.[12] Given Japan's peculiar situation, the driving force of that policy was understood to be economic assistance.

Japanese initiatives toward Indo-China stood out at the time, in part because the United States was rapidly becoming disenchanted with the region. In turn, America's low profile convinced Japanese policy-makers that it was time to formulate a somewhat 'autonomous' policy toward South East Asia without necessarily contradicting the fundamentally cooperative relationship with the United States. When the Carter administration set out to negotiate diplomatic normalization with Vietnam in the spring of 1977, the international environment appeared ripe to start a new Japanese diplomacy toward Vietnam. Simply put, Japanese policy-makers expected that improved relations between Vietnam and both Japan and the United States would encourage Vietnam to maintain an independent position between China and the Soviet Union. Such a 'strategic' positioning of Vietnam was understood to be the precondition for the success of Japan's new diplomatic initiative toward Vietnam in particular, and South East Asia in general.

Prime Minister Fukuda Takeo, who formed a Cabinet in December 1976, had from the early 1970s expressed his determination to lead Japan on a 'historically unparalleled path', attempting to make Japan an economic power without becoming a military power. The culmination of this vision was the announcement of an 'omnidirectional diplomacy', by which Fukuda expressed his preference for the diplomatic role of Japan as a bridge between conflicting countries or sub-regions, without depending on military imperatives. For Owada Hisashi, who was seconded from the Foreign Ministry as Fukuda's secretary, Japan as a world power should have a major doctrine. As Owada put it, the Fukuda Doctrine was 'a serious attempt to define the future role of Japan with respect to this part of the world, and by extension, to a wider world, not in terms of abstract philosophy, but in terms of a specific policy direction for Japan to follow'.[13]

Thus, Japan's policy as represented by the Fukuda Doctrine had two distinct characteristics: first, it was fundamentally conditioned by Japan's postwar aversion to involvement in politically sensitive issues, not to mention in areas where the elements of strategic and military rivalry among the major powers were salient; and second, it represented a Japanese aspiration for a

---

[12] Tomoda Seki, *Nyumon: Gendai Nihon-gaiko [Introduction to Contemporary Japanese Diplomacy]* (Tokyo: Chuo Koron-sha, 1988), p. 58.

[13] Owada Hisashi, 'Trilateralism: A Japanese Perspective', *International Security*, 5 (1980/81), p. 24.

larger political role in regional politics in the post-Vietnam War phase. As seen above, however, international realities gradually turned against Japan's wishes in the second half of 1978, and the Vietnamese invasion of Cambodia in December frustrated them completely.

In the lead-up to the invasion, Hanoi engaged in exceptionally active diplomacy, and Japan was an important target. From December 1977 to January 1978, Foreign Minister Nguyen Duy Trinh went to Malaysia, the Philippines, and Thailand; and in July 1978, Vice-Foreign Minister Pham Hien visited Singapore, Malaysia, Thailand, Australia, New Zealand, and Japan. In September–October, Prime Minister Phan Van Dong visited all five ASEAN nations. In December, shortly before the Vietnamese invasion of Cambodia, Foreign Minister Nguyen Duy Trinh visited Tokyo, and conferred with the newly established Ohira Masayoshi government. Tokyo understood these moves by Hanoi according to its own expectations, i.e., as demonstrations of Hanoi's intention to pursue an 'independent diplomacy' and its willingness to open dialogue with ASEAN. Although Tokyo started to feel some concern over the political situation in Indo-China, it continued to take Hanoi's pledges at face value and decided to give a 10 billion yen loan in July, and a 14 billion yen loan in December. Tokyo was still hoping to carry out the Fukuda Doctrine, as demonstrated by Foreign Minister Sonoda's explicit request to Hanoi to purchase as much of ASEAN's products as possible.[14] Thus, Japan was a captive of its own aspiration. To be more precise, Japan's strong aspiration for a political role, without being prepared to become a full-fledged political and strategic player, resulted in the policy-makers in Tokyo interpreting the situation according to their own wishes.

7.1.3. Japan's Diplomatic Response (2): Japan–China Peace and Friendship Treaty

An even more vivid example of this pattern of Japanese diplomacy is the impact of the Japan–China Peace and Friendship Treaty signed in August 1978 in the middle of a rapidly changing international political situation. The treaty was controversial because of the so-called 'anti-hegemony' clause that was widely understood to be anti-Soviet. The Japanese government, fully aware of its implications, initially resisted the inclusion of the clause. With the tenacity of the Chinese determination, however, it agreed to it but only in tandem with the so-called 'third country' clause. Articles 2 and 4 of the 'Treaty of Peace and Friendship Between Japan and the People's Republic of China', signed on 12 August 1978 respectively read as follows:

---

[14] Sudo Sueo, *The Fukuda Doctrine and ASEAN: New Dimensions in Japanese Foreign Policy* (Singapore: Institute of South East Asian Studies, 1992), p. 199.

The Contracting Parties declare that neither of them should seek hegemony in the Asia-Pacific region or in any other region and that each is opposed to efforts by any other country or group of countries to establish such hegemony.

The present Treaty shall not affect the position of either Contracting Party regarding its relations with third countries.

This treaty is often interpreted as signifying Japan's strategic China tilt along the line of American (particularly Brzezinski's) strategic thinking *vis-à-vis* China and the Soviet Union. Brzezinski understood the Japanese move in this strategic context and even as signifying the Japanese government's concurrence to his persuasion on his way back from China in May 1978.[15] Also, both China and the Soviet Union interpreted the major implications of the treaty in the same vein. As stated, however, Japanese motives lay elsewhere, and the Japanese government subsequently came to argue that the third country clause negated the treaty's anti-Soviet nature and brought the treaty in conformity with Fukuda's omni-directional diplomacy.

In fact, the Fukuda administration did not feel any US pressure in deciding to conclude the Japan–China Peace and Friendship Treaty, whose central motives were to solidify friendly and stable relations with China and thus were basically 'non-strategic' in thinking. There was no indication from the policy debate in Tokyo that the American attitude was much of a concern, and Fukuda decided by March 1978, well before Brzezinski's trip to China and Japan, on the terms of negotiations over the anti-hegemony clause and the third country clause.[16] Moreover, the Japanese government under the Miki Takeo administration had already agreed to the inclusion of the anti-hegemony clause in November 1975: it proposed its draft treaty, including the anti-hegemony clause, to the Chinese. In doing so, the Miki government had attempted to neutralize its anti-Soviet strategic implications by incorporating the four Japanese conditions, conveyed to Chinese Foreign Minister Qiao Quanhua by Foreign Minister Miyazawa Kiichi: (1) hegemony will be opposed not only in the Asia-Pacific region but also anywhere else, (2) anti-hegemony is not directed against a specific third party, (3) anti-hegemony does not mean any common action by Japan and China, (4) a principle that is in contradiction to the spirit of the United Nations Charter cannot be accepted.[17]

In 1978, therefore, the issue was not whether Japan would comply with the anti-hegemony clause, but whether China would agree to the third country clause desperately wanted by the Japanese side. When the Japanese government proposed its draft treaty in November 1975, the Chinese side was not yet ready to negotiate over the third country clause. In both Japan and China, 1976 was a year of political turmoil: the Miki cabinet was preoccupied with

[15] Brzezinski, *Power and Principle*, pp. 216–18.
[16] Ogata, *Normalization with China*, pp. 88, 95.
[17] Ibid., p. 84; Nagano, *Ten'no to To Shohei no Akushu*, p. 164.

the handling of the Lockheed scandal and had to resign after a fatal defeat in the Lower House elections in December, and China was bogged down in the leadership struggle with the deaths of Zhou Enlai and Mao Zedong. The return of Deng Xiaoping to power in July 1977 became an important turning point, just as it did in the process of US–China diplomatic normalization.

The final negotiations in Beijing from 21 July to 8 August 1978 centred on the third country clause. The agreed clause in the treaty's Article 4 was a result of the compromise between the Japanese proposal and the Chinese version which respectively read: 'The present Treaty is not directed against any specific third country' and 'The present Treaty is not directed against any third country that does not seek hegemony.'[18] Thus, the 'Treaty of Peace and Friendship Between Japan and the People's Republic of China' was signed on 12 August 1978 by Sonoda Sunao and Huang Hua, Foreign Ministers of Japan and China.

Subsequently, the Japanese government pretended, primarily to the domestic audience, that the third country clause effectively freed Japan from entanglement in the Sino-Soviet rift. The problem was, of course, that the realities did not unfold according to the Japanese government's expectations. The Chinese acceptance of the third country clause was nothing but an indication of its eagerness to conclude the Japan–China Peace and Friendship Treaty in the overall strategic consideration which was anti-Soviet in nature.

By the same token, the Vietnamese invasion of Cambodia and the Chinese invasion of Vietnam were a decisive blow to Japan's non-political posture. To Tokyo's dismay, the Chinese ambassador to Japan asked the Japanese government in January 1979 to support the Khmer Rouge government in Cambodia in accordance with the anti-hegemony clause of the Japan–China Peace and Friendship Treaty.[19] Soon after, the Soviet embassy in Tokyo issued a statement saying that if Japan stopped aid to Vietnam the USSR would regard it as a joint action with China based on the anti-hegemony clause of the treaty.[20] In February 1979, the Vietnamese party newspaper *Nhan Dan* began to talk about a 'Beijing–Washington–Tokyo axis', and to criticize Tokyo.[21] After the Soviet invasion of Afghanistan in December 1979, the international community's opposition to the Soviet–Vietnamese alliance became unequivocal. Thus, Japan was in fact entangled in Asian power politics, despite its proclaimed diplomatic orientation.

This gap was an important source of the difficulties that Japanese diplomacy faced in the 1970s. This, however, was also an indication of the distinct pattern of Japanese diplomacy that sought to retain autonomy in form and

---

[18] Ogata, *Normalization with China*, p. 91.
[19] *Asahi Shinbun*, 17 January 1979.
[20] *Asahi Shinbun*, 22 January 1979.
[21] Shiraishi, Masaya *Japanese Relations with Vietnam: 1951–1987* (Ithaca: South East Asia Program, Cornell University, 1990), pp. 79, 129.

substance. In the 1970s, Japan's trade relations with China developed in this prevailing mood to foster friendly relations with China, in which the legacies of the pre-normalization institutions and individuals played an important role.

7.2. TRADE RELATIONS IN THE 1970S

7.2.1. Continuity and Change

The Japanese diplomatic orientation to seek its own autonomous stance *vis-à-vis* China amid a strategic flux in the US–China–Soviet triangle received the strong support of pro-China institutions and individuals. Recall that they had resisted the Japanese government's policy to comply with the American strategy to 'contain' China in the previous two decades, and that they interpreted, in a rather self-serving fashion, the post-normalization political situation as having become compatible with their beliefs in the importance of China. To the extent that the promotion of Japan–China trade was congruent with US strategic objectives, there was not much chance for serious conflict with the United States either, although Japan's pro-China elements did not share US strategic interests. Under these circumstances, the legacies of the pre-normalization trade institutions and individuals of Japan continued to remain effective in the new trade relationship.

TABLE 7.1. Japan's trade with China, Taiwan, and South Korea, 1971–1982

Year	China[a]	%	Taiwan[a]	%	South Korea[a]	%
1971	901	17.8	1,209	23.9	1,130	22.3
1972	1,100	17.5	1,513	24.1	1,406	22.4
1973	2,014	18.9	2,533	23.7	2,996	28.1
1974	3,289	22.0	2,964	19.8	4,224	28.2
1975	3,790	25.9	2,633	18.0	3,556	24.3
1976	3,034	17.8	3,470	20.4	4,741	27.9
1977	3,486	17.7	3,841	19.5	6,193	31.4
1978	5,079	18.9	5,335	19.9	8,594	32.0
1979	6,654	20.6	6,843	21.2	9,606	29.8
1980	9,402	26.3	7,439	20.8	8,365	23.4
1981	10,387	26.6	7,927	20.3	9,047	23.2
1982	8,863	25.3	6,699	19.1	8,135	23.2

[a] $ million)

% Share out of Japan's trade with China, Taiwan, Hong Kong, South Korea, North Korea, and the Soviet Union.

Source: *Tsusho Hakusho*, respective years.

In fact, the normalization of diplomatic relations in 1972 did not have as much of an impact on Japan's China trade as the conventional wisdom would suggest. True, in monetary terms, Japan–China trade jumped remarkably from $1.1 million in 1972 to $2 million in 1973. But Japan's trade with Taiwan and South Korea also increased substantially in the same two-year period, by 67.4 per cent and 113.1 per cent, respectively. In terms of the share occupied by Japan–China trade in Japan's overall trade with North East Asia (China, Taiwan, Hong Kong, South Korea, North Korea, and the Soviet Union), we do not see a very drastic increase during the 1970s. Not until 1975 did this share reach its 1960s' peak level (26.0 per cent in 1966), and it dropped again in the second half of the 1970s, before a come-back in 1980.

These figures shown in Table 7.1 imply a very interesting continuity in postwar Japan–China relations. This continuity, however, must be assessed against the background of changes in Japan–China trade that occurred in the post-normalization decade. One conspicuous change in the trade pattern can be traced in the composition of major items, particularly machinery (including industrial plant) and fossil fuels (petroleum and coal). This new trend in Japan–China trade in the post-normalization era is vividly shown in Table 7.2. The central role of these two major items in Japan–China trade is underscored by the fact that fluctuations in total Japan–China trade are mainly accounted for by changes in machinery and fuel trade. For example, trade in

TABLE 7.2. Machinery and fuel in Japan–China trade, 1968–1982

Year	Machinery[a]	% in export	Fuel[a]	% in import
1968	33.9	10.1	5.4	2.4
1969	48.3	12.4	4.9	2.1
1970	119.2	20.9	6.4	2.5
1971	90.7	15.7	9.3	2.9
1972	78.8	12.9	7.6	1.6
1973	186.3	17.9	42.7	4.4
1974	554.5	27.9	429.5	32.9
1975	695.9	30.8	763.6	49.9
1976	329.7	23.6	571.5	43.1
1977	217.3	11.2	684.5	44.2
1978	636.9	20.9	818.7	40.3
1979	1,124.6	30.4	1,188.7	40.2
1980	2,146.7	42.3	2,376.6	55.0
1981	2,433.4	47.8	2,935.1	55.5
1982	1,067.1	30.4	3,061.4	57.2

[a] $ million

Source: *Tsusho Hakusho*, respective years.

machinery and fuel combined decreased by $495.3 million in 1976, when total Japan–China trade declined by $756.2 million; the down-swing in machinery and fuel trade thus accounted for 65.5 per cent of the total decline. Again, in 1982, the $1,366.3 million down-turn in machinery exports alone accounted for almost 90 per cent of the $1,524.1 million decline in total Japan–China trade.

On the other hand, Tables 7.1 and 7.2 show that total trade with China from 1979 to 1981 expanded rapidly, and that the sharp growth coincides with a steady and noticeable rise in machinery and fuel trade. This was due to the Long Term Trade Agreement (LTTA) signed in February 1978, which provided an institutionalized framework for stabilizing trade of the two major items.

It is obvious from these figures that a new pattern of commodity exchanges, Japanese machinery for Chinese coal and petroleum, came into prominence in the post-normalization decade, and indeed almost dictated the overall pattern of Japan–China trade. But while this pattern was new, there were nonetheless substantial continuities in institutional arrangements, particularly in the creation of the LTTA framework. Within this framework, one finds the old trade elements still actively involved, maintaining a balance with new participants in China trade from big business. Before examining the case of the LTTA, let us take a look at this balance between the old and the new in China trade.

7.2.2. The Old and the New

This new balance between the old and the new in Japan's conduct of China trade was exemplified in the relationship between the Japan–China Association on Economy and Trade (JCAET) and Keidanren. Although the JCAET and Keidanren generally worked in concert to bring about the 1978 Long Term Trade Agreement, their philosophies about Japan–China trade diverged. This cleavage derived mainly from their differing organizational orientations and their different experiences in Japan–China trade before diplomatic normalization. The JCAET was organized by people who had started as promoters of China trade when governmental relations had been worsening, while Keidanren, which saw itself as responsible for the economic activities of the entire nation, had during those years naturally sided with the government. They were on opposite sides of the fence for two decades, and so it is not surprising that their basic characteristics did not change easily. In the second half of the 1970s, however, their interests in China trade converged and they came to form a cooperative relationship in the promotion of Japan–China trade in the new era.

Given its role, Keidanren had understandably been skeptical of the four conditions announced by Zhou Enlai in April 1970. For instance, the chairman Uemura Kogoro declared in the Japan–Korea Economic Cooperation

Committee on 15 June 1970 that he would ignore Zhou's four conditions. In January 1972, he also bluntly criticized the Doyukai leadership, which had played a leading role in the Tokyo business people's delegation to China in November 1971. Keidanren's view was well expressed in a remark by Uemura to Gerald Curtis: 'Sometimes they cause us trouble because after we go through the painstaking task of building a consensus, Doyukai leadership makes a pronouncement that reflects a different position and succeeds only in confusing the issue. Sometimes I wish they would think a little more carefully about what they say.'[22]

Chinese leaders were therefore very cautious, at least in the early 1970s, in drawing Keidanren into the scheme of Japan–China economic cooperation.[23] This cautiousness explains their preference for the JCAET over a plan to create the 'Japan–China Economic Cooperation Committee', which had been developed by Keidanren and the rest of the *zaikai* leadership. Nagano Shigeo was particularly enthusiastic about this plan. He had played a central role in creating such committees with Australia, the Pacific Basin, the Soviet Union, and India,[24] and clearly was attempting to draw the new Japan–China trade into his own bailiwick. Uemura also supported the Economic Cooperation Committee idea vigorously in a similar attempt to take the leadership in the new era of Japan–China trade. Uemura had broken his reserved posture on the China issue for the first time on 12 August 1972, when in a meeting with Sun Pinghua in Tokyo he expressed a hope to establish a Cooperation Committee between Japan and China.[25] On 29 September 1972, the day when the joint communiqué to establish diplomatic relations between Japan and China was signed in Beijing, Uemura stated in a press conference that he would like to visit China at an appropriate time in order to promote the plan to establish the Cooperation Committee. He intended to put the subject of Chinese oil onto the agenda of the *zaikai*'s 'resource diplomacy' through the channel of the Cooperation Committee.[26]

Despite this eagerness among the *zaikai* leaders, the Chinese eventually turned down this Japanese initiative, presumably because it preferred the arrangement through the JCAET. On 18 September 1973, Liu Xiwen, who was heading a Chinese economic and trade delegation to Japan, said in Osaka that China considered a Cooperation Committee unnecessary for the moment.[27] It was against this background that Keidanren gradually came to side

---

[22] Gerald L. Curtis, 'Big Business and Political Influence', in Ezra F. Vogel (ed.), *Modern Japanese Organization and Decision-making* (Berkeley: University of California Press, 1975), p. 59.
[23] Watanabe Interview.
[24] William E. Bryant, *Japanese Private Economic Diplomacy: An Analysis of Business–Government Linkages* (New York: Praeger, 1975), Chapter 5.
[25] *Asahi Shinbun*, 13 August 1972.
[26] *Asahi Shinbun*, 30 September 1972; *Mainichi Shinbun*, 30 September 1972.
[27] *Nihon Keizai Shinbun*, 19 September 1973.

with the JCAET in its resource diplomacy, leading to Keidanren's participation in the process toward the conclusion of the Long Term Trade Agreement in February 1978. Before that, there was an undercover struggle between the old, those who established the JCAET, and the new, represented by Keidanren, over the leadership of Japan–China trade in the post-normalization era.[28]

As its chances for the Cooperation Committee faded away, Keidanren chose to work with the JCAET. But Keidanren's role was quite distinct from the JCAET in China trade, because it was simultaneously pursuing resource diplomacy with the Soviet Union. The channel was the Japan–Soviet Business Cooperation Committee, which had been established in 1965 and was co-chaired by Uemura and Nagano.[29] At the fifth joint meeting of this committee in Tokyo in February 1972, the Soviet Union presented five proposals including Japanese participation in the development of oil in Tyumen and natural gas in Yakutsk. Negotiations over the development of the Yakutsk natural gas were held in Tokyo in July 1973, and those over the Tyumen oil in Moscow in August 1973.[30] In the following month, Keidanren dispatched its first delegation to China. In February 1974, the sixth joint meeting of the Japan–Soviet Business Cooperation Committee was held in Moscow, and Uemura and Nagano visited Moscow in March to meet with Secretary General Brezhnev.[31] Keidanren's second delegation to China visited Beijing in October 1975, followed a year later by the first delegation from Keidanren to the Soviet Union in August 1976.[32] The seventh joint meeting of the Japan–Soviet Business Cooperation Committee ensued in September 1977 in Tokyo.

But for a variety of economic and political reasons, the Tyumen project negotiations had reached a virtual standstill by the spring of 1974.[33] One cause was the growing prospect of stable imports of Chinese oil in a long-term framework; as Nagano said later, it would be easier and cheaper to buy already developed Chinese oil.[34] Thus, from the viewpoints of the Chinese and the Russians, Keidanren indeed became a target in Sino-Soviet economic competition.

Keidanren's role derived from its strong interest in resource diplomacy, the crux of which lay in diversifying the countries supplying Japan's natural resources. Its basic stance was summarized in the words of one executive: 'We

[28] A number of people interviewed admitted this struggle, especially between Inayama and Nagano, in the early 1970s.

[29] This committee included members from both Keidanren and the Japan Chamber of Commerce and Industry, and had become a part of the Keidanren structure. Gerald L. Curtis, 'The Tyumen Oil Development Project and Japanese Foreign Policy Decision-Making', in Scalapino (ed.), *The Foreign Policy of Modern Japan*, p. 155.

[30] *Zaikai*, 15 September 1973, p. 30.

[31] *Zaikai*, 1 May 1974, pp. 34–46.

[32] *Zaikai*, 15 September 1976, pp. 40–41.

[33] Curtis, 'The Tyumen Oil Development Project', p. 158.

[34] *Toyo Keizai*, 24 July 1976, p. 15.

can't choose between China and the Soviet Union, but will deal with both of them. Whenever we have to choose between them, we will leave it to the government.'[35] Keidanren thus came into China trade simply because China became a realistic target for its private economic diplomacy.

In contrast, the JCAET is an organization which specializes in economic relations with China, and it inherited a sense of reciprocity as its organizing principle through its predecessor's experiences of Japan–China trade during the 1960s. It was indeed this sense of reciprocity that sustained Japan–China trade throughout the postwar years. The JCAET's character as an organization committed to China trade is fully spelled out in 'the tenor and the purpose of establishment' in the JCAET's manual:

> . . .The tenor of the establishment [of the JCAET] lies in contributing to the economic development of both Japan and China, through smooth economic exchanges and establishing a friendly good-neighbour relationship between the two countries.
>
> . . .To pursue the economic development of both countries through mutual understanding and on the basis of reciprocity and mutual complimentality, holds quite significant implications for the peace and development of not only Japan and China but also of Asia.

This is not a statement agreed with the Chinese, but was written by the Japanese side on its own. The legacy of the LT/MT institution and principle is thus alive in the JCAET, and it still maintains its distinct function in Japan's trade relations with China.

7.3. LONG TERM TRADE AGREEMENT

The Long Term Trade Agreement (LTTA) was signed on 16 February 1978. The underlying principles and formula of the LTTA closely resembled the old LT Trade agreement or even the long-term steel trade agreement of 1958. For example, the principle of balanced trade was adopted: each side was to export about $10 billion over the eight-year period. During the initial five years, Japan was expected to export $7–8 billion worth of technology and plant and $2–3 billion of construction materials and machinery. China in return was to export during the same period a total of 47.1 million metric tons of crude oil, 5.15–5.3 million metric tons of coking coal, and 3.3–3.9 million metric tons of steam coal.

Over this five-year period, the trade under the LTTA agreement reached $12,481 million, less than expected. Nonetheless, it was very significant that

---

35 Cited in 'Siberia Kaihatsu to Nihon no Shutaisei' [Siberian Development and Japanese Autonomy], *Sekai*, 343 (1974), p. 193. For an analysis of the Soviet Union's negative reactions to Japanese business' 'balanced diplomacy', see Allen S. Whiting, *Siberian Development and East Asia: Threat or Promise?* (Stanford: Stanford University Press, 1981), pp. 130–34. The author sees China as not a serious constraint on Japan's business relations with the Soviet Union, see pp. 145, 175.

the LTTA exchange occupied 30.9 per cent of total Japan–China trade—$40,385 million in five years—despite the great disturbances caused by Chinese economic readjustment policies. Also, Japanese plant exports unquestionably led to a substantial trade in related machinery outside the agreement, as suggested by the figures in Table 7.2.

It is hard to estimate objectively the extent to which the LTTA itself caused the conspicuous increase in Japan–China trade after 1978. Given the major changes in Chinese economic policy in the late 1970s, Japan–China trade would have improved a great deal even without the LTTA. It is quite important, however, that this long-term framework of trade embodied what otherwise would have remained an elusive concept: the fundamental principle of reciprocity.

Reciprocity refers not only to the economic compatibility between the two countries, but also entails a sense of obligation and commitment to the expansion of Japan–China trade. This sense of reciprocity virtually became a norm in postwar Japan–China trade, if only among those who were most actively engaged. In fact, this principle of reciprocity embodied LT/MT Trade, reflecting both economic compatibility and the sense of commitment felt by the Japanese in the pro-China group. This underlying principle persisted into the post-normalization era and proved to be an important factor behind the conclusion of the LTTA.

7.3.1. Japanese Actors

It is more than just symbolic that the pro-China JCAET, which inherited the legacy of LT/MT Trade, was the main promoter of the LTTA. Inayama (president of the JCAET) was especially enthusiastic. As early as 1958, he had led a steel delegation to China and signed a long-term barter trade agreement, although this was aborted along with all other trade transactions by the Nagasaki flag incident in May of that year. He had long hoped to revive such an agreement, and naturally hoped to include steel as one of Japan's export items to China.[36]

The JCAET itself had established divisions on energy and plant in 1973, and on steam coal in 1974, and thus started to play an active role in preparations for a long-term plan to exchange industrial plant for energy resources. These divisions provided a forum for consultation among Japanese suppliers and consumers of these items, and thus gathered basic information for the content of the LTTA.

The MITI, largely working through its Natural Resources and Energy Agency (NREA) established in July 1973, was also actively involved in preparations for the LTTA. The position of the NREA and the MITI was expressed

---

[36] *Nihon Keizai Shinbun*, 9 January 1976.

in a report on 'Energy Stabilizing Policy in the Showa 50s', compiled in August 1975 by the Overall Energy Research Council, a MITI advisory committee.[37] As the strategy for stability in energy over the coming decade, this report called for decreasing Japanese dependence on overseas resources, mainly oil. For example, the target figure for the oil share among all energy sources in 1980 was given as 68.9 per cent, compared with the actual figure of 77.4 per cent in 1973. (Incidentally, the policy embodied in this report proved effective, since the oil share in 1980 actually fell to 66.4 per cent.) Nonetheless, the report went on, Japan would still be much more dependent on imported oil than the western countries, and so its oil supply would have to be stabilized by diversifying its supplying countries. This policy was endorsed formally by the cabinet decision on 'the Basic Direction of the Overall Energy Policy' on 19 December 1975.[38] This energy strategy dictated the NREA's approach to the question of Chinese oil, and it reflected the consensus in the business community as well.

When the prospect for signing the agreement emerged in the spring of 1977, all the concerned actors supported the creation of the Japan Committee for the Promotion of Japan–China Long Term Trade Agreement. This committee was established in October 1977 as a forum for building a consensus among related firms, industries, and economic organizations, to promote the signing of the agreement. Inayama became chairman of the Committee, and Doko Toshio (president of Keidanren) and Fujiyama Aiichiro (president of the JAPIT) were engaged as advisors. The Committee included a general section, an oil section, a coking coal section, a steam coal section, an export section, and a finance and accounting section. On 31 January 1978, when the signing of the agreement came in sight, this committee was renamed the Japan Committee for the Long Term Trade Agreement.

Keidanren was totally supportive of the JCAET and the LTTA Committee, for the reasons explained above. The LTTA was indeed a product generated through combined efforts by these actors. Everyone agreed on a very simple and straightforward strategy: Japan would export industrial plant and construction materials to help China's modernization programmes, in exchange for Chinese coal and oil to stabilize Japan's energy supply. As the previous section demonstrated, however, there were reasons why Keidanren and the JCAET were not totally in harmony.

The key point, again, is that Keidanren was new to Japan–China trade, and was motivated not by a pro-China attitude but by seeing China as a realistic target within its economic diplomacy. Its main concern in the LTTA arrangements was thus the importation of Chinese energy resources, especially after the 'oil shock' in late 1973. Keidanren was also approaching the Soviet Union

---

[37] The report was published as *Showa 50-nendai no Enerugi: Antei Kyokyu no Tameno Sentaku* [*Energy in the Showa 50s: A Choice for Stable Supply*] (Tokyo: Tsusho Sangyo Chosa-kai, 1975).

[38] For the whole text of the decision, see *Nihon Keizai Shinbun*, 19 December 1975 (evening).

in search of energy resources. In contrast; the JCAET was a pro-China organization by nature, having inherited the old LT/MT Trade personnel and its principle of reciprocity. This character was an important factor in the JCAET becoming the central promoter of the LTTA. It initially paved the way for the LTTA, and often functioned as a bridge between the Chinese and Keidanren leaders. The JCAET actually became the Japanese negotiator for the details of the trade agreement.

7.3.2. Process

The LTTA was achieved through a series of economic missions from Japan, as shown in Table 7.3.

These missions were not solely concerned with the LTTA, except for the LTTA Committee visits in 1977 and 1978. Nonetheless, they established channels of communication, through which a consensus gradually was formed between Japan and China. As noted above, the Inayama mission of August 1972 had in mind a long-term plan for exchanging Chinese natural resources with Japanese industrial goods and plant. Zhou Enlai hinted to this mission the possibility of providing oil, and Idemitsu Keisuke, president of Idemitsu Oil, saw good possibilities.[39] When China decided to export oil to Japan one month after diplomatic normalization, Zhou conveyed this decision to Kimura Ichizo, who then worked to establish Kokusai Sekiyu (the International Oil Corporation) as a window organization for the imports.

The MITI and the JCAET sent a joint delegation led by MITI Minister Nakasone Yasuhiro and JCAET president Inayama Yoshihiro in January 1973. Very importantly, when Nakasone conferred with Zhou Enlai on 18 January, Zhou promised to examine the possibility of oil exports to Japan and the purchase of Japan's technology and equipment for the development of

TABLE 7.3. China visits by the LTTA actors

Inayama mission	23–31 August	1972
MITI, JCAET	17–21 January	1973
Keidanren	1–7 September	1973
JCAET	13–17 January	1975
NREA	22–30 January	1975
Keidanren	16–27 October	1975
MITI	17–19 November	1975
JCAET	18–22 January	1976
JCAET	2–6 February	1977
Keidanren	30 March–4 April	1977
LTTA Committee	26–29 November	1977
LTTA Committee	14–16 February	1978

39 *Asahi Shinbun*, 3 September 1972.

Chinese offshore oil.[40] When Keidanren dispatched its first mission to China in September 1973, Zhou remarked that when China developed enough natural resources it could supply Japan in exchange for Japanese industrial goods.[41] By this time, therefore, a clear consensus had developed between the Chinese leaders and the Japanese government and business leaders that Japan–China trade in the post-normalization era would develop by expanding Chinese natural resources exports to Japan. The fact that oil accounted for 33.2 per cent of Chinese exports to Japan as early as 1975 demonstrated its central position in Japan–China trade.

Inayama led another JCAET delegation in January 1975 and proposed an annual exchange of ideas with the JCAET. China welcomed this idea, and it was agreed that consultations about the balanced expansion of Japan–China trade would be repeated on a regular basis.[42]

Subsequently, the first oil delegation, headed by the deputy director of the NREA, was sent to China at the end of January 1976. It reached an agreement with the Chinese Ministry of Foreign Trade and Ministry of Petroleum and Chemical Industries that it was in the interests of both countries to ensure a long-term and stable supply of Chinese oil.[43] In April 1975, the NREA, the JCAET, and several petroleum and power companies held a joint discussion on the importation of Chinese oil. They agreed on 3 April that a framework for long-term, stable imports should replace the yearly negotiations.[44]

As the expectation of a trade agreement grew, the JCAET-affiliated promoters of the trade agreement such as Inayama began an attempt to alter the Chinese attitude toward Keidanren, because they thought the involvement of the business mainstream was indispensable in the long-term scheme to exchange key commodities.[45] Their efforts, coupled with the Chinese concerns about Keidanren's simultaneous approach toward the Soviet Union, produced a concrete result: in the spring of 1975, the CCPIT invited a delegation from Keidanren. Doko Toshio, president of Keidanren, stated before his departure in October that Japan should import Chinese oil to diversify supply. Vice-Premier Li Xiannian responded with his personal opinion that China could make a long-term contract for oil.[46]

In the meantime, the NREA, MITI's outer agency, was preparing plans for a long-term agreement on importing Chinese oil, in consultation with the private sector as well as the JCAET. In general, the Japanese industries which

[40] *Asahi Shinbun*, 22 January 1973.

[41] *Keidanren Hochu Daihyo-dan Hokoku-sho* [*Report of Keidanren Delegation to China*] (hereafter cited as *Keidanren Report*) (1974), p. 12.

[42] 'Nitchu Memo' [Japan–China Memo], *NKKK*, 21 (1975), p. 50; Tanaka Shujiro, 'Nitchu Keizai Kyokai Daihyo-dan no Hochu' [China Visit by the JCAET Delegation], *NKKK*, 22 (1975), p. 37.

[43] *Nihon Keizai Shinbun*, 29 January 1975.

[44] *Nihon Keizai Shinbun*, 4 April 1975.

[45] Watanabe Interview.   [46] *Keidanren Report* (February 1976), p. 19.

would have to buy most of the oil were most cautious. The government and business leaders were eager to import more oil than the industries wanted, partly to facilitate the diversification of supply and partly to ease the trade imbalance of China with Japan. When the NREA held a consultation about a long-term plan for importing Chinese oil in January 1976, several industries voiced strong opposition. The plan proposed to import 10 million metric tons in 1977, increasing to 15 million tons in 1981, whereas the industries' projected requirements did not exceed 9 million tons yearly over the same period.[47] Their reluctance reflected both gradually declining demand for oil in Japan and insufficient facilities for refining Chinese heavy oil.

The JCAET delegation nonetheless presented this plan to China in January. However, political turmoil and natural disasters in 1976 did not offer China a favourable environment to respond to the proposal immediately. The Chinese leaders later explained that the delay was due to the destructive activities that the Gang of Four inflicted on the resource production and transportation systems.[48] In addition to these developments in Chinese domestic politics, three great leaders passed away in 1976: Zhou Enlai in January, Zhu De in July, and Mao Zedong in September. Symbolically enough, the 1976 JCAET delegation which brought the concrete plan arrived in Beijing only four days after the funeral of Zhou Enlai.

The passing of Mao, however, unexpectedly opened the way for marked progress in LTTA negotiations. Hua Guofeng, who succeeded Zhou as Premier, and his associates suddenly arrested the Gang of Four in October, one month after Mao's death, and Hua simultaneously assumed the chairmanship of the CCP. Thereafter, Hua's efforts to advance Zhou's four modernization programs, which eventually led to his ambitious ten-year plan, became a catalyst for signing the LTTA.

In February 1977, the JCAET delegation paid its regular yearly visit, and exchanged opinions with Chinese leaders, including Vice-Premier Gu Mu and Foreign Trade Minister Li Qiang.[49] The Chinese side agreed in principle to move toward a long-term agreement for stable exports of Chinese oil, but did not give the impression that an agreement could be concluded quickly. Instead, China asked for another mission from Keidanren. Thus Keidanren sent its third economic mission in March–April 1977. When this mission met Minister of Foreign Trade Li Qiang, he stated, to the great surprise of the delegation members, that China would now accept a long-term trade agreement.[50]

---

47 *Nihon Keizai Shinbun*, 13 January 1976.
48 See, for example, remarks made by Vice-Minister Gu Mu, Minister of Foreign Trade Li Qiang, and Chairman of China–Japan Friendship Association Liao Chengzhi, to the JCAET delegation in February 1977, in 'Nitchu Memo' [Japan–China Memo], *NKKK*, 46 (1977), pp. 58–61.
49 Ibid.
50 *Keidanren Report*, pp. 15, 47.

On the basis of this agreement, the Japanese side established the LTTA Committee in October to prepare a draft plan. The plan was formulated on 24 November and presented by the LTTA Committee of Japan to its Chinese counterpart in Beijing on 29 November. After final consensus on the Japanese side was reached at the end of January 1978, the LTTA Committee dispatched another delegation on 14 February, which signed the Japan–China Long Term Trade Agreement with the China Committee for the China–Japan Long Term Trade Agreement, headed by Vice-Minister of Foreign Trade Liu Xiwen.

A key issue here was Japan's imports of Chinese oil in order to guarantee Japan's whole plant exports. Table 7.4 shows the content of draft plans prepared for the LTTA by Japan and China, and the final agreement.

The difference in the 1982 figures in the Japanese plan was a 'political addition', and Doko and Inayama were to be responsible for its disposal.[51] The Chinese side explained that it was capable of exporting 30 million metric tons in 1982, so it could guarantee 15 million tons to Japan.[52] Apparently, to finance the imports of Japanese industrial goods, the Chinese wanted to export more oil than was wanted by the Japanese. Thus, the political addition was accepted by Doko and Inayama to accommodate Chinese demands.

As it happened, the Chinese estimate proved overly optimistic: in the first half of the 1970s, Chinese oil production had increased by about 20 per cent per year, but the rate dropped to 11.1 per cent in 1978 and 1.9 per cent in 1979,[53] while domestic consumption steadily increased. Thus, in September 1980, the Chinese side asked that the figures for 1981 and 1982 be reduced to 8.3 million tons, and Japan concurred two months later. This revision was officially recorded in the discussion record of the third regular meeting between the two LTTA Committees signed on 24 July 1981 in Tokyo.[54]

TABLE 7.4. Oil and the LTTA (millions of metric tons)

	Japanese Plans.		Chinese Plan (29 Nov)	LTTA (16 Feb 78)
	(24 Nov 77)	(29 Nov)		
1978	6.8	6.8	6.8–7	7
1979	7.6	7.6	7.6–8	7.6
1980	8	8	8.5–9.5	8
1981	9.4	9.4	9.5–11	9.5
1982	11.3	15	15	15

Source: Nitchu Keiho, 107 (1978), pp. 355–7.

[51] *Nitchu Keiho,* 107 (1978), p. 356.   [52] *Ibid.,* p. 357.
[53] Nitchu Choki Boeki Kyogi Iinkai [Japan–China Long Term Trade Agreement Committee], *Nitchu Choki Boeki Torikime 5-nen-kan no Ayumi* [*5 Years of Japan–China Long Term Trade Agreement*] (1983), p. 31.
[54] *Ibid.,* pp. 56–7.

7.3.3. Oil Imports and Plant Exports

After diplomatic normalization, two Japanese window organizations for importing Chinese crude oil were established. One is Kokusai Sekiyu (the International Oil Corporation) established in March 1973, and the other is Nihon Chugoku Sekiyu Yunyu Kyogikai (the Japan–China Oil Import Council) established in July 1974. The former has connections with the JAPIT-Kansai, and the latter with the JAPIT-Tokyo.

The origin of the International Oil Corporation dates back to October 1972. At a banquet held especially for Japanese non-governmental people and organizations in celebration of diplomatic normalization, Zhou Enlai asked Kimura Ichizo to make arrangements to import Chinese oil.[55] Kimura then established a window company, which would make a lump-sum negotiation over volume and price with the Chinese National Chemicals Import and Export Corporation. Kimura, while holding the position of chief director of the JAPIT-Kansai, became vice-president of the International Oil Corporation, and the nominal chairmanship was assumed by Matsubara Yosomatsu (chairman of the JAPIT-Kansai; advisor to Hitachi Shipbuilding Corporation). Later, Inayama Yoshihiro took over as president, but Kimura continued to be the man in charge. He also brought in several staff members from the JAPIT-Kansai. The stock holders were the actual purchasers of Chinese oil through the Corporation, including six major 'indigenous' oil companies, nine power companies, and six steel corporations.

In July 1974, a total of fourteen minor oil companies and affiliates of foreign oil companies plus eight trading corporations, which were all excluded from the International Oil Corporation, formed the Japan–China Oil Import Council. Later, the membership expanded to seventeen and nine respectively. The JAPIT-Tokyo took the lead here, motivated by rivalry with the JAPIT-Kansai. However, the JAPIT-Tokyo then clashed with the participating oil companies over control of the Council. Eventually they reached a compromise: the Council would be managed primarily by the oil companies, and they would become members of the JAPIT-Tokyo. Nonetheless, the JAPIT connection remained more than symbolic because the vice-presidency was assumed by a managing director of Toko Bussan, an important old friendly firm and an influential member of the JAPIT-Tokyo. Hasegawa Ryutaro, president of Asia Oil, became president.[56]

When Inayama headed a delegation from the JCAET in January 1976, he proposed that these two windows be amalgamated into a new organization, but the Chinese side was inclined to keep them intact.[57] Thus, as with many aspects of Japan–China trade, multiple channels were maintained in the case

55 Kimura Interview.
56 *Nihon Keizai Shinbun*, 13 July 1974; *KS Repoto* [*KS Report*] (International Oil Corporation, Tokyo), 4 (1980), pp. 17–18.
57 *Nihon Keizai Shinbun*, 13 January 1976.

of oil imports as well. Table 7.5 shows the shares of imported oil between the two organization.

The pattern of plant sales from Japan to China has basically been a function of Chinese economic decisions. Each contract is concluded on a case-by-case basis with individual companies, not through comprehensive negotiations. Typically, business starts with a technical exchange. If the Chinese are satisfied, they send an inquiry and the Japanese company provides detailed explanations of its technology and equipment. If the Chinese decided to buy the plant, tough negotiations over price ensue.[58]

Even the lump-sum agreement on plant in the LTTA did not change this basic pattern, in which Chinese conditions dictated the general trend of plant trade. For instance, plant sales were severely shaken by the economic adjustment policies by China in 1979 and 1980/81.[59] Consequently, the per centage of Japan's share in the total Chinese plant purchase, measured in monetary terms, decreased from 77.9 per cent in 1979 to 20.5 per cent in 1981, respectively representing the highest and the lowest rates in the post-normalization decade. This dramatic fluctuation obscures an impressive average figure of 44.2 per cent in this category during the post-normalization decade (1972–81).

This volatile aspect of the plant trade seemed to convey an important message to both Japan and China. Most characteristically, it brought home

TABLE 7.5. Two windows of oil imports and their contracts, 1973–1982 (thousands of tons)

Year	International Oil	Oil Import Council	Total
1973	1,000	0	1,000
1974	3,000	1,000	4,000
1975	5,700	2,100	7,800
1976	3,500–5,500	2,320	5,820–7,820
1977	3,440–3,940	2,310–2,610	5,750–6,550
1978	4,360	2,820	7,180
1979	4,550	2,970	7,520
1980	5,090	3,030	8,120
1981	5,236	3,064	8,300
1982	5,236	3,064	8,300

Source: *Nitchu Keiho*, no. 188 (April 1983), p. 358.

58 *Nitchu Keiho*, 27 (1974), pp. 66–72.
59 Kokubun Ryosei, 'Chugoku no Taigai Keizai Seisaku Kettei no Seiji-teki Kozo: Puranto Keiyaku Chudan Kettei no Baai' [Political Structure of Chinese Economic Foreign Policy Making: Cancellation of Plant Contracts], in Okabe Tatsumi (ed.), *Chugoku Gaiko: Seisaku Kettei no Kozo* [*Chinese Diplomacy: Structure of Policy Making*] (Tokyo: Nihon Kokusai Mondai Kenkyu-jo, 1983); Kokubun Ryosei, 'The Politics of Foreign Economic Policy-making in China: The Case of Plant Cancellations with Japan', *The China Quarterly*, 105 (1986).

that one could not expect a dramatic increase in Japan–China trade. The rosy expectations for the LTTA withered at the end of the initial five-year period; Japan's plant exports barely reached $4 billion, less than a half of the originally projected figure.

With all these caveats in mind, we are still inclined to conclude that the LTTA had a favourable impact on the overall pattern of plant sales from Japan to China. First, China imported in 1978 $1,236 million worth of plant from Japan or 36.2 per cent of total plant imports, compared with $53 million in the previous year. These figures jumped in 1979 to $3,008 million and 77.9 per cent respectively. Second, Japanese plant sales registered a marked increase during the initial five-year period of the LTTA compared with sales by western countries, as shown in Table 7.6

The legacy from the 1960s is also visible in plant trade in the post-normalization era. The Yoshida letter of 1964 had been issued in response to Taiwan's pressure against the extension of Export–Import Bank credits to Kurashiki Rayon's chemical fibre plant. The letter, or rather its broad interpretation by the Sato government, precluded subsequent plant sales to China until diplomatic normalization. In July 1972, the MITI announced the extension of Export–Import Bank credits for Japanese plant exports to China for the first time since the Yoshida letter was sent to Taiwan.[60] In this respect, whole plant sales in the 1970s began a new area for Japan–China trade, and they gradually came to occupy a central place.

Nonetheless, it is interesting to note that Japanese old friendly firms were often listed as contractors in plant sales to China. In many contracts, one of the Japanese vendors was an old friendly firm. Such cases numbered 3 out of 4 contracts in 1974, 3/6 in 1975, 4/6 in 1976, 1/2 in 1977, 22/45 in 1978, 4/25 in 1979, 11/40 in 1980, 1/14 in 1981, and 7/17 in 1982.[61] This pattern basically reflects the Chinese policy to respect old friends in Japan–China trade. It is striking that this legacy persists even in this new area of trade, which was on

TABLE 7.6. China's plant imports from major countries ($ million)

Years	Japan	Germany	France	England	USA	Total[a]
73–77	1,060	581	643	266	316	1,806
78–82	5,725[b]	1,964	552	804	671	3,991
Total	6,785	2,545	1,195	1,070	987	5,797

[a] Total of West Germany, France, England, and USA.
[b] Includes spot contracts outside of the LTTA.

Source: *Nitchu Keiho*, no. 118 (April 1983), p. 305.

[60] *Asahi Shinbun*, 26 July 1972 (evening).
[61] *Nitchu Keiho*, 43 (1975), pp. 70–73; 64 (1976), p. 72; 87 (1977), p. 76; 107 (1978), pp. 124–25; 124 (1979), pp. 132–44; 141 (1980), pp. 77–83; 158 (1981), pp. 278–87; 173 (1982), pp. 310–15; 188 (1983), pp. 292–7.

a large scale and could not be carried out without big firms occupying the central place. In this way, old friends were carefully protected by the Chinese, and constituted part of a pluralistic structure in Japan's conduct of China trade.

In sum, two legacies from the pre-normalization period were handed down to the new era: institutional continuity, and a sense of reciprocity as an organizing principle. Ostensibly, both Friendship Trade and LT/MT Trade ended after normalization. The composition of trade also shifted substantially in the 1970s. But both friendly firms and the JAPIT continued to maintain their identities as formed through the experiences in the 1950s and 1960s, and the old LT/MT actors established their own channel of China trade after normalization. Thus, the source of structural pluralism basically remained intact in the 1970s. Moreover, a sense of reciprocity continued to motivate pro-China individuals and organizations, and they maintained their distinct role in Japan's economic diplomacy with China. The source of their independence from the strategic framework therefore also remained intact. In essence, pro-China Japanese believed that the political environment changed in such a way as to be compatible with the values held by those who continuously promoted Japan–China cooperation throughout the postwar years.

8
Conclusion

The conventional wisdom is that international politics dictated the course of postwar Japan–China relations. This study, however, has stressed the fact that Japan–China trade during the three postwar decades was more stable and constant than the argument presupposing the primacy of security factors suggests. The study has demonstrated that three distinct foreign policy orientations held by the Japanese and the rise of Japanese non-governmental actors as the architects of Japan–China trade gave rise to structural pluralism in Japan's trade relations with China, and that this structure produced a significant extent of stability and continuity in the postwar Japan–China relationship. In concluding this study, we will review the pattern of structural pluralism in Japan's trade relations with China, and discuss its implications in the overall context of Japanese diplomacy in the postwar years.

8.1. STRUCTURAL PLURALISM IN JAPAN–CHINA TRADE

8.1.1. The Japanese Government's Policy before Normalization

Before the US–China *rapprochement* in 1971/72, the Japanese government's China policy had been severely constrained by US policy in East Asia. To cope with this external environment, the Japanese government adopted the separation of politics from economics as an official policy. Under this basic policy, however, attitudes toward China trade differed among Prime Ministers, depending on their foreign policy orientations and the place of China in their overall diplomacy.

For Yoshida Shigeru and Ikeda Hayato, the principle promoters of 'collaboration' diplomacy with the United States under the intensifying Cold War, China was important only in the long-term perspective. It was in this long-term calculation that Yoshida resisted American pressure to choose Taipei over Beijing. Ikeda responded favourably to the promotion of LT Trade in the same vein. As we saw, Ikeda was blessed with favourable political situations both inside and outside Japan. Both Yoshida and Ikeda thought that, under the predominant system of Pax Americana, a pursuit of diplomatic 'autonomy' would not do much good, or would even be detrimental, to Japan's postwar recovery and economic growth.

On the other hand, diplomacy by Hatoyama Ichiro, Ishibashi Tanzan, Kishi Nobusuke, and Sato Eisaku was more aggressive in seeking to expand the margins of diplomatic autonomy. Of course, their political beliefs and international perspectives were not identical. Nonetheless, Pax Americana was so predominant that the outcome of their personal proclivities stopped short of affecting the structure of the predominant international system, and was simply an attempt to expand the margins of autonomy within Pax Americana.

In the case of Hatoyama, his quest for diplomatic autonomy was motivated primarily by his sense of political rivalry against Yoshida Shigeru who had laid the groundwork for the collaboration line. For Hatoyama, diplomatic normalization with China was important as a major modification of Yoshida's pro-US diplomacy; but of course, the international realities did not allow such an ambitious policy. Ishibashi was also strongly motivated by his sense of frustration against Yoshida's diplomatic stance, but was unique as a postwar Prime Minister in that he held a liberal view toward international politics. He was a strong proponent of an alternative international order to the Cold War, and saw China as important in his visionary world order. It is hard to imagine, however, that Ishibashi could have realized his vision even if he had stayed longer as Prime Minister. After all, Ishibashi could put his belief into action only from outside the government.

Kishi and Sato disclosed a strong sense of nationalism in their diplomacy. Kishi's energy of diplomatic autonomy was discharged with the United States and South East Asia, and not with China. For Kishi, who wished to use his Asian diplomacy as a leverage to gain an 'equal partnership' with the United States, approaching China was out of the question; it was not only contrary to his anti-communist ideology but also would surely have invited US suspicion. Sato was more proactive in his China policy at the beginning, but as international and domestic politics turned against his wishes, Sato also looked to the United States and South East Asia as targets of opportunities to carry out his aspiration for diplomatic autonomy.

Before diplomatic normalization, these differing attitudes of Prime Ministers were an important factor affecting the political atmosphere of Japan–China relations. Also, these factors influenced the pattern of 'division of labour' between the Japanese government and non-governmental actors. Particularly, the difference between the autonomy orientation and the 'independence' orientation that existed among the non-governmental pro-China actors was important. The group of people who were motivated by an aspiration for diplomatic autonomy *vis-à-vis* the United States tended to accept the realities of predominant Pax Americana and aspired to make Japan's relations with both the United States and China compatible. To the extent that they understood the importance of the United States, there was room to establish a relationship of division of labour with the Japanese government in China trade. The Japanese government was naturally more interested in China trade promoted by the autonomy advocates than by the independence proponents who challenged the basic governmental policy to live in Pax Americana.

8.1.2. Non-Governmental Actors

Under this pattern of division of labour, however, a further pluralistic structure in the Japanese non-governmental sector was crucial in producing con-
sistency and resilience in Japan–China trade with the exception of several
years following the Nagasaki flag incident, while governmental attitudes fluc-
tuated depending on Prime Ministers and in response to changing political
factors. As we saw, non-governmental actors did not form a single channel of
Japan–China trade and were divided into several distinct institutions. In the
1950s, there were four major institutions oriented toward China trade. Two
were associated with governmental organizations: the Japan–China Importers
and Exporters Association (JCIEA) with the MITI, and the Japan–China
Trade Promotion Diet Members League (JCTPDML) with the Diet. But
this governmental connection affected them adversely at a time when governmental relations were uncongenial. However, the other two, the Japan–China
Trade Promotion Association (JCTPA) and the Japan Association for the
Promotion of International Trade (JAPIT), continued to be central to the
evolution of Japan–China trade in the 1950s and the 1960s.

For one thing, a central factor making these two pro-China organizations
distinct actors in China trade was their diplomatic orientations. During the
1950s, the JCTPA was strongly motivated by the independence line of diplomacy with a view of freeing Japan from US control, whereas the JAPIT was
motivated by the aspiration to seek diplomatic autonomy *vis-à-vis* the United
States and within the confines of Pax Americana.

As governmental relations between Japan and China became frozen, particularly after the Nagasaki flag incident in May 1958, however, the JAPIT's
diplomatic stance had begun to shift closer to the independence line. Okazaki
Kaheita and Takasaki Tatsunosuke, the central promoters of the LT Trade
arrangements in the 1960s, had initially joined the JAPIT, but dissociated
themselves as it gradually made manifest its anti-governmental stance. This
pluralistic configuration of Japanese pro-China elements became a foundation on which two separate trade channels, Friendship Trade and LT Trade,
were opened in the early 1960s. This structure was reinforced further by the
Chinese policy to take advantage of their political differences. LT Trade was
established on the basis of an understanding of mutual political differences
between Japan and China, whereas Friendship Trade was founded on Japanese unilateral compliance with Chinese political demands. This structural
pluralism at the non-governmental level provides an important explanation
why Japan–China trade survived the politically volatile 1960s: it was because
Friendship Trade offset the decline in LT/MT Trade.

These patterns persisted in the post-normalization era. The Chinese took
measures to protect the old Friendship Trade institutions. In the 1960s,
Friendship Trade tended to outdo LT/MT Trade at times of bilateral political

difficulties. These old Friendship Trade elements continued to retain loyalty to China after diplomatic normalization. The LT/MT Trade individuals made institutional transition into the Japan–China Association on Economy and Trade (JCAET) in the post-normalization decade. They carried with them a sense of reciprocity into the post-normalization era, which was demonstrated most typically by a commitment to the Long Term Trade Agreement of 1978.

The central norm motivating Japanese non-governmental, pro-China actors was this sense of reciprocity, which was generated by the combination of a belief in 'Asianism', personal encounters with China, and a sense of guilt over the war. Reciprocity was embodied in the institutionalized bilateral trade channels in both pre- and post-normalization periods, and thus became an important driving force for bilateral cooperation. The importance of this factor can be understood if we take note that the same institutionalized pattern of reciprocity was hardly imaginable in the case of Japan–Soviet trade relations.

Thus, the explanation of Japan's postwar trade with China is not complete without taking its non-governmental elements into full account. These actors became an important integral part of the pluralistic trade structure, which produced a significant amount of resilience in bilateral trade. The government's role in this context was to encourage, give *ex post facto* approval, and to make the best use it could of non-governmental initiatives.

Moreover, a *fait accompli* initiated by Japanese non-governmental actors was often incorporated into policy by the Chinese government. This made it all the more necessary for the Japanese government to take non-governmental initiatives into account in making policy on China trade. For example, we have seen that the initiative by the LT Trade elements for plant exports with deferred payments in the 1960s developed into a political issue between the two governments. In the post-normalization era also, pre-normalization patterns were central in structuring Japan–China trade, not only because of Japanese conditions but also because of the Chinese policy to respect their old friends.

8.2. JAPANESE DIPLOMACY AND CHINA

Even though our analysis has focused primarily on the evolution of the structure and process of postwar Japan–China trade as seen from the Japanese side, these findings also have important implications for the study of Japanese diplomacy. For one thing, they suggest a pluralistic rather than a monolithic perspective. To be concrete, our findings caution us against viewing Japan's trade behaviour toward China from the perspective of consensus building between government and business, either before or after normalization. It is true that consensus was reached easily when the fundamental interests of government and non-governmental actors were congruent, but before diplomatic normalization, non-governmental actors wanted to push China trade more than the government wished. Such moves often facilitated the development of bilateral trade.

Here, an important distinction has to be made between consensus as a cause of a development and *post facto* consensus. *Post facto* consensus may be necessary for a smooth implementation of policy, but the initiatives for the policy may lie elsewhere. In the case of Japan–China trade, we found examples of consensus building between business and government in such cases as the LT agreement and the Long Term Trade Agreement. But our analysis revealed that, very often, by the time a consensus was formed, non-governmental initiatives had already been made, and in most cases these initiatives prevailed in the end.

The making of Japan's China policy was therefore much more complex than many of the western writings tend to argue. Japan was not a unitary actor. The government and various groups of non-governmental actors perceived issues differently and felt diverse motivations. This study has demonstrated that differences among the Japanese actors, both at the governmental and non-governmental levels, over three distinct diplomatic orientations, were important sources of pluralism in postwar Japanese economic diplomacy toward China. To describe all this complexity as a purposeful act of the government oversimplifies Japanese diplomacy at best, and renders Japan's China policy no more than a 'conspiracy' by 'Japan Incorporated' at worst.

Finally, our analysis has suggested that Japan's political approach to China was conditioned by the Japanese aspiration for autonomous diplomacy, particularly since the time of diplomatic normalization. We have defined autonomous diplomacy as an expression of a Japanese wish to conduct the kind of diplomacy that was not derivative of international strategic imperatives including US strategy.

Such diplomacy was not the result of Japan's strategic choice, but was a reflection of the peculiar political situations that confronted Japan in the postwar years. Anti-military pacifism in domestic politics was a real obstacle for the Japanese government in developing a policy to cope with the dominant security environment, often causing paralysis in the decision-making process. This was further reinforced by prevailing memories of Japan's wartime aggression in Asia. Therefore, the Japanese government often aspired for autonomous diplomacy only in such a way as not to become entangled in a complicated regional security situation. Japanese actions, nonetheless, were regarded as significant by other regional countries.

Such peculiar diplomacy was not necessarily unpopular among many Japanese including traditional pro-China individuals. In general, the Japanese public tended to perceive US Cold War strategy as an artificial scheme placing unnecessary security burdens on Japan. It was in this dominant mood that the establishment of a friendly relationship with China received popular support. The US–China *rapprochement* in 1971/72 was both popular and shocking in this context: popular because it cleared the way for diplomatic normalization, and shocking because the United States betrayed Japan and treated it so lightly despite the fact that Japan had obediently followed the US strategy against its dominant public mood and wishes. It was believed, therefore, that Japan should pursue a new diplomacy in the 1970s, an autonomous diplomacy which should not be dictated by the strategic interests of the United States and other major powers. To the extent that the governmental approach to China aspired to create a stable and friendly relationship following the Japanese logic, as was the case with the signing of the Peace and Friendship Treaty, it received support from the public including pro-China Japanese who gathered under the JCAET and promoted the Long Term Trade Agreement.

The paradox was that, while, in theory, a truly autonomous diplomacy would require Japan to be a full-fledged player of political and security games in the region, in reality, Japan pursued an autonomous diplomacy precisely because it lacked conditions to become such a full-fledged country. In reality, therefore, Japanese autonomous diplomacy in the 1970s was merely an expression of its wishes conditioned by the peculiar political conditions prohibiting Japan from becoming a truly autonomous country, and the sustained Japan–US political and security relationship continued to be the core element in Japan's coping with real political and security issues in the region. Thus, autonomous diplomacy, which appealed to the sentiments of many Japanese, was possible only in tandem with the continuation of the alliance relationship with the United States, and if the two came into conflict the latter prevailed. Incidentally, this is why and how Japanese attitudes toward the United States have often been mixed and ambivalent.

This study examined two cases where Japanese diplomacy exhibited such a pattern: Japan's Indo-China policy exemplified by the Fukuda Doctrine and the signing of the Japan–China Peace and Friendship Treaty. In both cases, Japan attempted to solidify its relations with these sub-regions free from the logic of the triangle relationship among the United States, China, and the Soviet Union, but in the end was entangled into its strategic dynamism.

Japan's autonomous diplomacy was thus an incomplete diplomacy. Although it is well beyond the scope of this study, it is pertinent to point out that the post-Cold War changes in the Asia-Pacific provide Japan with a host of opportunities to develop a complete diplomatic strategy. In fact, there are some signs that Japan has been heading in this direction in the 1990s. Such a shift, however, requires a 'paradigm' change in Japanese diplomacy and a fundamental redefinition of the role of the Japan–US relationship in a new international context. Given the magnitude of the changes currently sweeping the world as well as inside Japan, this paradigm change is not altogether impossible. We do not know when and how it will happen, but it is certain that China, as well as the United States, will continue to be the key external factor.

BIBLIOGRAPHY

MEMOIRS AND PERSONAL ACCOUNTS

Brzezinski, Zbigniew (1983). *Power and Principle: Memoirs of the National Security Advisor, 1977–1981*. New York: Farrar, Strause and Giroux.

Carter, Jimmy (1982). *Keeping Faith: Memoirs of a President*. New York: Bantam Books.

Chang, Chun (1980). *Nikka: Huun no 70-nen [Japan–China: Seventy Stormy Years]*. Tokyo: Sankei Shuppan.

Chiang, Kai-shek (1985). *Sho Kaiseki Hiroku (Ge) [Secret Stories of Chiang Kaishek, Vol. 2]*. Tokyo: Sankei Shinbun-sha.

Fujiyama, Aiichiro (1972). 'Pekin Kosho no Kiso' [Basis of Negotiations in Beijing]. *Chuo Koron*, 87.

—— (1976) *Seiji Waga-Michi [Politics My Way]*. Tokyo: Asahi Shinbun-sha.

Furui, Yoshimi (1972). 'Nitchu Kokko Seijoka no Hiwa' [Secret Stories of Japan–China Diplomatic Normalization]. *Chuo Koron*, 87.

—— (1978) *Nitchu 18-nen: Seijika no Kiseki to Tenbo [Eighteen Years of Japan–China: the Past and the Future of a Politician]*. Tokyo: Makino Shuppan.

—— (1986) 'Nitchu wa Korekara ga Hajimarida' [Now is the Beginning of Japan–China Relations]. *Sekai*, 488.

Hara, Kichihei (1985). 'Nichibo Puranto Shodan Tenmatsu-ki' [A Story of Nichibo's Plant Negotiations]. In Kawakatsu, Den. *Yuko Ichiro: Watashi no 'Nitchu' Kaiso-ki [The Way to Friendship: My Memoirs of 'Japan–China']*. Tokyo: Mainichi Shinbun-sha.

Hatoyama, Ichiro (1957). *Hatoyama Ichiro Kaikoroku [Memoirs by Hatoyama Ichiro]*. Tokyo: Bungei Shunju-sha.

Hirano, Yoshitaro (1963). 'Nitchu Boeki Undo no Hajimari: "Chunichi Boeki Sokushin-kai" no Junbi Jidai' [The Beginning of Japan–China Trade Movements: Preparation Years of 'China–Japan Trade Promotion Association']. *Ajia Keizai Junpo*, 526–527.

Hoashi, Kei (1952). *Soren-Chugoku Kiko [A Trip to the Soviet Union and China]*. Tokyo: Kawade Shobo.

—— (1953) *Mitekita Chugoku [China that I Saw]*. Tokyo: Iwasaki.

Hoashi, Kei, and Wakimura, Yoshitaro (1952). 'Chukyo Boeki wa Kano ka' [Is China Trade Possible?]. *Sekai*, 81.

Ikeda, Masanosuke (1962). 'Nitchu Boeki Kosho ni Omou' [My Reflections on Japan–China Trade Negotiations]. *Seisaku Geppo*, 82.

—— (1963) 'Nitchu Boeki Kosho Hiroku' [Secret Stories of Japan–China Trade Negotiations]. *Naigai Karento*, 3.

—— (1969) *Nazo no Kuni: Chukyo Tairiku no Jittai [A Mysterious Country: True Situation in Communist China]*. Tokyo: Jiji Tsushin-sha.

Inayama, Yoshihiro (1986). *Watashi no Showa Tekko-shi [My Showa History of Steel]*. Tokyo: Toyo Keizai Shinpo-sha.

Ishibashi, Tanzan (1962). 'Nitchubeiso-Domei no Teisho' [I Urge for Japan–China–U.S.–Soviet Alliance]. *Chuo Koron*, 77.

Ishibashi, Tanzan (1970) *Ishibashi Tanzan Zenshu, Dai-14-kan [Complete Works of Ishibashi Tanzan, Vol. 14]*. Tokyo: Toyo Keizai Shinpo-sha.

Ishii, Mitsujiro (1976). *Omoide no Ki, III [Recollections, III]*. Tokyo: Karucha Shuppan.

Iwasa, Saneatsu (1990). *Kaiso 80-nen: Gurobarisuto no Me [Recollections of 80 years: An Eye of a Globalist]*. Tokyo: Nihon Hosei-gakkai.

Kawai, Ryoichi (1972). 'Nitchu Keizai Koryu wo Tenbo-suru' [Observing the Future of Japan–China Economic Exchange]. *Zaikai*, 20.

Kawai, Ryosei (1961). 'Nitchu Hukko no Toki' [The Time of Japan–China Normalization]. *Chuo Koron*, 76.

—— (1965) 'Nitchu Kankei wo Kataru' [Talking about Japan–China Relations]. *Sekai*, 231.

Kawakatsu, Den (1985). *Yuko Ichiro: Watashi no 'Nitchu' Kaiso-ki [The Way to Friendship: My Memoirs of 'Japan–China']*. Tokyo: Mainichi Shinbun-sha.

Kennan, George F. (1967). *Memoirs 1925–1950*. Boston: Little, Brown.

Kimura, Ichizo (1963). 'Wagakuni no Tsusho Gaiko Seisaku no Tenkan wo Hakare: Nitchu Boeki Kakudai wa Hitsuzen no Michi' [Our Trade and Foreign Policies need to be Reconsidered: Expansion of Japan–China Trade is Inevitable]. *Ajia Keizai Junpo*, 544.

—— (1970) 'Shu Onrai Sori no Teiki-shita Yon-komoku no Joken' [Four Conditions Presented by Premier Zhou Enlai]. *Ajia Keizai Junpo*, 802.

Kishi, Nobusuke (1983). *Kishi Nobusuke Kaikoroku: Hoshu Godo to Anpo Kaitei [Memoirs by Kishi Nobusuke: Unification of Conservative Parties and Revision of Japan–U.S. Security Treaty]*. Tokyo: Kosaido Shuppan.

Kishi, Nobusuke, Yatsugi, Kazuo, and Ito, Takashi (1981). *Kishi Nobusuke no Kaiso [Recollections of Kishi Nobusuke]*. Tokyo: Bungei Shunju-sha.

Kissinger, Henry (1979). *White House Years*. Boston: Little, Brown.

Kora, Tomi (1952). 'Kokoro ni Nokotta Koto: Nihon ni Kaette' [What Remains in My Heart: On Returning to Japan]. *Sekai*, 81.

—— (1952) *Watashi wa Mitekita Soren Chukyo [I Saw the Soviet Union and Communist China]*. Tokyo: Asahi Shinbun-sha.

—— (1983) *Ahinsa wo Ikiru: Kora Tomi Jiden [Living Non-Violence: Autobiography of Kora Tomi]*. Tokyo: Domesu Shuppan.

Kurogane, Yasumi (1970). 'Matsumura Hochudan Zuiko Nisshi' [Travel Diary of the Matsumura Delegation to China]. *Asahi Janaru*, 12.

—— (1971) 'Fujiyama Hochu Zuiko Nisshi' [Travel Diary of Fujiyama Visit to China]. *Asahi Janaru*, 13.

Matsumoto, Shunichi (1968). 'Nihon Gaiko to Nitchu Kankei' [Japanese Diplomacy and Japan–China Relations]. *Ajia Keizai Junpo*, 728.

—— (1971) 'Chugoku no Kokusai Ninshiki to Nihon Gaiko' [Chinese Perception of the World and Japanese Diplomacy]. *Sekai*, 310.

Matsumura, Kenzo (1960). 'Nitchu Kankei wo Do Dakai Suruka' [How to Break the Deadlock in Japan–China Relations]. *Asahi Janaru*, 2.

—— (1962) 'Chugoku kara Kaette' [On Returning from China]. *Asahi Janaru*, 4.

—— (1962) 'Nitchu Kankei no Shindankai' [New Stage of Japan–China Relations]. *Chuo Koron*, 77.

—— (1963) 'Watashi no Ajia-kan: Nitchu Kankei wo Chushin-ni' [My View of Asia: In Relation to Japan–China Relations]. *Shiso*, 463.

Matsumura, Kenzo, and Kazami, Akira (1960). 'Chugoku wa Ikaga Deshitaka' [How was China?]. *Chuo Koron*, 75.

Matsumura, Kenzo, Okazaki, Kaheita, Nishi, Haruhiko, Matsumoto, Shigeharu, and Uchida, Kenzo (1964). 'Chugoku Mondai to Nihon no Gaiko: Dai-3-ji Matsumura Hochu' wo Oete' [The China Issue and Japanese Diplomacy: After the 'Third Matsumura China Visit']. *Sekai*, 223.

Matsumura, Kenzo, Takenaka, Yutaro, Okazaki, Kaheita, and Uchida, Kenzo (1966). 'Nitchu Kankei eno Teigen: "Dai-4-ji Matsumura Hochu" wo Megutte' [Suggestions for Japan–China Relations: Concerning the 'Fourth Matsumura China Visit']. *Sekai*, 249.

Murata, Shozo (1955). 'Shu Onrai to Atte' [Meeting with Zhou Enlai]. *Sekai*, 112.

—— (1955) 'Nitchu Kankei no Genjo wo Ureu' [Worrying about the Present Situation of Japan–China Relations]. *Sekai*, 119.

—— (1972) *Nitchu Kakehashi no Ichi-kiroku [A Record of Bridging Japan and China]*. Tokyo: Osaka Shosen Mitsui Senpaku.

Nagano, Shigeo (1982). *Waga Zaikai Jinsei [My Zaikai Life]*. Tokyo: Daiyamondo-sha.

Nan, Hanchen, and Kawai, Ryosei (1964). 'Atarashii Nitchu Kankei no Tameni' [For New Japan–China Relations]. *Ekonomisuto*, 42.

Ogawa, Heishiro (1977). *Pekin no 4-nen [Four Years in Beijing]*. Tokyo: Saimaru Shuppan-kai.

—— (1981) *Chugoku Saiho: Hurikaette Mita 8-nen [Revisiting China: Eight Years Reconsidered]*. Tokyo: Saimaru Shuppan-kai.

Ohara, Soichiro (1963). 'Tai-Chugoku Puranto Yushutsu ni Tsuite' [About the Plant Export to China]. *Sekai*, 213.

Okada, Akira (1983). *Mizudori Gaiko Hiwa: Aru Gaikokan no Shogen [Secret Stories of Waterfowl Diplomacy: Testimony of a Diplomat]*. Tokyo: Chuo Koron-sha.

Okazaki, Kaheita (1962). 'Nitchu Boeki eno Kangaekata' [How to Think About Japan–China Trade]. *Asahi Janaru*, 4.

—— (1963) 'Chugoku no Genjo to Nitchu no Shorai' [The Present Situation in China and the Future of Japan–China]. *Ajia Keizai Junpo*, 529.

—— (1966) 'Nitchu Kankei no Shorai to Yoshida Shokan' [The Future of Japan–China Relations and the Yoshida Letter]. *Sekai*, 252.

—— (1968) 'Nitchu Oboegaki Boeki wo Musunde, (Jo), (Ge)' [On Concluding Japan–China Memorandum Trade, (1), (2)]. *Ajia Keizai Junpo*, 716, 717.

—— (1971) 'Oboegaki Boeki no Kigengire wo Maenishite Omou' [My Thought Facing the Expiration of the Memorandum Trade]. *Sekai*, 302.

—— (1971) 'Shogai to Tenbo to Kakushin to: Nitchu Oboegaki Boeki Kosho wo Oete' [Obstacle, Prospect, and Confidence: After the Memorandum Trade Negotiations]. *Sekai*, 306.

—— (1971) *Chugoku Mondai eno Michi [My Approach to the China Issue]*. Tokyo: Shunju-sha.

—— (1972) 'Chugoku ni Kaketa Waga Hansei no Ki' [Records of My Life Devoted to China]. *Chuo Koron*, 87.

—— (1976) 'Shu Onrai Sori no Omoide' [Memories of Premier Zhou Enlai]. *Sekai*, 364.

—— (1976) 'Shu Onrai Sori no Omoide: Hoi' [Memories of Premier Zhou Enlai: Supplement]. *Sekai*, 365.

Okazaki, Kaheita (1979) *Watashi no Kiroku [My Records]*. Tokyo: Toho Shoten.

—— (1984) *Owari-naki Nitchu no Tabi [Endless Journey between Japan and China]*. Tokyo: Hara Shobo.

Okazaki, Kaheita, and Tagawa, Seiichi (1972). 'Yatto "Sono Hi" ga Otozureta' [At Last 'The Day' Has Come]. *Gekkan Ekonomisuto*, 3.

Saeki, Isamu (1971). 'Nitchu Seijoka to Zaikai no Yakuwari' [Japan–China Normalization and the Role of Big Business]. *Ekonomisuto*, 49.

Samejima, Keiji (1971). *Hachi-oku no Yujin-tachi: Nitchu Kokko Kaihuku eno Michi [800 Million Friends: A Road to Japan–China Diplomatic Normalization]*. Tokyo: Nihon Keizai Shinbun-sha.

Sebald, William J., and Russel Brines (1965). *With MacArthur in Japan: A Personal History of the Occupation*. New York: W.W. Norton.

Shimakura, Tamio (1972). *Pekin Nikki [Beijing Diary]*. Tokyo: Nihon Keizai Shinbun-sha.

Shukutani, Eiichi (1961). 'Nitchu Boeki wo Do Hatten Saseruka' [How to Promote Japan–China Trade]. *Sekai*, 189.

Soma, Tsunetoshi (1968). 'Nitchu Boeki ni Seii wo' [Sincerity to Japan–China Trade]. *Ekonomisuto*, 46.

Sun, Pinghua (1985). 'Zhong-Ri Youhao Suixiang-lu (12), (14)' [Recollections of China–Japan Friendship (12), (14)]. *Shijie Zhishi*, 20, 22.

Suzuki, Haruo (1972). 'Imakoso Chugoku eno Ninshiki wo' [Now is the Time to Consider the China Issue]. *Ekonomisuto*, 50.

Suzuki, Kazuo (1959). 'Ishibashi Tanzan Shi to Tomo-ni' [Together with Mr. Ishibashi Tanzan]. *Sekai*, 167.

—— (1960) 'Nitchu Kankei to Shu Hatsugen' [Japan–China Relations and the Statement by Zhou]. *Sekai*, 179.

—— (1962) 'Nitchu Boeki Kakudai eno Michi' [A Way to the Expanded Japan–China Trade]. *Ekonomisuto*, 40.

—— (1965/6) 'Bosoku Undo ga Ayunda Michi: Suzuki Kazuo Shi ni Kiku, (1), (2), (3), (4)' [Looking Back on Trade Promotion Movements: Interview with Mr. Suzuki Kazuo, (1), (2), (3), (4)]. *Ajia Keizai Junpo*, 619, 621, 622, 637.

—— (1972) 'Kakezuri Mawatta Nitchu Boeki "Sosoki" no Koto' [About the Beginning Years of Japan–China Trade]. *Gekkan Ekonomisuto*, 3.

Tagawa, Seiichi (1969). 'Nitchu Kankei Dakai no Tame no Teigen: Nitchu Oboegaki Boeki Kosho wo Oete' [Suggestions for Breaking the Deadlock in Japan–China Trade: After the Japan–China Memorandum Trade Negotiations]. *Asahi Janaru*, 11.

—— (1971/2) 'Matsumura Kenzo no Hansei, (Jo), (Chu), (Ge)' [Life of Matsumura Kenzo, (1), (2), (3)]. *Sekai*, 313, 314, 315.

—— (1972) 'Nisshi: Matsumura Kenzo Shi no Sogi Zengo (46/8/21–9/1)' [Diary: Before and After the Funeral of Mr. Matsumura Kenzo (21 August 1971–1 September)]. *Sekai*, 316.

—— (1972) *Matsumura Kenzo to Chugoku [Matsumura Kenzo and China]*. Tokyo: Yomiuri Shinbun-sha.

—— (1973) *Nitchu Kosho Hiroku: Tagawa Nikki—14-nen no Shogen [Secret Stories of Japan–China Negotiations: Tagawa Diary—Testimony of Fourteen Years]*. Tokyo: Mainichi Shinbun-sha.

—— (1980/1) 'Nitchu Hukko Butai-ura no Hitotachi (1)–(13)' [People behind the Stage of Japan–China Normalization, (1)–(13)]. *Nitchu Keizai Kyokai Kaiho*, 82–94.

—— (1983) *Nitchu Koryu to Jimin-to Ryoshu-tachi [Japan–China Exchange and the LDP Leaders]*. Tokyo: Yomiuri Shinbun-sha.

Takasaki, Tatsunosuke (1953). *Manshu no Shuen [The Collapse of Manchuria]*. Tokyo: Jitsugyo no Nihon-sha.

—— (1961) 'Watashi no Mita Chugoku' [China that I Saw]. *Asahi Janaru*, 3.

—— (1961) 'Shu Onrai to Kaidan-shite' [Meeting with Zhou Enlai]. *Chuo Koron*, 76.

—— (1962) 'Chugoku ni Tsukai-shite' [My Mission to China]. *Jitsugyo no Nippon*, 65.

Utsunomiya, Tokuma (1960). *Heiwa Kyozon to Nihon Gaiko [Peaceful Coexistence and Japanese Diplomacy]*. Tokyo: Kobundo.

—— (1961) 'Nitchu Hukko to Kyokuto no Heiwa' [Japan–China Normalization and Peace in the Far East]. *Sekai*, 189.

—— (1963) *Nitchu Kankei no Genjitsu [Real Situation of Japan–China Relations]*. Tokyo: Hutsu-sha.

—— (1964) *Nana-oku no Rinjin [700 Million Neighbors]*. Tokyo: Tocho-sha.

Vance, Cyrus (1983). *Hard Choices: Critical Years in America's Foreign Policy*. New York: Simon and Schuster.

Watanabe, Yaeji (1974). 'Nitchu Kankei no Ayumi to Hoko' [Past and Future of Japan–China Relations]. *Boeki Seisaku*, 177.

—— (1980) 'Chugoku no Kindaika to Wagakuni no Kyoryoku' [Chinese Modernization and Japanese Cooperation]. *Boeki Seisaku*, 251.

(1986). 'Watanabe Yaeji Shi' [Mr. Watanabe Yaeji]. In Tsusho Sangyo Chosa-kai (ed.) *Sangyo Seisaku-shi Kaiso-roku, Dai-36-bunsatsu [Recollections on Industrial Policies, Vol. 36]*. Tokyo: Sangyo Chosa-kai.

Yamamoto, Kumaichi (1957). 'Nitchu Boeki to Nichi-Bei Kankei' [Japan–China Trade and Japan–U.S. Relations]. *Sekai*, 139.

—— (1958) 'Trade Problems with People's Republic of China.' *Contemporary Japan*, 25.

Yamashita, Seiichi (1977). 'Asu wo Mitooshita Kikawada Kazutaka Shi' [Mr. Kikawada Kazutaka Who Foresaw the Future]. *Nitchu Keizai Kyokai Kaiho*, 48.

Yatsugi, Kazuo (1973). *Waga Ronin Gaiko wo Kataru [Talking of My Lone Diplomacy]*. Tokyo: Toyo Keizai Shinpo-sha.

Yonezawa, Hideo (1964). 'Takasaki Tatsunosuke Shi wo Omou' [Memories of Mr. Takasaki Tatsunosuke]. *Ajia Keizai Junpo*, 568.

Yoshida Shigeru (1951). 'Japan and the Crisis in Asia.' *Foreign Affairs*, 29.

—— (1957) *Kaiso Junen (3 Vols.) [Recollections of Ten Years]*. Tokyo: Shincho-sha.

—— (1963) *Sekai to Nippon [The World and Japan]*. Tokyo: Bancho Shobo.

OTHER PRIMARY SOURCES

'Ajia Mondai Kenkyu-kai' [Asian Problem Study Group]. *Ekonomisuto*, 43 (1965).

Asahi Shinbun-sha (ed.) (1972) *Shiryo: Nihon to Chugoku, 1945–1971 [Sources: Japan and China, 1945–1971]*. Tokyo: Asahi Shinbun-sha.

Chugoku Kenkyu-jo [China Research Institute]. *Ajia Keizai Jumpo* (Tri-monthly).
—— *Chugoku Nenkan, Shin Chugoku Nenkan [China Yearbook, New China Yearbook]* (Annual).
—— (ed.) (1955). *Nitchu Boeki Handobukku [Japan–China Trade Handbook].* Tokyo: Yuhikaku.
'Chugoku Seisaku wo Towareru Hoshu-Kakushin' [Conservative and Progressive Parties Challenged by the China Policy]. *Ekonomisuto*, 43 (1965).
Gaimu-sho Ajia-kyoku Chugoku-ka [China Section, Asia Bureau, Ministry of Foreign Affairs] (ed.) (1970). *Nitchu Kankei Kihon Shiryo-shu, 1949–1969 [Compilation of Basic Materials on Japan–China Relations, 1949–1969].* Tokyo: Kazan-kai.
Hirai, Hakuji (1971). *Nitchu Boeki no Kiso Chishiki [Basic Knowledge on Japan–China Trade].* Tokyo: Tabata Shoten.
—— (1972) *Nitchu Boeki no Jitsumu Chishiki [Practical Knowledge on Japan– China Trade].* Tokyo: Nihon Jitsugyo Shuppan-sha.
Horikoshi, Teizo (1957). 'Dai-1-kkai Nikka Kyoryoku Iinkai' [The First Japan–China (Taiwan) Cooperation Committee]. *Keidanren Geppo*, 5.
—— (1958) 'Dai-2-kai Nikka Kyoryoku Iinkai Hokoku' [A Report on the Second Japan–China (Taiwan) Cooperation Committee]. *Keidanren Geppo*, 6.
—— (1959) 'Nikka Keizai Kyoryoku Iinkai Dai-5-kai Sokai Hokoku' [A Report on the Fifth General Meeting of the Japan–China (Taiwan) Cooperation Committee]. *Keidanren Geppo*, 7.
Ishikawa, Tadao, Nakajima, Mineo, and Ikei, Masaru (eds.) (1970). *Sengo Shiryo: Nitchu Kankei [Postwar Materials: Japan–China Relations].* Tokyo: Nihon Hyoron-sha.
Ito, Masaya (1986). *Ikeda Hayato to Sono Jidai [Ikeda Hayato and His Time].* Tokyo: Asahi Shinbun-sha. (Originally published as *Ikeda Hayato: Sono Sei to Shi [Ikeda Hayato: His Life and Death].* Tokyo: Shiseido, 1966.)
Japan External Trade Organization (1972). *How to Approach the China Market.* Tokyo: Press International CTP.
"Kazeni Soyogu Nitchu Boeki" [Japan–China Trade Trembling in the Wind]. *Asahi Janaru*, 8 (1966).
KS Repoto. (Kokusai Sekiyu [International Oil Corporation].) (Monthly).
Keidanren [Japan Federation of Economic Organizations]. *Keidanren Geppo* (Monthly).
—— (1974, 1976, 1977) *Hochu Hokoku [Reports of China Visits].*
'Konransuru Nitchu Boeki-shosha no Uchimaku' [Inside Stories of Japan–China Trade Firms in Disarray]. *Toyo Keizai*, 3366 (1967).
Kusuda, Minoru (ed.) (1983). *Sato Seiken 2797-nichi (Jo), (Ge) [2797 Days of the Sato Government, Vol. 1, Vol. 2].* Tokyo: Gyosei Mondai Kenkyu-jo.
Ministry of Foreign Affairs (1951). 'Daresu-komon Honichi ni Kansuru Ken' [On the Japan Visit by Mr. Dulles]. Foreign Ministry Archive, Microfilm B'-0009.
Ministry of Foreign Affairs (1951). 'Sori no Daresu-ate Shokan' [Prime Minister's Letter to Dulles]. Foreign Ministry Archive, Microfilm B'-0009.
Ministry of International Trade and Industry (1963). 'Biniron Puranto no Chugoku-muke Yushutsu ni Tsuite: Kakugi Hokoku' [On the Chemical Fiber Plant Export to China: A Report to the Cabinet].
Ministry of International Trade and Industry. *Tsusho Hakusho* (Annual).

Miyake, Takeo (1961). 'Nitchu Boeki no Genjo to Shorai' [Present and Future States of Japan–China Trade]. *Chuo Koron*, 76.

'Nan Kanshin no Yonju-nichi' [Forty Days of Nan Hanchen]. *Ekonomisuto*, 42 (1964).

Nihon Boeki Shinko-kai [Japan External Trade Organization] (1971). *Nitchu Boeki Handobukku: Chugoku Shijo eno Apurochi [Japan–China Trade Handbook: An Approach toward the China Market]*. Tokyo: JETRO.

Nihon-Chugoku Koryu Nenshi [Annual Records of Japan–China Exchange] (1957–1972). Tokyo: Minshushugi Kenkyu-kai.

Nihon Gaiko Shuyo Monjo-Nenpyo (2) 1961–1970 [Major Documents and Chronology of Japanese Diplomacy (2) 1961–1970] (1984). Tokyo: Hara Shobo.

Nihon Kokusai Boeki Sokushin Kyokai [Japan Association for Promotion of International Trade]. *Kokusai Boeki* (Weekly).

—— *Kokusai Boeki* (Monthly).

—— *Nitchu Boeki Kankei Kigyo Meibo [Directory of Japan–China Trade Firms]* (1984).

Nihon Kokusai Boeki Sokushin Kyokai Hochu Yuko Daihyo-dan [The Japan Association for Promotion of International Trade Friendship Delegation to China] (1967). *Puroretaria Bunka Daikakumei to Nitchu Boeki no Tenbo: Hochu Hokoku [The Great Proletarian Cultural Revolution and the Prospects of Japan–China Trade: The Report of China Visit]*.

Nihon Kokusai Boeki Sokushin Kyokai, Kansai Honbu [The Kansai Headquarters of the Japan Association for Promotion of International Trade] (1974). *20-nen no Ayumi [Twenty-Year History]*.

Nihon Kyosan-to Jiten [Encyclopedia of the Japan Communist Party]. Tokyo: Zenbo-sha (1978).

Nihon Ryuan Kogyo-shi [History of Japan Ammonium Sulphate Industry]. Tokyo: Nihon Ryuan Kogyo Kyokai (1968).

Nihon Tekko Yushutsu Kumiai 20-nen-shi [Twenty-Year History of the Japan Steel Export Association]. Tokyo: Nihon Tekko Yushutsu Kumiai (1974).

Nitchu Boeki Sokushin Giin Renmei [Japan–China Trade Promotion Diet Members League]. *Nitchu Giren Shiryo Geppo [Monthly Reports of the JCTPDML Materials]*.

Nitchu Boeki Sokushin-kai [Japan–China Trade Promotion Association] (1966). *Nitchu Boeki Sokushin-kai Yuko Daihyo-dan Hochu Hokoku-sho [Report of the China Visit by the JCTPA Friendship Delegation]*.

'Nitchu Boeki Sokushin-kai Kaisan Seimei' [Statement of Dissolution of the Japan–China Trade Promotion Association]. *Ajia Keizai Junpo*, 664 (1966).

Nitchu Choki Boeki Kyogi Iinkai [Japan–China Long Term Trade Promotion Committee] (1983). *Nitchu Choki Boeki Torikime 5-nen-kan no Ayumi [Five Years of Japan–China Long Term Trade Agreement]*.

Nitchu Keizai Kyokai [Japan–China Association of Economy and Trade]. *Shiryo: Nitchu Keizai [Sources: Japan–China Economy]* (Monthly).

—— *Nitchu Keizai Kyokai Kaiho [Bulletin of the Japan–China Association of Economy and Trade]* (Monthly).

—— *Nitchu Keiho [Japan–China Economic Report]* (Annual and irregular).

—— *Jigyo Hokoku-sho [Business Report]* (Annual).

—— (1975). *Nitchu Oboegaki no 11-nen [Eleven Years of Japan–China Memorandum]*. Tokyo: Nitchu Keizai Kyokai.

Nitchu Kokko Kaihuku Sokushin Giin Renmei [Diet Members League for the Promotion of Japan–China Diplomatic Normalization] (ed.) (1972). *Nitchu Kokko Kaihuku Kankei Shiryo-shu [Compilation of Materials Related to Japan–China Diplomatic Normalization].* Tokyo: Nitchu Kokko Shiryo Iinkai.

Nitchu Yuko Kyokai Zenkoku Honbu [National Headquarters of Japan–China Friendship Association]. *Nihon to Chugoku [Japan and China].* (Renamed in June 1966 *NitchuYuko Shinbun [Japan–China Friendship Newspaper].*) (Weekly).

—— (ed.) (1975, 1980) *Nitchu Yuko Undo-shi [History of Japan–China Friendship Movements].* Tokyo: Seinen Shuppan-sha.

Nitchu Yushutsunyu Kumiai [Japan–China Importers and Exporters Association] (1957). *Nitchu Boeki Jitsumu Dokuhon [Trade with China: A Practical Guide].* Nitchu Yushutsunyu Kumiai.

—— (1958). *Nitchu Boeki Hakusho: Boeki Chudan ni Saishite [White Paper of Japan–China Trade: Facing Trade Disruption].* Tokyo: Daido Shoin Shuppan.

Nixon, Richard M. (1970). *US Foreign Policy for the 1970s: A New Strategy for Peace.* Washington, DC: US Government Printing Office.

Oa Kyokai (ed.) (1965). *Chuso Ronso Shuyo Bunken-shu [Compilation of Major Sources of Sino-Soviet Dispute].* Tokyo: Nikkan Rodo Tsushin-sha.

Showa 50-nendai no Enerugi: Antei Kyokyu no Tameno Sentaku [Energy in the Showa 50s: A Choice for Stable Supply]. Tokyo: Tsusho Sangyo Chosa-kai (1975).

Sugioka, Isao (1957). 'Nitchu Boeki to "Kato Kyoso" ' [Japan–China Trade and 'Excessive Competition']. *Ajia Keizai Junpo,* 331.

Takahashi, Shogoro, and Tanaka, Shujiro (1968). *Nitchu Boeki Kyoshitsu [Japan–China Trade Classroom].* Tokyo: Seinen Shuppan-sha.

Takemoto, Yasuo (1966). 'Chugokuten Mondai to Nitchu Boeki Sokushin-kai' [The Question of Chinese Exhibitions and the Japan–China Trade Promotion Association]. *Ajia Keizai Junpo,* 659.

Tanaka, Hiroshi (1971). 'Chugoku Sekkin wo Mosaku-suru Zaikai' [Big Business in Search of Access to China]. *Ekonomisuto,* 49.

Tanaka, Shujiro (1967). 'Soren ga Kokusai Bosoku to Kankei Danzetsu Shita Shin no Riyu: Nisso Boeki Sokushin-shi Josetsu' [True Reason Why the Soviet Union Terminated Relations with the JAPIT: History of Japan–Soviet Trade Promotion]. *Kokusai Boeki,* July 1967.

—— (1975). 'Nitchu Keizai Kyokai Daihyo-dan no Hochu' [China Visit by the Japan–China Association of Economy and Trade]. *Nitchu Keizai Kyokai Kaiho,* 22.

Tokyo Ginko Chosa-bu (1958). *Nitchu Boeki Gaikan [Overview of Japan–China Trade].* Tokyo: Tokyo Ginko.

Yonezawa, Hideo (1954). 'Kokusai Boeki Sokushin Kyokai no Jigyo' [Business of the Japan Association for Promotion of International Trade]. *Ajia Keizai Junpo,* 231.

—— (1956) 'Saikin no Nitchu Boeki Sokushin Undo' [Japan–China Trade Promotion Movements in Recent Years]. *Ajia Keizai Junpo,* 279.

Yoshimura, Katsumi (1985). *Ikeda Seiken, 1575-nichi [The Ikeda Government, 1575 Days].* Tokyo: Gyosei Mondai Kenkyu-jo.

Yoshimura, Toshio (1971). 'Kansai Zaikai Hochu Misshon Doko-ki' [Travel Records of the Kansai Big Business Mission to China]. *Zaikai,* 1 November 1971.

'Yuko Boeki no Saihensei' [Restructuring of the Friendship Trade]. *Ekonomisuto,* 44 (1966).

'Yuko wo Meguru Shosha no Anyaku' [Behind-the-Scene Movements of Trading Firms over Friendship]. *Ekonomisuto*, 39 (1961).

SECONDARY SOURCES AND STUDIES

Japanese

Asahi Shinbun-sha (ed.) (1973). *Nihon Kyosan-to [Japan Communist Party]*. Tokyo: Asahi Shinbun-sha.

Besshi, Yukio (1980). 'Nitchu Kokko Seijoka no Seiji Katei: Seisaku Kettei-sha to Sono Kodo no Haikei' [Political Process of Japan–China Diplomatic Normalization: Decision Makers and Backgrounds of Their Behaviors]. *Kokusai Seiji*, 66.

—— (1980) 'Sato Naikaku Koki no Nitchu Kankei: "Kettei Chushin" no Kenkyu' [Japan–China Relations in the Late Stage of the Sato Cabinet: Study of the 'Decision Center']. *Hogaku Seijigaku Kenkyu (Seikei University)*, 2.

—— (1983) 'Sengo Nitchu Kankei to Hiseishiki Sesshoku-sha' [Postwar Japan–China Relations and Informal Negotiators]. *Kokusai Seiji*, 75.

Eto, Shinkichi (ed.) (1967). *Chukaminkoku wo Meguru Kokusai Kankei [International Relations Surrounding the Republic of China]*. Tokyo: Tokyo-daigaku Shuppan-kai.

—— (1987). *Sato Eisaku*. Tokyo: Jiji-Tsushin-sha.

Fujita, Isao (1972). 'Beichu Shinjidai-ka no Nihon Zaikai' [Japanese Big Business in the New Era of U.S.–China Relations]. *Keiei Mondai*, 10.

Fukui, Haruhiro (1972). 'Jimin-to no Gaiko Seisaku to Sono Kettei Katei: Chugoku Mondai wo Chushin to Shite' [LDP's Foreign Policy and Its Decision Process: A Case of the China Issue]. *Kokusai Mondai*, 145.

—— (1970). *Jiyuminshu-to to Seisaku Kettei [LDP and Policy-Making]*. Tokyo: Fukumura Shuppan.

Furukawa, Mantaro (1981, 1988). *Nitchu Sengo Kankei-shi [History of Postwar Japan–China Relations]*. Tokyo: Hara Shobo [Revised Version, 1988].

Hayashi, Shigeru (1964). 'Nitchu Boeki Jugo-nen-shi (Jo), (Chu), (Ge)' [Fifteen-Year History of Japan–China Trade (1), (2), (3)]. *Ajia Keizai Junpo*, 566, 567, 568.

Hiwatari, Yumi (1990). *Sengo-seiji to Nichibei-kankei [Postwar Politics and Japan–U.S. Relations]*. Tokyo: Tokyo-daigaku Shuppan-kai.

Horie, Fukashi, and Araki Y (1980). 'Nihon Kyosan-to no Gaiko-rosen: Jishu-Dokuritsu-rosen to Miyamoto-taisei no Kakuritsu-katei' [Foreign Policy of the Japan Communist Party: Process of the Establishment of the Self-Reliance and Independence Line and the Miyamoto Regime]. In Horie, Fukashi, and Ikei, Masaru (eds.) *Nihon no Seito to Gaiko-seisaku [Japanese Political Parties and Foreign Policy]*. Tokyo: Keio Tsushin.

Horie, Fukashi, and Ikei, Masaru (eds.) (1980). *Nihon no Seito to Gaiko Seisaku [Japanese Political Parties and Foreign Policy]*. Tokyo: Keio Tsushin.

Hosoya, Chihiro (1982). 'Yoshida Shokan to Bei-Ei-Chu no Kozo' [The Yoshida Letter and the Structure of the U.S.–Britain–China Relations]. *Chuo Koron*, 97.

Hosoya, Chihiro, and Watanuki, Joji (eds.) (1977) *Taigai-seisaku Kettei-katei no Nichibei Hikaku [Comparative Study of Japanese and American Foreign Policy Making Process]*. Tokyo: Tokyo Daigaku Shuppan-kai.

Ikei, Masaru (1974). 'Sengo Nitchu Kankei no Ichi Kosatsu: Ishibashi, Kishi Naikaku Jidai wo Chushin to Shite' [A Study of Postwar Japan–China Relations: The Ishibashi and Kishi Cabinets]. *Kokusaiho Gaiko Zasshi*, 73.

—— (1980) 'Nikka Kyoryoku Iinkai: Sengo Nittai Kankei no Ichi Kosatu' [The Japan–China (Taiwan) Cooperation Committee: A Study of Postwar Japan–Taiwan Relations]. *Hogaku Kenkyu (Keio University)*, 53.

Jijitsushin-sha (ed.) (1972). *Dokyumento: Nitchu Hukko [Document: Japan–China Normalization]*. Tokyo: Jijitsushin-sha.

Kamiya, Fuji (1989). *Sengo-shi no Naka-no Nichi-bei Kankei [Japan–U.S. Relations in the Postwar History]*. Tokyo: Shincho-sha.

'Kansai Zaikai to Chugoku: Sono Dento to Senkusha Gunzo' [Kansai Zaikai and China: Its Tradition and Pioneers]. *Kokusai Keizai*, 16 (1979).

Kida, Shojiro (1982). *Gendai Chugoku-gaiko Kenkyu Bunken Mokuroku, 1949–1980 [Bibliography of Studies on Contemporary China's Foreign Policy in Japan]*. Tokyo: Ryukei Shosha.

Kokubun, Ryosei (1983). 'Chugoku no Taigai Keizai Seisaku Kettei no Seiji-teki Kozo: Puranto Keiyaku Chudan Kettei no Baai' [Political Structure of Chinese Foreign Economic Policy Making: Cancellation of Plant Contracts]. In Okabe, Tatsumi (ed.) *Chugoku Gaiko: Seisaku Kettei no Kozu [Chinese Diplomacy: Structure of Policy Making]*. Tokyo: Nihon Kokusai Mondai Kenkyu-jo.

Kusano, Atsushi (1980). 'Dai-4-ji Nitchu Boeki Kyotei to Nikka Hunso' [The Fourth Japan–China Trade Agreement and Japan–Taiwan Conflict]. *Kokusai Seiji*, 66.

'Kyosan-ken Boeki no Paionia <Matsubara Yosomatsu>' [A Pioneer in Communist Trade <Matsubara Yosomatsu>]. In Yomiuri Shinbun-sha (ed.) *Nihon no Jinmyaku: Zaikai [Japanese Personal Networks: Big Business]*. Tokyo: Yomiuri Shinbun-sha (1972).

Mainichi Shinbun-sha Seiji-bu (ed.) (1979). *Tenkan-ki no Anpo [Security in Transition]*. Tokyo: Mainichi Shinbun-sha.

Nagano Nobutoshi (1983). *Tenno to To Shohei no Akushu [Shake-hands by the Emperor and Deng Xiaoping]*. Tokyo: Gyosei Mondai Kenkyu-jo.

Nagashima, Katsusuke (1972). 'Takasaki Tatsunosuke to Chugoku' [Takasaki Tatsunosuke and China]. *Sekai*, 317.

Nihon Kokusai-seiji Gakkai (ed.) (1983). *Nihon Gaiko to Hiseishiki Channeru [Informal Channels in Japanese Diplomacy]. Kokusai Seiji*, 75.

Nomura, Kosaku (1978). *Okazaki Kaheita Ron [On Okazaki Kaheita]*. Tokyo: Raihu-sha.

Ogata, Sadako (1977). 'Nihon no Taigai-seisaku Kettei-katei to Zaikai: Shihon Jiyuka, Nitchu Kokko Seijoka Katei wo Chushin ni' [Japanese Foreign Policy Making Process and the Business Community: Cases of Capital Liberalization and Japan–China Diplomatic Normalization]. In Hosoya, Chihiro, and Watanuki, Joji (eds.) *Taigai-seisaku Kettei-katei no Nichibei Hikaku [Comparative Study of Foreign Policy Making Process between Japan and the United States]*. Tokyo: Tokyo-daigaku Shuppan-kai.

—— (1981) 'Tai-Chu Kokko Seijoka Katei no Nichi-Bei Hikaku' [Comparative Study of Diplomatic Normalization Process with China between Japan and the United States]. *Kokusai Mondai*, 254.

—— (1992) (Translated by Soeya Yoshihide) *Sengo Nitchu-Beichu Kankei [Postwar Japan–China/US–China Relations]*. Tokyo-daigaku shuppan-kai.

Okabe, Tatsumi (1976). *Chugoku no Tainichi Seisaku [Chinese Policy toward Japan]*. Tokyo: Tokyo-daigaku Shuppan-kai.

Okabe, Tatsumi (ed.) (1983). *Chugoku Gaiko: Seisaku Kettei no Kozu [Chinese Diplomacy: Structure of Policy Making]*. Tokyo: Nihon Kokusai Mondai Kenkyu-jo.

Okamoto, Saburo (1971). *Nitchu Boeki Ron [Japan–China Trade]*. Tokyo: Toyo Keizai Shinpo-sha.

Oshima, Kiyoshi (1972). 'Ohara Soichiro to Chugoku' [Ohara Soichiro and China]. *Sekai*, 316.

Osu, Kenichi (1972). 'Taiwan Robi no Doyo to Anyaku' [Unrest and Behind-the-Scene Movements of the Taiwan Lobby]. *Gendai*, Me 13.

Sakata, Masatoshi (1986). 'Kowa to Kokunai-seiji: Nitchu Boeki tono Kanren wo Chushin ni' [Peace Treaty and Domestic Politics: In Relation to the Japan–China Trade Issue]. In Watanabe, Akio, and Miyazato, Seigen (eds.) *Sanhuranshisuko Kowa [San Francisco Peace Treaty]*. Tokyo: Tokyo-daigaku Shuppan-kai.

Sasamoto, Takeharu, and Shimakura, Tamio (eds.) (1977). *Nitchu Boeki no Tenkai Katei [Evolution of Japan–China Trade]*. Tokyo: Ajia Keizai Kenkyu-jo.

Shimizu, Chojiro (1972). 'Tenkan-suru Kokusai Seiji to Zaikai' [World Politics in Transition and Big Business]. *Sekai*, 318.

Shirai, Hisaya (1973). *Kiki no Naka no Zaikai [Big Business in Crisis]*. Tokyo: Saimaru Shuppan-kai.

Soeya, Yoshihide (1995). *Nihon-gaiko to Chugoku, 1945–1972 [Japanese Diplomacy and China, 1945–1972]*. Tokyo: Keio University Press.

Takamura, Naosuke (1982). *Kindai Nihon Mengyo to Chugoku [Modern Japanese Cotton Industry and China]*. Tokyo: Tokyo-daigaku Shuppan-kai.

Takemi, Keizo (1980). 'Kokko Danzetsu-ki ni Okeru Nittai Kosho Channeru no Saihen Katei' [Reorganization Process of the Japan–Taiwan Negotiation Channel at the Rupture of Diplomatic Relations]. In Kamiya, Fuji (ed.) *Hokuto Ajia no Kinko to Doyo [Balance and Disturbance in North East Asia]*. Tokyo: Keio Tsushin.

—— (1981) 'Jiyuminshu-to to Nitchu Kokko Seijoka: Hukugo-teki Seisaku Kettei ni Okeru Dakyo no Kozo' [The LDP and Japan–China Diplomatic Normalization: Structure of Compromise in Complex Policy Making]. *Hogaku Kenkyu (Keio University)*, 54.

Tanaka, Akihiko (1991). *Nitchu Kankei, 1945–1990 [Japan–China Relations, 1945–1990]*. Tokyo: Tokyo-daigaku Shuppan-kai.

Tanaka Takahiko (1993). *Nisso Kokko-kaifuku no Shiteki-kenkyu [A Historical Study of Japan–Soviet Diplomatic Normalization]*. Tokyo: Yuhikaku.

Tomoda, Seki (1988). *Nyumon: Gendai Nihon-gaiko [Introduction to Contemporary Japanese Diplomacy]*. Tokyo: Chuo Koron-sha.

Uchida, Kenzo (1963). 'Matsumura, Takasaki Hochu no Seika to Haikei: Hoshu-to no Tai-Chugoku Seisaku wo Miru' [Achievements and Backgrounds of the Matsumura and Takasaki China Visits: China Policy of the Conservative Party]. *Sekai*, 205.

—— (1970) 'Nichi-Nichi Mondai to shiteno Nitchu Mondai' [The Japan–China Issue as the Japan–Japan Issue]. *Asahi Ajia Rebyu*, 2.

Ueno, Hideo (1971, 1974). *Gendai Nitchu Kankei no Tenkai [The Evolution of Modern Japan–China Relations]*. Tokyo: Hutaba Shoten.

Ueno, Hideo (1972, 1973) 'Bunka Dai-kakumei to Nitchu Boeki, (1), (2)' [The Cultural Revolution and Japan–China Trade, (1), (2)]. *Hikaku Hosei (Kinki University)*, 1, 2.

Usami, Shigeru (1972). 'Jimin-to Seiken no Tai-Chu Seisaku no Hensen' [The Evolution of China Policy of the LDP Government]. *Kokusai Mondai*, 153.

Watanabe, Tamao, and Ogawa, Kazuo (1972). *Nitchu Boeki Nyumon: Keizai Koryu no Genjo to Shorai [Introduction to Japan–China Trade: The Present Situation and the Future of Economic Exchanges]*. Tokyo: Nihon Keizai Shinbun-sha.

Yamada, Reizo (1970). 'Shiren ni Tastu Nitchu Kisha Kokan' [Japan–China Exchange of Reporters in an Ordeal]. *Chugoku*, 75.

Yamamura, Yoshiharu, and Yamamoto, Tsuyoshi (1972). 'Mitsubishi Gurupu no Kareinaru Tenshin' [Conversion of the Mitsubishi Group]. *Chuo Koron*, 87.

Yanagida, Kunio (1983). *Nihon wa Moete-iruka [Is Japan Flaring?]*. Tokyo: Kodansha.

Yashiki, Hiroshi (1964). *Nitchu Boeki Annai [Guide to Japan–China Trade]*. Tokyo: Nihon Keizai Shinbun-sha.

Yasuhara, Yoko (1982). 'Amerika no Tai-kyosanken Kinyu Seisaku to Chugoku Boeki no Kinshi, 1945–50' [American Policy of Embargo against the Communist Bloc and Prohibition of China Trade]. *Kokusai Seiji*, 70.

—— (1986) 'Chugoku Iinkai (Chinkomu) no Seiritsu to Nippon' [Birth of the China Committee (CHINCOM) and Japan]. *Tokyo Daigaku Kyoyo Gakubu Kyoyo Gakka Kiyo*, 18.

English

Akler-Karlson, Gunner (1968). *Western Economic Warfare, 1947–1969: A Case Study in Foreign Economic Policy*. Stockholm: Almquist & Wiksell.

Barnett, A. Doak (1977). *China and the Major Powers in East Asia*. Washington, DC: The Brookings Institution.

Bedeski, Robert E. (1983). *The Fragile Entente: The 1978 Japan–China Peace Treaty in a Global Context*. Boulder: Westview Press.

Borden, William S. (1984). *The Pacific Alliance: The United States Foreign Economic Policy and Japanese Trade Recovery, 1947–1954*. Madison: University of Wisconsin Press.

Brown, David G. (1972). 'Chinese Economic Leverage in Sino-Japanese Relations.' *Asian Survey*, 12.

Bryant, William E. (1975). *Japanese Private Economic Diplomacy: An Analysis of Business–Government Linkages*. New York: Praeger.

Curtis, Gerald L. (1975). 'Big Business and Political Influence.' In Vogel, Ezra F. (ed.) *Modern Japanese Organization and Decision-making*. Berkeley: University of California Press.

—— (1977) 'The Tyumen Oil Development Project and Japanese Foreign Policy Decision-Making.' In Scalapino, Robert A. (ed.) *The Foreign Policy of Modern Japan*. Berkeley: University of California Press.

Doi, Akira (1958). 'Ten Years Exchange with China.' *Japan Quarterly*, 5.

Dower, John W. (1979). *Empire and Aftermath: Yoshida Shigeru and the Japanese Experiences, 1878–1954*. Cambridge: Harvard University Press.

Eckstein, Alexander (1977). *China's Economic Revolution.* Cambridge: Cambridge University Press.

Eto, Shinkichi (1972). 'Japan and China: A New Stage.' *Problems of Communism,* November–December.

—— (1980) 'Recent Development in Sino-Japanese Relations.' *Asian Survey,* 27.

—— (1983) 'Evolving Sino-Japanese Relations.' *Journal of International Affairs,* 37.

Fukui, Haruhiro (1970). *Party in Power: the Japanese Liberal-Democrats and Policy-Making.* Berkeley: University of California Press.

—— (1977) 'Tanaka Goes to Peking: A Case Study in Foreign Policymaking in Contemporary Japan.' In Pempel, T. J. (ed.) *Policymaking in Contemporary Japan.* Ithaca: Cornell University Press.

Garthoff, Raymond L. (1985). *Detente and Confrontation: American-Soviet Relations from Nixon to Reagan.* Washington, DC: The Brookings Institution.

Hellmann, Donald C. (1969). *Japanese Foreign Policy and Domestic Politics: The Peace Agreement with the Soviet Union.* Berkeley: University of California Press.

—— (1972). *Japan and East Asia: The New International Order.* New York: Praeger.

—— (1974) 'Japan and China: Competitions in a Multipolar World?' In Clapp, Priscilla, and Halpein, Morton H. (eds.) *United States-Japanese Relations, the 1970s.* Cambridge: Harvard University Press.

—— (1976) *China and Japan: A New Balance of Power.* Lexington: Lexington Books.

Hersh, Seymour M. (1983). *The Price of Power: Kissinger in the Nixon White House.* New York: Summit Books.

Hoadley, J. Stephen, and Hasegawa, Sukehiro (1971). 'Sino-Japanese Relations, 1950–1970: An Application of the Linkage Model of International Politics.' *International Studies Quarterly,* 15.

Hsiao, Gene T. (1974) 'The Sino-Japanese Rapprochement: A Relationship of Ambivalence.' *The China Quarterly,* 57.

—— (1974) 'Prospects for a New Sino-Japanese Relationship.' *The China Quarterly,* 60.

—— (1977) *The Foreign Trade of China: Policy, Law, and Practice.* Berkeley: University of California Press.

Hudson, G. (1973). 'Japanese Attitudes and Policies Toward China in 1973.' *The China Quarterly,* 56.

Huntington, Samuel P. (1973). 'Transnational Organizations in World Politics.' *World Politics,* 25.

Ijiri, Hidenori (1990). 'Sino-Japanese Controversy since the 1972 Diplomatic Normalization.' *The China Quarterly,* 124.

Iriye, Akira (1974). *The Cold War in Asia: A Historical Introduction.* Englewood Cliffs: Prentice-Hall.

—— (1990) 'Chinese–Japanese Relations, 1945–1990.' *The China Quarterly,* 124.

—— (1992) *China and Japan in the Global Setting.* Cambridge: Harvard University Press.

Ishikawa, Tadao (1974). 'The Normalization of Sino-Japanese Relations.' In Clapp, Priscilla, and Halpein, Morton H. (eds.) *United States-Japanese Relations, the 1970s.* Cambridge: Harvard University Press.

Jain, Rajendra Kumar (1977). *China and Japan, 1949–1976.* New Delhi: Radiant.

—— (1981) *China and Japan, 1949–1980.* Oxford: Martin Robertson.

Jan, George P. (1969). 'The Japanese People and Japan's Policy Toward Communist China.' *The Western Political Quarterly*, 12.

—— (1969) 'Japan's Trade with Communist China.' *Asian Survey*, 9.

—— (1971) 'Public Opinion's Growing Influence on Japan's China Policy.' *Journalism Quarterly*, Spring.

—— (1971) 'Party Politics and Japan's Policy toward Communist China.' *Orbis*, 14.

Jansen, Marius B. (1975). *Japan and China: From War to Peace, 1894–1972*. Chicago: Rand-McNally College Publishing.

Johnson, Chalmers (1986). 'The Patterns of Japanese Relations with China, 1952–1982.' *Pacific Affairs*, 59.

Keohane, Robert O. (1986). 'Reciprocity in International Relations.' *International Organization*, 40.

—— (ed.) (1986) *Neorealism and Its Critics*. New York: Columbia University Press.

Kim, Young C. (1975). 'Sino-Japanese Commercial Relations.' Joint Economic Committee, Congress of the United States. China: A Reassessment of Economy. Washington, DC: United States Government Printing Office.

Kokubun, Ryosei (1986). 'The Politics of Foreign Economic Policy-making in China: The Case of Plant Cancellations with Japan.' *The China Quarterly*, 105.

Langdon, Frank C. (1988). 'Japanese Liberal Democratic Factional Discord on China Policy.' *Pacific Affairs*, 41.

Lee, Chae-Jin (1969). 'The Politics of Sino-Japanese Trade Relations.' *Pacific Affairs*, 42.

—— (1976) *Japan Faces China: Political and Economic Relations in the Postwar Era*. Baltimore: The Johns Hopkins University Press.

—— (1979) 'The Making of the Sino-Japanese Peace and Friendship Treaty.' *Pacific Affairs*, 52.

—— (1984) *China and Japan: New Economic Diplomacy*. Stanford: Hoover Institution Press.

Maeno, John R. (1973) Postwar Japanese Policy Toward Communist China, 1952–1972: Japan's Changing International Relations and New Political Culture. *Ph.D. Dissertation*, University of Washington.

Matsumoto, Shigeharu (1965). 'Japan and China: Domestic and Foreign Influence on Japan's Policy.' In Halpern, A. M. (ed.) *Policies Toward China: Views from Six Continents*. New York: Council of Foreign Relations.

Mueller, Peter G., and Ross, Douglas A. (1975). *China and Japan: Emerging Global Powers*. New York: Praeger.

Mendl, Wolf (1978). *Issues in Japan's China Policy*. London: MacMillan.

Nakasone, Yasuhiro (1961). 'Japan and the China Problem: A Liberal-Democratic View.' *Japan Quarterly*, 8.

Ogata, Sadako (1965). 'Japanese Attitudes Toward China.' *Asian Survey*, 5.

—— (1977) 'The Business Community and Japanese Foreign Policy: Normalization of Relations with the People's Republic of China.' In Scalapino, Robert A. (ed.) *The Foreign Policy of Modern Japan*. Berkeley: University of California Press.

—— (1988) *Normalization with China: A Comparative Study of US and Japanese Processes*. Berkeley: Institute of East Asian Studies, University of California.

Ogura, Kazuo (1979). 'How the "Inscrutables" Negotiate with the "Inscrutables": Chinese Negotiating Tactics Vis-a-Vis the Japanese.' *The China Quarterly*, 79.

Okabe, Tatsumi (1984). 'Japan–China Relations.' In Hosoya, Chihiro (ed.) *Japan and Postwar Diplomacy in the Asia-Pacific Region*. Urase: International University of Japan.

Oksenberg, Michel (1982). 'A Decade of Sino-American Relations.' *Foreign Affairs*, 61.

Owada, Hisashi (1980/81). 'Trilateralism: A Japanese Perspective.' *International Security*, 5.

Park, Yung H. (1975). 'The Politics of Japan's China Decision.' *Orbis*, 19.

Puthenveetil, John (1979). 'Strategic Options Behind Sino-Japanese Trade Relations.' *International Studies*, 18.

Radtke, Kurt Werner (1990). *China's Relations with Japan, 1945–83: The Role of Liao Chengzhi*. Manchester: Manchester University Press.

Scalapino, Robert A. (ed.) (1977). *The Foreign Policy of Modern Japan*. Berkeley: University of California Press.

Schaller, Michael (1985). *The American Occupation of Japan: The Origins of the Cold War in Asia*. New York: Oxford University Press.

Sebald, William J., and Brines, Russel (1965). *With MacArthur in Japan: A Personal History of the Occupation*. New York: W. W. Norton.

Shiraishi, Masaya (1990). *Japanese Relations with Vietnam: 1951–1987*. Ithaca: South East Asia Program, Cornell University.

Soeya, Yoshihide (1993). 'Japan's Policy Towards South East Asia: Anatomy of "Autonomous diplomacy" and the American Factor.' In Chandran, Jeshurun (ed.) *China, India, Japan and the Security of South East Asia*. Singapore: Institute of South East Asian Affairs.

—— (1994) 'Japanese Diplomacy and China: The Impact of Historical Legacies.' *Keio Journal of Politics (Keio University)*, 7.

—— (1994) '*Jishu Gaiko* in Action: Japanese Diplomacy and Vietnam.' The Woodrow Wilson Center, Asia Program, Occasional Paper, Number 64.

—— (1997) 'Vietnam in Japan's Regional Policy.' In Morley, James, and Nishihara, Masashi (eds.). *Vietnam Joins the World*. New York: M. E. Sharpe.

Sudo, Sueo (1992). *The Fukuda Doctrine and ASEAN: New Dimensions in Japanese Foreign Policy*. Singapore: Institute of South East Asian Studies.

Tucker, Nancy Bernkopf (1984). 'American Policy Toward Sino-Japanese Trade in the Postwar Years: Politics and Prosperity.' *Diplomatic History*, 8.

White, Nathan Newby (1971). An Analysis of Japan's China Policy Under the Liberal Democratic Party, 1955–1970. *Ph.D. Dissertation*, The University of California, Berkeley.

Whiting, Allen S. (1981). *Siberian Development and East Asia: Threat or Promise?* Stanford: Stanford University Press.

—— (1989) *China Eyes Japan*. Berkeley, University of California Press.

Yang, A. Ching-An (1969). The Policy-Making Process in Japan's China Policy Toward the People's Republic of China: The Making of the Liao-Takasaki Trade Agreement. *Ph.D. Dissertation*, Columbia University.

Yasuhara, Yoko (1984). Myth of Free Trade: Cocom and Chincom, 1945–1952. *Ph.D. Dissertation*, University of Wisconsin-Madison.

Yasuhara, Yoko (1986) 'Japan, Communist China, and Export Controls in Asia, 1948–1952.' *Diplomatic History*, 10.

Zagoria, Donald S. (1962) *The Sino-Soviet Conflict, 1956–1961*. Princeton: Princeton University Press.

Zhao, Quangshen (1993). *Japanese Policymaking: The Politics Behind Politics—Informal Mechanisms and the Making of China Policy*. New York: Praeger.

INDEX